STUDIES ON ETHNIC GROUPS IN CHINA

Stevan Harrell, Editor

STUDIES ON ETHNIC GROUPS IN CHINA

Cultural Encounters on China's Ethnic Frontiers
Edited by Stevan Harrell

Guest People: Hakka Identity in China and Abroad
Edited by Nicole Constable

Familiar Strangers: A History of Muslims in Northwest China
Jonathan N. Lipman

*Lessons in Being Chinese: Minority Education
and Ethnic Identity in Southwest China*
Mette Halskov Hansen

*Manchus and Han: Ethnic Relations and Political Power
in Late Qing and Early Republican China, 1861–1928*
Edward J. M. Rhoads

Ways of Being Ethnic in Southwest China
Stevan Harrell

Governing China's Multiethnic Frontiers
Edited by Morris Rossabi

*On the Margins of Tibet: Cultural Survival
on the Sino-Tibetan Frontier*
Åshild Kolås and Monika P. Thowsen

The Art of Ethnography: A Chinese "Miao Album"
Translation by David M. Deal and Laura Hostetler

*Doing Business in Rural China:
Liangshan's New Ethnic Entrepreneurs*
Thomas Heberer

DOING BUSINESS IN RURAL CHINA

Liangshan's New Ethnic Entrepreneurs

THOMAS HEBERER

UNIVERSITY OF WASHINGTON PRESS

Seattle and London

PUBLICATION OF *DOING BUSINESS IN RURAL CHINA* IS SUPPORTED IN
PART BY A GENEROUS GRANT FROM THE VOLKSWAGEN FOUNDATION.

University of Washington Press
P.O. Box 50096, Seattle, WA 98145 U.S.A.
www.washington.edu/uwpress

All photographs by Thomas Heberer unless noted otherwise.

Library of Congress Cataloging-in-Publication Data
Heberer, Thomas.
Doing business in rural China: Liangshan's new ethnic
entrepreneurs / Thomas Heberer.
p.   cm. — (Studies on ethnic groups in China)
Includes bibliographical references and index.
ISBN-13: 978-0-295-98729-3 (hardback : alk. paper)
ISBN-10: 0-295-98729-4 (hardback : alk paper)
1. Businessmen—China—Liangshan Xian (Sichuan Sheng)
2. Entrepreneurship—China—Liangshan Xian (Sichuan Sheng)
3. Ethnic groups—China—Liangshan Xian (Sichuan Sheng)
4. Liangshan Xian (Sichuan Sheng, China)—Economic conditions.
5. Liangshan Xian (Sichuan Sheng, China)—Ethnic relations.
6. Liangshan Xian (Sichuan Sheng, China)—Social conditions.   I. Title.
HC428.L37H43 2007   330.951'38—dc22   2007016249

The paper used in this publication is acid-free and 90 percent recycled from
at least 50 percent post-consumer waste. It meets the minimum requirements
of American National Standard for Information Sciences—Permanence of
Paper for Printed Library Materials, ANSI z39.48–1984.♾♻

CONTENTS

FOREWORD

The publication of Thomas Heberer's *Doing Business In Rural China* marks at least three mileposts for the University of Washington Press series on Studies on Ethnic Groups in China, its editor, and its authors. This is the tenth book in the series, and it appears in the first return of the Year of the Pig, which saw the inaugural volume *Cultural Encounters on China's Ethnic Frontiers*. And it appears in the *dinghai* Year of the Golden Pig, the birth year and thus sixtieth birthday year both for my dear friend and age mate Thomas Heberer and for me.

Professor Heberer is justly known for re-introducing the study of the Nuosu, or Yi of Liangshan, to the scholarly literature in Western languages. As an editor and translator for *Peking Rundschau* (the German edition of the Chinese government magazine *Peking Review*) in the late 1970s and early 1980s, he was granted what was then rare access to the minority areas of southwest China, in particular the Liangshan Yi Autonomous Prefecture in southwestern Sichuan. His visits to the prefectural capital of Xichang and to the counties of Zhaojue, Meigu, Xide, and Yuexi led to the publication, in 1984, of his pioneering work *Nationalitätenpolitik und Entwicklungspolitik in den Gebieten Nationaler Minderheiten in China* (Nationality politics and development politics in national minority areas of China). This was his first monograph and the first work in a European language to treat the Nuosu in detail since Lin Yaohua's 1947 *Liangshan Yijia* (translated into English as *Lolo of Liangshan* in 1962). The general and theoretical sections of Heberer's monograph appeared in a very abridged, but nonetheless informative and influential English edition, *China and Its National Minorities: Autonomy or Assimilation* (1987), but the rich ethnographic and empirical sections dealing with his initial research in Liangshan remained inaccessible to those unable to read German.

Since that first book, Thomas Heberer has written or edited a long series of monographs and volumes of essays, on topics as diverse as the political legacy of Mao Zedong, corruption in China, women's political participation in Asia, and Chinese rock music. But he has never given up his interest in Liangshan or the Nuosu people who live there, and in the intervening years he has published many articles in German, English, and Chinese, as well as organized two museum exhibits of Nuosu arts and crafts. He was a participant in the First International Conference on Yi Studies, held in Seattle in 1995, and organized the Second International Conference at his former University of Trier in 1998. Most notably, he secured the funding to endow a large elementary school in the county seat of Meigu, where the opening ceremonies were held for the Fourth International Conference in 2005. In the years from 1999 to 2002, he had the opportunity to return to his scholarly roots in Liangshan and to collaborate with colleagues at the Liangshan Prefecture Nationalities Research Institute in a four-year study of an important, emerging phenomenon—the rise of entrepreneurs among a people for whom business and commerce were previously despised occupations. Through four summers of rain, mud, jeeps, and drink, Heberer and his colleagues visited almost all of Liangshan's seventeen counties, interviewed more than a hundred Nuosu and Han entrepreneurs, and collected reams of statistics on local economic development and the role of entrepreneurs in the local economy and society.

When Professor Heberer approached me about including a prospective monograph on Liangshan entrepreneurs in the Studies on Ethnic Groups in China series, I was enthusiastically receptive. Because of differing styles of writing and editing in German- and English-language scholarly publications, and because of the vagaries of translation, it has taken longer than any of us wished to bring the book to fruition. But it has been well worth the wait. This is the first study in a Western language of minority entrepreneurs anywhere in China, and one of the most detailed ethnographic accounts of any facet of Nuosu life or culture. In it, Heberer combines his scholarly training as a political scientist with his natural talent as an ethnographer to present us with both the daily life of Nuosu entrepreneurs and the larger social, political, and developmental contexts in which they live and work. His discussions of entrepreneurship and poverty, entrepreneurship and development, entrepreneurship and ethnicity have implications far beyond the detailed study of one remote region in China, shedding light on the role of entrepreneurs in economic peripheries all over today's globalizing world.

What makes this work so special is perhaps best expressed by my memory of a conversation with the author and his wife, Jing, about the benefits of doing long-term fieldwork in China. *Man lernt so viel,* he said, "One learns so much." *Von Thomas Heberer haben wir alle so viel gelernt.*

STEVAN HARRELL
Seattle, April 2007

ACKNOWLEDGMENTS

This book would not have been possible without the support of many individuals and institutions. The Institute of Nationalities Studies of Liangshan Yi Autonomous Prefecture in Xichang (research partner with the Institute of East Asian Studies at the University of Duisburg-Essen) received the funding and equipment for the research project through a generous grant from the German Volkswagen Foundation. Moreover, four Yi scholars had the opportunity to receive further training in empirical research methods at the Institute of East Asian Studies in 2000 and 2001 through funding by the Volkswagen Foundation, which also funded my research trips to Liangshan.

Above all, I would like to express my heartfelt appreciation to my Yi colleagues at the Institute of Nationalities Studies, who worked with undoubted commitment and did their utmost to enable the implementation of this project on the ground. During our joint field research, they shared not only scholarly success and happy events with me, but also hardships and difficulties. Without their guidance, I would not have been able to understand many of the socioeconomic structures and processes in Liangshan. I am therefore very grateful to Luohong Zige (Luo Cong), director of the Institute, and his deputy, Mgebbu Lunzy (Ma Erzi), as well as senior research fellows Bajie Rihuo and Gaga Erri. I am also grateful to Li Jin and Dong Hongqing, two Han scholars from Liangshan Agricultural College who participated in our research, for their support. Wang Bin, from Meigu County, also contributed notably to the project. My sincere gratitude goes as well to the Party committees and governments of the counties of Butuo, Ganluo, Jinyang, Meigu, Mianning, Puge, Yanyuan, and Zhaojue, without whose support this research project could not have been so successfully managed. I am very grateful, too, to the large number of officials and entrepreneurs who, through their various efforts, facilitated the success of this research.

I would like to express special thanks to Stevan Harrell for his valuable comments and advice, and for the opportunity to publish this book in the series Studies on Ethnic Groups in China. Lorri Hagman at the University of Washington Press was particularly supportive and provided fruitful advice throughout the publishing process. Further thanks go to Timothy J. Gluckman, who translated most of the text from German into English, and especially to Victoria Polling who brought the English text into splendid form. Finally, I would like to thank Rene Trappel, Peter in der Heiden, Julian Schollmeyer, and Michael Petzold, who helped format the manuscript.

THOMAS HEBERER
Duisburg, March 2007

DOING BUSINESS IN RURAL CHINA

MAP 1. *China*

Introduction

Liangshan and Its Entrepreneurs

....

In Liangshan Prefecture in the mountainous far south of Sichuan Province, many members of the Yi, or Nuosu, ethnic group have become entrepreneurs in the past two decades.[1] These entrepreneurs operate under conditions that differ significantly from those obtained in China's coastal areas. The world market, internationalization, and globalization do not yet determine the structure and development of entrepreneurship in Liangshan. Instead, connections with the local and ethnic community and to local development are the significant forces in an entrepreneur's success. As one of the entrepreneurs interviewed for this volume stated, "We operate in a completely different setting here. Just look at the work of our county government and try to understand it." In addition, Nuosu entrepreneurs operate according to different values, and have different goals and priorities, from entrepreneurs belonging to the Han majority ethnic group in most of China. To understand Nuosu entrepreneurs and their place in local society, we must understand the society itself, including the social and political structures within which the entrepreneurs and their activities are embedded and the values that guide the entrepreneurs.

A WORLD APART WITHIN THE CHINESE STATE

At the beginning of the third millennium, Liangshan still showed few traces of globalization as defined by Anthony Giddens: an intensification of worldwide social relationships through which distant places are connected, so that events in one place are stamped by processes that happen in another place many miles away (Giddens 1995: 85). In 2001, it took us sixteen hours in an off-road vehicle to travel fewer than 100 miles from Xichang, the seat of the prefectural government, to one of the counties where we conducted research. We drove along mountain tracks that had been blocked by rock-slides, traversed flooded streams that thundered down to the valley below, and passed trucks that had skidded in the mud and fallen over the precipice. In the small, poor, and grimy market town whose population was 97 percent Yi , we met people from distant hamlets and high mountains who had hiked downhill for many days to reach that county town at over 6,000 feet above sea level. They carried baskets filled with agricultural goods to trade for handicrafts or industrial products at the market. There was little entre-preneurship to be seen in this town. Because there were only a few large-size entrepreneurs here, I had some time to observe the county government's everyday routines and working operations. In my travel diary I noted:

> The county government headquarters stands opposite the government guest-house. The doors are wide open; I can see without difficulty into the offices and have counted 18 office rooms. It is afternoon, 2.30 P.M., still two and a half hours to go before the end of the official workday. Some offices are unoccu-pied. Most of the male and female officials present are busy talking, reading, knitting, washing their clothes, staring into space while sunk into thought, or smoking. None of them appear to be carrying out administrative tasks. One of them has just carried an empty beer crate out of his office and put it in the corridor. A telephone rings. After the phone-call, the tranquility is interrupted by hectic activity. Everywhere, people are sweeping and cleaning.
>
> A short time later, the director of the county government general office arrives and checks the premises for cleanliness. He notes the results and, seem-ingly satisfied, he goes away. Quietness settles on the offices. Now and again, visitors call in to chat or to smoke a cigarette with one of the civil servants. In the guesthouse courtyard, the deputy director of the tax office is playing cards with friends. He explains to me that today the county Party Secretary is absent; his chauffeur has driven him to Xichang, the prefectural capital, regarding an urgent matter: his sister needs to be taken to the train station there. Her holidays are over and she has to return to her school in Chengdu, the provincial capital. Considering the duration of the round trip, the earli-est he will return is tomorrow.
>
> The deputy mayor of the county walks by shortly afterwards. He calls out to me that he will not be able to keep me company for dinner and drinks tonight, because he is on his way to friends where one can eat and drink extremely well. He says that he deeply regrets this but, "everyone has his obligations." In the office building, it has become quieter; the end of the workday approaches grad-

ually. While locking up his office, an official tells me that he has worked from 9 to 12, and since 3 o'clock, so it is now high time for him to return home. The director of the Bureau for the Administration of Industry and Commerce (also its Party Secretary), who had me give him a German name yesterday (Felix or, as he pronounced it, Felicksäh), looks in and expresses his regrets that he, too, will be unable to entertain me tonight. A *bimo* (a priest) will be visiting him tonight to purify his house from evil spirits. As it is unknown exactly what type of evil spirits are present, a ritual to drive out unknown spirits will be performed. This ceremony will last until morning.

Meanwhile, in the courtyard, a lighthearted mood prevails. The deputy director of the tax office and his friends are drinking and singing songs while playing cards. In the office building, there is something going on as well; laughter breaks out and the mood has brightened. Empty beer bottles have been carted out to the door, and a female staff member is roasting corn for her colleagues. Around 4 P.M., most of them head home. 'Wo zoule' (I am leaving now) can be heard for a while until the last person has left the building.

How can this impoverished county with an average annual income of US$50 per person afford such an inefficient administration? On the streets, Yi men squat together in groups and abandon themselves to alcohol. Cloaked in

FIG. 1. *On the way to visit a village entrepreneur, Meigu County*

felt capes and otherwise inadequately garmented, they are immediately recognizable as extremely poor. There are mostly women at the market; the
men are out developing social contacts. This seemingly irrational behavior
of the county administration provides a window into the world in which
Nuosu entrepreneurs operate: the dual world of the Chinese state market
economy and the Nuosu clan-based society.

In fact, county authorities are not frequently called upon to address local
issues because the local population possesses its own organizational structure, the clans, which help to resolve everyday problems and regulate work
as well as social life. The administrative officials are perceived as instruments
of social control who had best be avoided, and the top-down administrative structure operates very differently from, and often in conflict with, local
organizational structures such as the clans.

Nuosu social organization includes many obligations to clan members,
both material and moral in nature. Dining and drinking together strengthens community and shared identities and, at the same time, is a method of
networking; it is expected social behavior and has little to do with corruption. Within this scheme, the fact that one of the men observed drinking
and playing cards works as a tax officer is insignificant. Social obligations
take priority over political or administrative obligations. That the Party Secretary could not be at work for several days because he had to take his sister to the station is accepted as his social duty and responsibility toward
his family. No one here would understand if he were he to neglect his duty
and such neglect would make him an outsider, someone who has become
like a "Han," a person with whom others would avoid contact.

Nevertheless, local authorities do provide some order, as in the hygiene
inspection I described above. The county government is responsible for clean-
liness in public spaces, an important factor in controlling disease epidemics.
Two years earlier, a cholera epidemic had broken out during my stay in another
county in the same region. Within a few hours, all the officials had been mobi-
lized; accompanied by medical personnel, they were allocated and dispatched
so that every village and township in the county was provided with treatment,
prophylaxis, and information. By threatening to hold the Party Secretary and
the mayor personally responsible for any further deaths, the higher Party
officials rapidly succeeded in bringing the epidemic under control.

It should be clear by now that entrepreneurial processes and local political patterns in Liangshan cannot be measured with the yardstick of rationality and efficiency alone. Our analysis must take into account a dualism:
most Yi perceive the (local) state to be a Han state, in spite of the fact that

most local officials are Yi. However, there also exist ethnic institutions in the form of clans and clan law that exert authority over social and political life. Different social systems and cultures cultivate different modes of rationality and contain distinct logics. Even the concept of morality, often considered universal, is interpreted differently depending on the culture. For instance, the majority of Yi entrepreneurs perceive Han entrepreneurs' quest for profit as a sign of moral decay, which validates their sense of Yi ethnic superiority. Yi attitudes toward the Han mode of doing business could be interpreted in terms of modernization theories as "yesterday's values." We could also argue that a trend toward individualization naturally occurs during civilization processes that eventually replace the moral economy with the market economy. However, the Yi people in Liangshan have made and promise to make no such transition. The moral economy and the state and market institutions exist in their present form because they are embedded in Nuosu society and consonant with Nuosu rationality, even if they seem irrational to an outsider. "Every society," writes Isaiah Berlin, "possesses its own positive points, its own values, its own kinds of creative activity that are not measurable by the same standard." Berlin argues that each society must be understood on its own terms—understood and not necessarily evaluated against a universal standard (Berlin 1995: 23).

In the interest of promoting and establishing their concept of modernization, the Chinese central government has promoted the elimination of traditional values and forms of organization and their replacement with more modern values. If we agree with Michael Walzer that liberty requires that we shake off involuntary fetters (Walzer 1999: 12), what will take the place of the eroding clan structures in this instance? Who or what will maintain social and economic security? If the clans ceased to exist, the result would be not "freedom" but the opposite state of captivity and defenselessness, because the clan generally represents the sole social, cultural, and symbolic capital that individuals and groups possess. In order to understand entrepreneurship in Liangshan, we must understand the social role played by local processes and their embeddedness in local knowledge, and that requires field research.

The problem for entrepreneurs and for local officials is that they are embedded and must assert themselves in two different albeit ambiguously defined worlds: the world of the Yi and the world of the Han. Though they stand in contradiction to each other, the two worlds are not very distant from one another. This volume is concerned with Liangshan Yi entrepreneurs in the historical context of changing national and regional economies, at a time when the two worlds coexist and the entrepreneurs must operate in both of them. The entrepreneurs' position is to be understood through using a combination of conceptual frameworks and new descriptive material gathered through field research. Before presenting the main ideas of our study, I shall briefly introduce the Liangshan Yi and the area in which we conducted our field research.

The Liangshan Yi (Nuosu) and Their Region

The Yi belong to the Tibeto-Burman language group and are the sixth-largest ethnic minority in China. There are about 8 million Yi people in China, primarily in the southwestern provinces of Sichuan, Yunnan, and Guizhou, with a small number in Guangxi. Approximately 2 million Yi, the Liangshan Yi in southern Sichuan Province and some Yi in northwestern Yunnan Province, call themselves Nuosu in their own language. I will switch from Yi to Nuosu when I am talking about specific features of Yi society in Liangshan such as clans, religion, and language. This is because our observations of Liangshan Nuosu Yi society do not necessarily apply to Yi in other areas, such as those in most of Yunnan and Guizhou. However, when I am talking about how they contrast with the Han, I shall use the term Yi. When referring to official data about the Liangshan Nuosu Yi, I use the term Yi, because that is the terminology that the authorities use; when referring to our own survey, I use Nuosu.

Up until the mid-1950s, the Nuosu in Liangshan had, to a large degree, managed to maintain their social, political, and cultural institutions. Liangshan was more or less independently controlled by various Nuosu clans, which played a particularly important role in Nuosu society, both as economic units and as a source of solidarity.

Even today, the Nuosu are embedded in clan groups whose members are descended from common ancestors. Members of a clan bear the same family name and regard themselves as related to each other by blood, which, as a rule, they genuinely are. Clan members commit themselves to the same obligations toward each other as immediate kin, such as the mutual duty to provide help and support. A clan may encompass tens of thousands of people, as with the Shaga clan in Ganluo, with more than 20,000 people and ten lineages (Ch: *fen zhi*). Some clans, such as the Shama Qubi, the Hielie, and the Jjike, are spread out across Liangshan. In rural areas, clan members often live near each other and form stable units with common spheres of economic activity, religious practice, and social solidarity.

Animism and animistic beliefs shape the religious thinking of the Nuosu; sickness, death, and unhappiness are all ascribed to the influence of spirits. Because spirits can bring evil, there are many rituals to keep them under control, and the bimo, as a priest and magician, serves as the intermediary between the spirits and the people (see Bamo 2001). The Nuosu have their own script, which was formerly used primarily by the bimo for ritual purposes.

The majority of the Nuosu live in Liangshan Prefecture, which encompasses 60,423 square km and includes 16 counties and one prefectural city (Xichang, the seat of the prefectural government). At the end of 2001, Liangshan had a population of 4,059,000; of this number, 43.4 percent were Yi and 52.9 percent Han. More than one-fifth of the Han live in Xichang. The remaining 3.7 percent belong to various other ethnic minority communities. "Tibetans" (Ch: Zangzu)[2] are the largest of these groups, with a population of 63,882 in 2001.

The Da Liangshan mountain ranges (Great Cool Mountains) close in on a lowland plain surrounding the Anning River north and south of Xichang, and they rise to a height of almost 12,000 feet; the average elevation is between 6,000 and 7,500 feet above sea level. Some of the Liangshan Nuosu also live in northwestern Yunnan province (primarily in Ninglang County) near the Sichuan border. Others live in Mabian and Ebian Autonomous Counties northeast of Liangshan Prefecture, in Hanyuan and Shimian Counties to the northwest of the prefecture, and in the area around the steel-producing city of Panzhihua to the south.

Liangshan is rich in mineral resources such as copper, iron ore, gold, silver, coal, lead, tin, zinc, and rare earth metals, and in water resources for generating energy. Since the 1950s, due to national policies, particularly during the Mao era, these resources have been tapped primarily for industrial use outside the prefecture. The autonomous prefecture itself has derived little benefit from resource extraction; the raw materials are transported to other regions at cheap prices, and the expensive finished products are beyond the means of the local population.

The Liangshan region was heavily forested in the past, too, but almost the entire forest stock was cut between 1950 and the early 1990s, and the timber was utilized for industrial purposes in other regions.[3] Nowadays most of the mountains are bare and for some years now, laborious attempts have been made to reforest them. Some of these attempts have been successful; many have not.

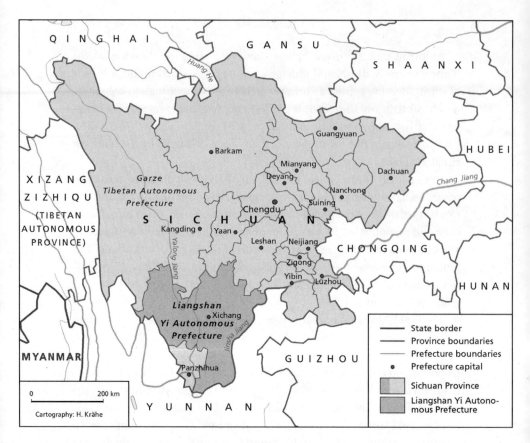

MAP 2. *Sichuan Province*

Poverty and Entrepreneurship

By national standards and in comparison to other minority areas, Liangshan Prefecture is among the poorest and least developed regions of China. This is particularly true if we disregard the industrial and cultural center Xichang, which has a predominantly Han population. At the end of the 1990s, 12 of the 16 counties in Liangshan Prefecture and 390 towns and townships (Ch: *zhen* and *xiang*) in those 12 counties were officially registered as "poor." In 1992, "poor" meant that the county population had an average annual per capita income of less than 200 yuan (approx. US$25). At that time, more than half of the Nuosu in Liangshan had a yearly income of less than 200 yuan and were counted as "very poor" (Jike Quri 1999: 39; Qubishimei and Yang 1992: 33). According to official reports, the situation clearly improved during the 1990s. At the end of 2001, 11 percent of the rural population in Liangshan, or 400,000 people, was still living below the subsistence level. However, these figures do not include those who had recently slipped below the poverty line (due to bad harvests, natural disasters, or a significant rise in medical costs); recent figures suggest that 1.84 million people, or 45.3 percent of the population of Liangshan, have an annual income of less than 1,200 yuan (approx. US$148) at their disposal, and 1.63 million people have an annual income of less than 1,000 yuan, which was considered the poverty line in 2002 (Xiao Lixin 2002: 10).

In 1997, half of Liangshan's population had no access to electricity and 95 percent of the villages were not integrated into the road network. The twelve poorest counties had an average annual income of 13 million yuan and had to be provided with 300 million yuan in state subsidies. Through the 1990s, these counties had difficulties paying wages, providing social welfare, and maintaining infrastructure (Sun Qingyou 1997: 61–62).[4] There were very few outside investors and, during our stay in Liangshan, many professionals told us that they intended to leave the area because of the poor economic conditions. Since the early 1990s, similar to other regions inhabited by ethnic minorities, Liangshan has faced a serious brain drain and an outflow of investments.

Most counties and townships in Liangshan are highly in debt, perpetuating conditions of continuous poverty. In August 2001, the regional newspaper, *Liangshan Ribao*, reported that in the year 2000, county and township governments had an average debt of 269,700 yuan, or an estimated 37.1 percent of the average annual fiscal revenue; the article claimed that the situation was very serious for the prefecture. In 2000, the combined debt of all 609 *zhen* and *xiang* was 164 million yuan, up from 41 million yuan in 1990; one township alone was 7.4 million yuan in the red (*Liangshan Ribao*, 8 August 2001).

The difficult traffic and transport conditions are a significant factor in the region's poverty, as is the lack of qualified labor. In 2002, for instance, sections of the Xichang-Ganluo, Xichang-Yanyuan, Xichang-Jinyang, Butuo-Zhaojue, Jinyang-Zhaojue, and Xichang-Meigu roads were in poor shape, and road construction between Xichang and Zhaojue and between Xichang and Butuo caused considerable travel delays during our period of research. Heavy storms during the rainy season had washed out many of the roads (the stretch between Xichang and Mianning was an exception) and in 2002, all of these stretches were under construction, with the goal of paving the most important connections between Xichang and individual counties. However, it is doubtful that the repair will ensure their safety from future floods, landslides, and rockslides. Though some roads are still in appalling shape, there is now a freeway from Mianning almost to Panzhihua; this road brings no practical benefit to the people living in the mountains.

As a rule in China, the areas inhabited by ethnic minorities (50%–60% of the total land area) are less developed and poorer than the regions where the ethnic majority (Han) lives. Nearly half the areas designated by the central government as "poor areas" are located in the so-called minority areas. There are few state firms in such areas and in those that do exist, the employees mostly come from Han regions. High unemployment is accompanied by poverty and corresponding social problems such as high crime rates, drug addiction, and migration. One Chinese study found the limited development of the private sector to be a major reason for the underdeveloped economy of Western China, and most of the minority areas are located in the West (Zhang Houyi and Ming 2000: 4). Conventionally, the poverty of the minority areas is attributed to the social backwardness of the people, which in turn is attributed to their remote location and their lack of contact with the more advanced economic and educational systems of the Han areas (see Zhao 2000: 5–19). But if we look at the policies followed by the Chinese Communist Party government in the last fifty years, we find that the effects of disadvantageous natural conditions have been greatly exacerbated by wrongheaded and misguided schemes of economic, educational, and cultural development.

Since the 1950s, Chinese national economic policies have paid little heed to specific local and regional conditions in regions such as Liangshan and have put promoted inappropriate policy measures such as the destruction of the organic foundations of life (including the forests), the one-sided emphasis on growing cereal crops, the ill-conceived development priority given to heavy industry, and, within the industry, an undue emphasis on making cheap raw materials available to interests in Central and East China. Because all of these factors have significantly contributed to perpetuating poverty in Liangshan, it is more than shortsighted of some social scientists to blame the Yi for causing their own poverty through their "backward-looking, traditional views and customs" (see, for instance, Li Wenhua 2000: 8). To remedy the poverty of minority regions, the central government decided as early as the beginning of the 1990s to support the founding of private enterprises in minority areas more than in other areas. However, the support merely consisted of simplifying the business license application process with the local authorities. Minority regions do not have the financial means to support private enterprises, and banks extend lines of credit to private individuals in these regions only in exceptional circumstances. This may change under the "Development of the West" program established by the Chinese leadership in 1999 that prioritizes the rapid development of China's western provinces (including Sichuan and, therefore, Liangshan). National integration and nation building are central aspects of this program directed at ethnic minorities and the regions in which they live.

In Liangshan, a large proportion of state-run and collective companies (those owned by villages, for instance) were closed down in the 1990s and government efforts to keep larger enterprises running have been unfruitful. For example, a Nuosu cadre in Xichang told us that the state had attempted to save the ailing steelworks in the prefectural capital by providing a subsidy of 100 million yuan but that this had not accomplished anything. He argued that this money would have been better spent on creating jobs for local Yi. State companies hardly employed any Yi, and if they did, then only a few and primarily as security staff. In the mid-1990s, only one of the 60 managers in charge of state companies in Liangshan was a Yi (Yang Hui 1995: 81). This cannot be explained simply by referring to deficiencies in formal education among the Yi; rather, in many areas, the charges against the minority cadres were that they lacked the "party spirit" and were ideologically and politically unreliable (see, for example, He Mingwei 1995).

The historical causes of poverty can more apparently be traced to the policies of the People's Republic of China (PRC) government in the last fifty years than to geographical remoteness or any supposed ethnic backwardness. Continuous poverty is an important reason why developing the private sector and an entrepreneurial stratum has emerged as the main economic strategy for Liangshan. As a key process in overcoming underdevelopment, poverty, and unemployment, both the prefectural leadership and the local population hope that that the private sector will help solve Liangshan Yi's economic and social problems. A large majority of the private entrepreneurs we interviewed professed that they believed either fully (Yi: 60.5%, Han: 42.9%) or partially (Yi: 53.1%, Han: 52.4%) that the private sector was the most important sector for economic development in Liangshan. Not a single Han and only four Yi entrepreneurs rejected this opinion.

The Comparative Context of Liangshan Entrepreneurship

In recent years, the role of entrepreneurs in development and transformation processes has become an important research topic not only in the field of economics but also in the social sciences (Birley and MacMillan 1997; Burns and Dewhurst 1996), and radical changes in Eastern Europe have contributed to this growing interest.[5] For example, Ivan Szelenyi (1988) investigated the reemergence of entrepreneurs in Hungary and Bernhard Lageman et al. (1994) studied the revival of entrepreneurship in Poland, Hungary, and the Czech and Slovak Republics. Rapid economic development in East Asia in the 1980s and 1990s, particularly in China, has also raised a host of questions. How significant is the emergence of entrepreneurship to political development? What are the preconditions for the emergence of this entrepreneurship? Besides their economic function, what role do entrepreneurs play in social and political processes of change?[6] The development of a "new middle class" and its sociopolitical functions have further stimulated this discussion, and the new entrepreneurship is credited with an important potential for creating economic and social change.[7] However, the extent to which the middle and entrepreneurial classes influence political change is sometimes overestimated; not only do members of these groups hold different political aims and opinions, but also, as in any authoritarian political constellation, the entrepreneurs operate less through conventional political channels and more through informal social and political participation. They may use their social relationships or networks to bargain informally with state officials, for instance, thus influencing values, attitudes, social and consumer behavior, which changes society as a whole. Until now, the discussion about the development of entrepreneurship has included little material on entrepreneurship among the autochthonous minorities in multinational states or on the consequences of the emergence of a modern, industrial entrepreneurship in otherwise non-industrialized societies. This is partly because ethnic minorities, who have limited access to capital, education, and other resources, often choose or are forced into the more marginal areas and niches of the economy, while the more modernized sectors are often the domain of the numerically or ethnically dominant group. On the other hand, as our findings among Yi entrepreneurs demonstrate, entrepreneurs from minority groups may accumulate experience and capital in the trade and informal sectors, which are characterized by informally organized and unregistered self-employment and where they can learn through trial and error, before venturing into more formal economic arenas.

What academic literature does exist on economic actors from minority ethnic communities can be divided into two categories: the first concentrates on immigrant groups and ethnic intermediaries, or middlemen, and the second concentrates on the trade and informal sector. Consequently, research on the economic behavior of ethnic minorities has focused on the more traditional domains such as agricultural or artisan activities, the eco-

nomic behavior of immigrant minorities, and on trading minorities, peasant peddlers, and professional traders. In contrast, our study combines
research on entrepreneurship among minorities with research on entrepreneurship as an aspect of social change.

The literature on China contains numerous studies of the private sector[8] as well as a few explorations of the private sector in areas where ethnic
minorities live,[9] but all these investigations are concerned only with Han
entrepreneurship. Studies of individual and private enterprises in areas with
minorities only refer to quantitative development in these regions or to political economy questions, such as how to encourage private trade in a certain area through administrative support. The published investigations are
neither sensitive to minority economic culture and values nor do they use
comparative and interdisciplinary methods for researching the new ethnic
entrepreneurship and its effects on the ethnic group's society. This study,
on the other hand, seeks to understand entrepreneurship in China by exam-
ining literature on the nature of entrepreneurs and ethnic entrepreneurship, and by understanding the role of entrepreneurs in contemporary China.

Entrepreneurs as Economic and Social Actors

For our particular purposes, it seems most fitting to consider the economic
and the social roles of entrepreneurs together. In this study, the term entrepreneurs refers to people who have founded and currently run private enterprises or who have taken over state or privately owned businesses that they
now manage and develop independently,[10] and among them, those who left
the secure state sector for situations that are economically, politically, and
socially risky, or even deviant, show a great deal of innovation in their work.

The ideal-type entrepreneur is the active *Homo economicus* who plans and
founds an enterprise that he owns and/or takes the initiative in leading independently and responsibly, while taking either personal or capital risks
(Gabler 1984; see 1768–69). The semantics of the word "entrepreneur" indicate an active subject, and entrepreneurial activities necessarily set dynamic
economic processes in motion. Joseph A. Schumpeter, one of the most
important theorists of entrepreneurship, attributes entrepreneurs with creative, innovative behavior and leadership qualities. Their function is to recognize and exploit new possibilities in the economy. He also points out that
entrepreneurs act more out of social or economic ambition than out of intellectual aims, and that they frequently have to defend themselves against accu-
sations of deviant and antisocial behavior (Schumpeter 1928, 1987a, 1987b).

Economic theories distinguish between those approaches to the study of entrepreneurship that emphasize the distribution of income, focus on market processes, and address entrepreneurs as economic innovators and creators, and those that examine the relationship between entrepreneurs and their enterprises (Casson 1990: xiii–xx). Our approach considers the interconnectedness of economy and society. Karl Polanyi points out that economic activities are embedded in social relations; in addition to securing individual interests in material ownership, they also secure social status and demand, and define social attitudes and values (see Polanyi 1977a: 68–79, 1977b). In agreement with Polanyi, who emphasizes the non-economic motives that operate within economic systems, the sociologist Mark Granovetter argues that economic action is embedded in interpersonal relations and institutions and is subject to informal norms. This embeddedness materializes in formal institutions (for example, in laws) or informal institutions (for example, in clans, lineages, families, ethnic communities, and social networks).[11] This insight is particularly important when we consider Nuosu entrepreneurs operating in the dual system of the Chinese state market economy and the Nuosu clan-based society outlined above.

The economic side of entrepreneurship[12] does not reveal anything about its social and political role. There is no doubt that collective activities undertaken by entrepreneurs produce processes of social and political change and that entrepreneurs are substantially involved in forming and influencing the entire system within which they operate, not just its economic aspects.

Far from acting autonomously or within a vacuum, they are embedded in their social environments and relationship structures. For entrepreneurs, social relationships are a necessary prerequisite for successful business dealings. Particularly if founding and directing an enterprise is regarded as a process not as an event, an entrepreneur's social and political commitments are critical to fulfilling the enterprise's economic functions (Birley 1996: 20). Because of the process-like nature of running a business, the entrepreneur has to act beyond the economic sphere in order to maintain, develop, and expand the enterprise. For Nuosu entrepreneurs, operating simultaneously in the growing quasi-capitalist Chinese economy and the social world of Nuosu clans and clan control, maintaining their business enterprises requires a particularly sensitive balancing of the requirements of these two worlds.

In addition, entrepreneurs rely upon several other relationships and social structures that provide security and minimize risk to their enterprises: a stable legal framework, individual relationships with politicians, bankers, and state authorities, and organization into interest groups. In particular, activities undertaken by interest organizations can be characterized as political activities because they attempt to secure advantageous situations for the interest group or enterprise in economic, legal, and political spheres. Thus, entrepreneurs' interests must reach far beyond the economic sphere, even if those interests ultimately serve to secure their economic activities, and, in maximizing their own interests, they also promote economic and social change. Again, Nuosu entrepreneurs must pay attention to and cultivate formal state structures at the same time that they maintain their contacts in the world of village and clan.

The anthropological distinction between "big men" and entrepreneurs might shed light on this balancing act (see Sahlins 1963; Finch 1997). "Big men" are local leaders who engage in business in order to meet their social obligations and preserve their social prestige, which they do through lavish gift-giving. In contrast to entrepreneurs, they are required to spend a significant part of their wealth on their supporters or factions. There is some similarity between Nuosu clan leaders and Melanesian "big men"; some of the Liangshan entrepreneurs, as leaders of their clans, indeed have significant moral obligations toward their clans. However, there are also marked differences between "big men" and Nuosu entrepreneurs, whose primary obligation is to the market and who fulfill moral obligations only as a secondary goal. An entrepreneur's accumulated wealth is largely reinvested rather than being consumed by supporters or traditional communities, as is the case with "big men." The majority of Nuosu entrepreneurs are aware of the contradiction between the demands of social obligations and those of the market, and they attempt to find a balance between the two. In this sense, Nuosu business people teeter uneasily between the roles of big man in local clan society and entrepreneur in the wider Chinese and world economy.

Ethnic Economy and Ethnic Entrepreneurs

An "ethnic economy" exists when an ethnic minority creates its own private economic sector, which includes employers, co-ethnic employees, and the self-employed (Light and Karageorgis 1994: 647–48). "Ethnic entrepreneurship" refers to the model of business deployed by entrepreneurs of an ethnic minority who rely on formal networks (ethnic institutions and organizations) within their ethnic community or informal support from friends and family in order to do business, and who use ethnic resources in their businesses. Ivan Light and Carolyn Rosenstein define ethnic resources as "sociocultural features of the whole group, which co-ethnic entrepreneurs actively utilize in business or from which their business passively benefits" (1995: 171). These sociocultural features include ethnic culture, ethnic networks, employees and management personnel from the same ethnic group, business relations with other members of the ethnic group, and ethnic identity and trust as social and symbolic capital in the sense in which Pierre Bourdieu uses the terms (Bourdieu 1998: 175; for details, see Light 1973). The concept of ethnic entrepreneurship is also restricted to businesses that operate within a limited environment, whether defined by the geographical territory where the business is located or by the area covered by the business.

This raises the question: Are there specific types of ethnically created economic behavior? N. Smelser and R. Swedberg argue that such behavior exists if "co-ethnicity influences economic choices" (1994: 650). Other authors have argued that a great number of field studies would be necessary to establish the role that cultural and structural factors play in encouraging or obstructing ethnic entrepreneurship and to determine how these factors should be understood and differentiated (see Aldrich, Jones, and McEvoy 1984: 236).

One controversial theoretical issue is the question of the social causes of the emergence of ethnic entrepreneurship and there are four theoretical models in the academic debate. Prejudice theories maintain that the dominant ethnic majority discriminates against minorities and blocks their chances of upward social mobility, forcing members of the minority into self-employment. Culture theories emphasize a society's cultural predispositions toward entrepreneurship; they ask, for example, whether a "merchant ideology" exists in the ethnic community and whether entrepreneurship is just a "way of making a living" or a "way of life" (Mars and Ward 1984). Context theories consider the social context and social, economic, and political institutions as crucial determinants of the development of entrepreneurship. And situation theories postulate that specific historical circumstances determine the emergence of ethnic entrepreneurship (Auster and Aldrich 1984). Frank Young (1971: 142) and Everett Hagen (1962: 215–31, 248) also argue that ethnic entrepreneurship is a group's reaction to the real or imminent loss of status, and call this response "reactive ethnicity." Ivan Light (1987: 207) argues that reactive ethnicity is not only a social movement in response to discrimination and the loss of status but that it also fosters entrepreneurship and solidarity within an ethnic group.

Do these theories explain Nuosu entrepreneurship? Theories about cultural tendencies can be easily discounted because there are no cultural expectations of entrepreneurship among the Nuosu; in fact, the clan system and its social obligations complicate life enormously for most Nuosu entrepreneurs. I prefer a mix of context theories (the institutional framework for entrepreneurship has changed with the beginning of reform policies), prejudice theories (entrepreneurship as an opportunity for upward mobility, an option blocked by policies during the Mao era), and situation theories (the reform situation as a starting point for entrepreneurial activity) to explain the emergence of entrepreneurship among the Nuosu. A reactive ethnicity emerges due to an unequal distribution of power between an ethnic minority and a majority. This may happen due to the denial of political rights and access to resources, capital, employment, and education to minority groups, or due to a demand on the minority to be integrated into and subordinated to the majority.[13] In the case of the Nuosu, we could also argue that self-employment is a result of a desire for individual autonomy and group independence, and it enables the minority to evade Han control. Ethnic entrepreneurship could then be viewed as an ethnic departure from the Han-dominated economy; however, this explanation is troubled by the fact that many Nuosu people consider entrepreneurial activity to indicate "Han-like" behavior (N: *hxiemgat sup*). So in order to understand Nuosu entrepreneurship, we must look to multiple explanations: traditional thought (disposition toward or against business and business thinking),[14] situational conditions (access to resources, poverty, unemployment), institutional circumstances, and social infrastructure, including incentives such as class mobility.

Entrepreneurship in China

Nuosu entrepreneurs engage in trade not only in the context of two cultural and institutional worlds, but also in the context of burgeoning entrepreneurship of all sizes and scales in China during the Reform era, from 1979 to the present. Entrepreneurship did not emerge as a theme in China, especially in remote Liangshan Prefecture, until a few years after the beginning of the reforms. New entrepreneurs have begun to emerge with the revival of private economic activities, now that a legal private sector has returned and restrictions on it have been lifted. For instance, in 1987 the limitations on the number of employees permissible on a business's payroll were removed and the legitimacy of this sector was legally safeguarded. At the outset, the private sector was seen only as a supplement to the state-owned economy, but a constitutional change in 1999 made the private sector legally equal to the state sector. The reasons for this shift included a crisis in state-run businesses, a simultaneous job shortage and surplus of people entering the workforce, as well as expectations of increased public income through taxes from the private sector. Pressure from a surplus of rural labor and, since the beginning of the 1990s, the attempt to resuscitate the state sector through large-scale layoffs and the closing of unprofitable businesses have resulted in the concentration of new jobs in the private sector.

According to official data, by the end of 2001, there were probably more than 100 million people in China working in the private economy—in "individual enterprises" (Ch: *getihu*, the "individual economy" or family-run businesses), with seven or fewer employees, and in "private enterprises" (Ch: *siying qiye*), with eight or more employees. The officially categorized "private entrepreneurs" alone accounted for 2.03 million people in a workforce of 22.5 million, and 24.33 million "individual entrepreneurs" employed 47.6 million workers. Urban-based businesses made up 67.3 percent of the private enterprises and 46.4 percent of the individual enterprises.[15] In 1978, when such enterprises were reauthorized, individual enterprises employed about 330,000 people; by the turn of the century, they employed more than one hundred million. However, although the private sector encompasses small-, medium-, and large-scale registered businesses, many entrepreneurs are not included in the official statistics.[16]

Unregistered enterprises comprise illegally run individual and private companies, people holding second jobs in addition to regular ones, rural collective enterprises that are actually in private hands, businesses nominally owned by straw men but actually owned by government officials, and the many non-rural companies that are nominally state-owned or collectives but are actually privately run. Added together, these unregistered groups working in the private sector of the Chinese economy totaled between 250 and 300 million, or 35–40 percent of the total workforce in 2001.

The reasons for the statistical underestimates are political, economic, and social. The need for political safety and correctness in a context in which state and collective firms are still ranked higher than private companies encourages misclassification, as does the desire to obtain membership in the Chinese Communist Party (CCP). Until the 16th Party Congress in November 2002, private entrepreneurs were ineligible to become Party members, an important entry point to political networks. Economic factors, such as better access to credit, tax advantages, more extensive information about markets and better support from local authorities, as well as higher social prestige also contribute to underestimating the number of entrepreneurs.

Among businesses not counted in the official statistics are enterprises with partial or total foreign investments, joint stock companies, limited liability companies, enterprises that are misregistered in terms of type of ownership (enterprises classified as collective and state businesses but privately run), or unregistered businesses (the shadow economy).[17]

Entrepreneurs in China are not a homogeneous group. Apart from the scale at which entrepreneurs operate—there are large, medium, and small businesses—entrepreneurs may be former local Party officials or state bureaucracy cadres[18] who continue to have connections with these institutions, or they may have no political background or official contacts. Werner Sombart distinguishes between "powerful" and "cunning" entrepreneurs. Former bureaucratic employees become "powerful" entrepreneurs by using resources available to them from previous jobs, such as cultural capital, connections, and networks. "Cunning" entrepreneurs behave like "conquerors" and tend to rely on their entrepreneurial trading potential (Sombart 1987, vol. 1, part 2: 839). Entrepreneurs also have different reasons for becoming self-employed. Dissatisfaction with the working conditions of their employment causes "push" entrepreneurs to start their own businesses, while "pull" entrepreneurs are attracted to social and financial opportunities and give up their jobs for this reason (see Amit and Muller 1996). Some entrepreneurs take the initiative to make use of existing market opportunities and incentives in urban areas or more developed regions while others find opportunities based on privileges or social connections with members of the local political elite and sub-elite. Entrepreneurship may also be the best choice when faced with a limited array of employment options, especially for those with blocked prospects of upward mobility, and for the unemployed and the pensioners. Li Fang's discussion of motivating factors is similar (Li Fang 1998: 87–88) but he distinguishes between three types of entrepreneurs: able rural people (Ch: *nengren*), urban speculators (Ch: *daoye*), and state administration employees who "dive into the sea" (Ch: *xia hai*), that is, become self-employed (ibid.: 58). However, this categorization is based on negative stereotypes, makes blanket judgments, places urban entrepreneurs on a level with speculators, and overlooks social strata within the group. Despite the limitations of such classifications of entrepreneurs in China, however, the different categories exist among the Nuosu and are, thus, potentially useful in understanding the specific role of Nuosu entrepreneurs in Liangshan.

Entrepreneurship in Liangshan

Having set up the local and comparative context for Nuosu entrepreneurship, we can return to the specific topic of this book: the impact of entrepreneurship on Nuosu society and social organization, on Nuosu group consciousness, and on local-level relations between Nuosu and Han. Our thesis is that the emergence of entrepreneurs has had an important effect on local politics, social change, and ethnic relations in Nuosu society.

Liangshan local politics are a multifaceted process determined by local Party officials and various other social actors who participate in debates, decision making, and shaping the implementation of local decisions. In this work, I am concerned with the social and political roles of Nuosu and Han entrepreneurship rather than with their economic and fiscal functions.[19] I explore the extent to which Nuosu entrepreneurship has had an impact on local officials and development, including development policies, by address-ing the following questions. Are an ethnic economy and "ethnic entrepre-neurship" with strong network structures developing as a result of economic reorganization according to market economy principles and structures? What role does the mobilization of ethnic resources play in this process? To what extent do entrepreneurs benefit from their ethnic surroundings? Do they enjoy advantages from ethnic solidarity with clans, co-ethnics, and/or officials that are denied to non-Yi in the Liangshan region? The inter-relationship between entrepreneurship and local governments is significant to these questions. Nuosu entrepreneurs distinguish between local and cen-tral governments; they primarily interact with local governments, composed mainly of Yi officials, but do not consider them as trustworthy and sincere as central government authorities.[20]

The development of an entrepreneurial stratum has had social conse-quences for Nuosu society, including for social organization, group con-sciousness, and social structures (the clan or lineage). In asking how institutions are changing in response to economic and social processes of change, I am primarily interested in the social relations in which Nuosu entrepreneurship is embedded and the changes that the entrepreneurship causes in these relations.

Their embeddedness in the dual system of social and economic relations presents Nuosu entrepreneurs with "the trader's dilemma"—the tension between making a profit and the moral obligation to share income with the clan community (see Evers 1994; Schiel 1994). On the one hand, they must give in to the market and ignore non-economic considerations, and, on the other, they must fulfill their obligations to their community, clan, and lin-eage. This is because the economy is embedded in a wider social context (see Polanyi 1977a, 1977b) or, in the words of Marcel Mauss, "exchange is not simply an economic transaction, but a total social phenomenon" (quoted in Schiel 1994: 16).

Recognizing entrepreneurs' dual role as social actors in the marketplace and as members of an ethnic group (Yi) enables us to understand the processes through which Nuosu social structures are changing. Individual Nuosu entrepreneurs possess what Mark Granovetter calls "multiple collectivities" (1974)—they simultaneously operate as individuals and as members of personal-relationship groups such as clans, and ethnic, regional, or language groups. Their market behavior cannot be entirely "rational," because they are embedded in a network of social interactions and affective behavior patterns that include kinship and social relationships, define social status, and involve values, norms, and trust (see Granovetter 1985; Evers 1995: 3ff). Hans-Dieter Evers calls this the "power of emotions in market transactions" (1995: 4).

Local Han entrepreneurs were included in our surveys, both to ascertain differences between Han and Yi economic and social behavior and to examine ethnic and economic segregation. Does entrepreneurship reinforce segregation, and is there a cultural division of labor between Yi and Han entrepreneurs? Are new ethnic tensions building up due to market competition and the growing possibility of being out-competed? To what extent do Yi and Han entrepreneurs differ in their entrepreneurial behavior and economic thinking? Does ethnic entrepreneurship strengthen ethnic identity and ethnicity? People who belong to the same ethnic group (Ch: *minzu*) share a common language and culture, which may encourage a degree of familiarity and empathy in their business relations. The Nuosu Yi language is important in this context because it not only facilitates networking but also activates exclusion mechanisms and strengthens feelings of separation between Nuosu and Han. Does this worsen the us-versus-them dichotomy and solidify barriers between the ethnic groups? Shared ethnicity may be successfully used as a business resource,[21] but is it true that development in a periphery "advances the bargaining position and organizational capacities of ethnic groups," and does this increase the ethnic group's mobilization potential against the central state (Olzak and Nagel 1986: 2)?

RESEARCH METHODS

This book is based on extensive field research conducted over a four-year period, from 1999 to 2002. The research was carried out in cooperation with the Institute for Nationalities Studies of the Liangshan Yi Autonomous Prefecture and the Faculty of Economics at the College for Agriculture in

FIG. 2. *The research team interviewing a Nuosu entrepreneur*
(third from left), Meigu County

Xichang, and was sponsored by the German Volkswagen Foundation. Field
research was conducted in 10 of the 16 counties that make up Liangshan
Prefecture. Our research team visited Ganluo and Mianning in 1999, Zhaojue and Yanyuan in 2000, Leibo, Meigu, Butuo, and Puge in 2001, and Xide
and Jinyang in 2002. The empirical part of this research was carried out using
a combination of qualitative and quantitative research methods that provide different types of information and are appropriate to particular aspects
of the research. For example, politically sensitive questions, such as those
related to ethnicity or ethnic identity, could not be posed in questionnaires.
Altogether, 138 private entrepreneurs were interviewed using a questionnaire
and qualitative interview techniques, for which a series of semi-standard-
ized, open-ended questions was prepared. In each county, 8 to 10 local
county, township, and village officials were interviewed, and statistical data
and written material were obtained from Party and government documents
and publications.

We collected information from 21 entrepreneurs each in Zhaojue and in Meigu, 17 each in Leibo and Yanyuan, 16 in Ganluo, 15 in Mianning, 13 in Jinyang, 9 in Butuo, 7 in Xide, and 4 in Puge. Because there were only a handful of enterprises in some counties, the number of entrepreneurs interviewed varied greatly among the counties and we also had to give up our original intent to interview only industrial entrepreneurs and decided to include some people with larger companies in the tertiary sector (department stores, restaurants, and shops).[22] Our interviewees included entrepreneurs from as many different lines of business as existed locally. Only 16 entrepreneurs were female; 3 of them were Han and they primarily owned businesses in the tertiary sector—trade, producing garments (particularly local Yi entrepreneurs), larger restaurants, etc.

Since we were interested in comparing Yi and Han entrepreneurs' economic and social behaviors, we included Han entrepreneurs in our study at a ratio of about 2 Yi : 1 Han, which enabled us to focus on Yi entrepreneurs and still collect enough information on Han entrepreneurs to make a comparison concerning differences in social and economic thinking and behavior, different uses of social and ethnic resources, and their perceptions about each other.

1

Nuosu Traditional Culture
and Social Change

....

According to official Chinese historiography, traditional Nuosu social structure was based on a two-class system comprising the "Black Yi" (N: *nuoho*), including nobility as well as land and slave owners, and a slave class encompassing three graded castes, known in Nuosu as *quho*, *mgajie*, and *gaxy*. The uppermost slave caste, *quho*, which comprised members of Yi clans, and those *mgajie* who also belonged to Yi clans represented the "White Yi." All individuals belonging to the three slave castes were considered their Nuosu masters' personal property. However, *quho* and some *mgajie* were allowed to own land and slaves, and are, therefore, more appropriately described as dependents of the Black Yi, whereas the *gaxy* were a more traditionally slavelike caste.

The official classification of Nuosu society as a slave-owning society is based on Stalin's "doctrine of socioeconomic formations" (see below) and is problematic for multiple reasons: the so-called slaves possessed their own so-called slaves, and members of the lower slave castes could rise to a higher caste. Also, the Nuosu understanding of their society is different from the Communist Party's understanding of social structures (see Hill 2001: 1035; Pan Jiao 1997: 108, 117). Among the Nuosu, strict segregation rules based on consanguinity (sharing common ancestors) separated the various classes and castes from each other; marriage between individuals belonging to different strata was prohibited. Although both class and caste existed in traditional Liangshan society, they neither coincided nor functioned in the same way; for example, it was possible to rise or fall in class status, but difficult to change caste, albeit members of the lower slave castes under certain conditions could rise to a higher caste.

Every clan occupied a defined territory. Farmland was *essentially* family

26

private property, though it was never really a commodity, whereas forests, pastures, and uncultivated land were jointly owned clan property. Clan members were bound by duty to assist each other and the clan functioned as a protective organization for its members. People with a Yi genealogy who were not Black Nuosu were members of White Nuosu clans, which were dependent on Black Nuosu clans. From the standpoint of European social history, *quho* and *mgajie* could be defined as "serfs," since they farmed land independently for their subsistence, rather than being provided with subsistence in return for non-free labor, as did *gaxy*, the true slaves. It is also important that *gaxy* and *mgajie* were not permanent statuses; though movement from *gaxy* to *mgajie* was more common, there was also some movement in the other direction.

Controversies over clan members' rights and interests were often settled by force, resulting in frequent clan feuds. Such feuds broke out for various reasons such as when somebody was murdered by a member of another clan and the murderer refused to pay compensation, when there was a robbery, or when a member of one clan was offended by a member of another clan. Because almost every clan had disputes with other clans, there was no sense of ethnic unity among the Liangshan Nuosu. If occasionally two or three clans allied with one another (in most cases, against Han attacks), the alliances were usually short-lived and would break apart when the immediate goal(s) had been achieved. When clans came together, it was often through affinal alliances.[1]

Though traditional social structures undoubtedly affected economic activity, being classified as a wealthy person (N: *suyy*) was not related to a particular class status; even *mgajie* could occasionally be *suyy* if they owned slaves.[2] There was also a lot of economic mobility, especially after the influx of silver from the opium trade in the twentieth century.

INTEGRATION INTO THE SOCIALIST PROJECT

In the early 1950s, the Communist Party did not interfere with conditions in minority areas, in marked contrast to Han regions, where the Party expropriated the property of large landowners and distributed the land amongst the peasantry. Obviously, the CCP and the government preferred to avoid exacerbating already existing conflicts with non-Han populations and among ethnic nations. In Yi areas, comprehensive reforms came into effect as late as 1956–1957, when the slave system was abolished and Beijing attempted to integrate the Yi into the socialist polity and society.

In the 1950s, the central government attempted to integrate and homogenize different ethnic groups by classifying them into "nationalities" (Ch: *minzu*) for which new names were arbitrarily created. According to Stevan Harrell, there is a threefold pattern of ethnic classification in China: ethnohistory, which is a scholarly discourse of the history of an ethnic group or an area; a state discourse of ethnic classification, which is the basis for official classification by Chinese authorities; and ethnic identity, which is the perception of one's own ethnicity (Harrell 1995a: 98). Names such as Yi are part of the state discourse of ethnic categorization; different groups that did not previously perceive themselves to be part of a unified ethnic group were classified under one officially recognized nationality or identity and the groups' own names for themselves were usually ignored. According to Nicholas Tapp, this classification of ethnic groups (Ch: *minzu shibie*) resembles "one of the great colonizing missions of the twentieth century, a huge internal 'self-Orientalizing' mission, designed to homogenize and reify internal cultural differences in the service of a particular kind of . . . cultural nationalism" (Tapp 2002: 65).[3]

The more than 50 groups lumped together as Yi did not perceive themselves as a unified ethnic group at the time of the state classification project, and even at the beginning of the twenty-first century, discrepancies exist between the state categorization and genuine self-understanding of identity. For example the Yala in southern Sichuan Province do not see themselves as Yi, speak a completely different language than the neighboring Nuosu Yi, and fundamentally reject marriage with members of the Nuosu (Harrell 1998: 1–2). Other groups, such as the *Sani* in northern Yunnan, have tried to withdraw from Yi nationality and establish themselves as an independent nationality. As the state retreats from many social domains, there are likely to be other consequences of the contradiction between objective (state) classification and subjective feelings of belonging. However, like other newly created nationalities, the Yi have increasingly begun to identify with the grouping implied by the new name. This conforms with Benedict Anderson's hypothesis that nationalities always represent imaginary constructs (imagined political communities).[4]

Although the initial gradual attempts to change Nuosu society in the early 1950s were quite successful, the radicalization of that process after 1956 provoked massive resistance; during the so-called Democratic Reforms (1956–1957), the traditional Nuosu power structure was eliminated. An armed uprising between 1956 and 1958 continued into the early 1960s in the form of a guerilla war against the official mission of eliminating the "reactionary, slave-holding society." Bimo and *suni* (shamans occupying a lower social position than bimo) activities were classified as "superstitious" and prohibited, and their practice led to harassment. In these times of political radicalization, bimo and suni were designated as "charlatans" and "class enemies" and were made direct targets of political persecution.

During the "Great Leap Forward" (1958–1960) the Chinese state pursued a policy of forced assimilation. The erroneous assumption that this was the final hour of the diverse ethnic groups accompanied the mistaken belief that communism, as a synonym for an ideal future arising out of socialism, was imminent. The so-called fusion of the nationalities brought about restrictions and even bans on many aspects of Nuosu life, including the use of the Nuosu language and script, cultivation of Nuosu literature, and the practice of Nuosu rites, customs, and religion. Ethnic social structures were also eliminated, and Nuosu religious practitioners and members of the former ruling strata were sentenced to forced physical labor. The most extreme forced assimilation and national oppression occurred during the Cultural Revolution (1966–1976) in the form of physical destruction and cultural annihilation. Nuosu today still remember this traumatic experience.[5]

For most Nuosu people, political campaigns and movements were phenomena that did not concern their immediate spheres of living. A Nuosu cadre explained:

> In the 50s, the Party told us, Gao Gang and Rao Shushi were bad guys and should be criticized; in the 60s Liu Shaoqi had to be criticized. Lin Biao, the deputy of Mao was at first magnificent, then an evil-doer. We even had to criticize Confucius. All those people were Han and we didn't know if they were good or bad; they had nothing to do with us.[6]

At the beginning of the 1980s, the Chinese leadership saw itself forced into a more moderate policy both because of discontent in non-Han areas and because of an interest in the economic development and modernization of these regions. The results of the Cultural Revolution had made it clear that the integration of non-Han people would be achieved—if at all—not by force, but through measures that were based on a broad consensus. The Constitution of 1982 improved the status of minorities, and the 1984 Autonomy Law formally extended to them the most far-reaching freedoms since the founding of the People's Republic: decisions and directives of higher bodies that did not reflect or recognize the conditions within the autonomous region no longer had to be carried out, although only as long as the higher bodies gave their permission! The autonomous regions' leading cadres were required to be members of the autonomous nationality they represented, and the autonomous areas received a larger package of rights in respect to planning, economic development, protection and exploitation of resources, foreign trade, education, finance, public health, and in other sectors.

However, most of the Autonomy Law's clauses are so vaguely worded that they can not be implemented. It is a *soft law* for setting state policy goals and it provides no reference to an effective system for protecting autonomy. There are no legal measures to enforce the implementation of this law, and, not surprisingly, people complain that local authorities do not respect the Autonomy Law. This piece of legislation does not address minority leaders' demands for far-reaching and genuine autonomy.

In recent years, there has been some academic discussion concerning more extensive rights and greater political participation by ethnic minorities. The discussion initially concentrated on the defects of the Autonomy Law and established an urgent need for revision. Some of the participating scholars argued that the Autonomy Law had not had significant effects because its specifications were not legally binding and neither the authorities in the autonomous regions nor their superiors acted in accordance with them. According to one scholar, the administration of nationalities' affairs should be defined in legal terms and unambiguous laws for particular spheres (economics, education, financial administration, control of resources, scripts and languages, culture, religion, and ethnic customs) needed to be passed and implemented through formal institutions (Wu Zongjin 1998: 2ff.; Song 1998). Other scholars say that legal institutions and administrative laws should be established to penalize breaches of the Autonomy Law (Yue and Yuan 1998; Chen Lipeng 1998). The autonomous regions have begun to demand laws similar to those applied to special economic zones, as these appear to be much more effective than the autonomy laws.[7]

Other scholars pushed for a greater degree of political participation through the expansion of self-administration laws (see Zhou Ping 1997), arguing that the conditions were not yet favorable for the development of a state under rule of law. However, they saw progress in the fact that, although unenforced, the hegemonic state's activities did have legal boundaries and a revision to the Autonomy Law was passed in 2001 although it has not brought about appreciable changes.[8] In fact, the People's Congresses did strengthen the ability of the autonomous regions' parliaments to approve and make decisions. However, the parliaments were supposed to obtain even greater decision-making privileges, for example the power to establish local regulations and laws, as well as local development policies, or to site industrial development. Again, this draft is a soft law without specific legal mechanisms for implementation.[9]

An existing, limited affirmative action policy toward non-Han ethnic groups that resulted in special laws for minorities being passed in the 1950s and in the 1980s recognizes different ethnic groups' existence, prohibits discrimination, provides aid to minority areas, guarantees special representation, allocates special benefits regarding population policy and university entrance examinations, and provides the freedom to choose an ethnic identity. However, these affirmative action policies are not always implemented and often do not achieve their aims.

Autonomy is not only related to political decisions but also to economic strength. China's recent development demonstrates that genuine self-administration rights require an economic foundation. The bigger the economy of a region, the greater its maneuvering room or independence vis-à-vis the center. Correspondingly, the more dependent a region is on the center, in this case the province, the smaller its maneuvering room. Thus, economic growth in the private sector could enhance autonomous rights.

THE REVITALIZATION OF TRADITIONAL INSTITUTIONS

The reform process has not led to acculturation or cultural homogenization; instead, the partial withdrawal of the state has brought about a resurgence of local traditions because in periods of rapid social change, people turn to their own traditions in order to maintain their identity as a group. For example, despite three "marriage reforms," Nuosu in Liangshan mostly still marry within their own caste, although the caste system was officially eliminated in 1957 and its material basis (land and dependent castes) was also abolished (see Baqie Rihuo 1998: 9–10). There are many other examples of the renewal of traditional practices, for instance, the resurgence of clan activities and customary law as well as a renewal of bimo activity; in fact, local religious systems have been revitalized everywhere. Nowadays shamans as well as traditional priests and healers enjoy a growing popularity in rural as well as urban areas.

The bimo are socially prestigious priests and healers in Nuosu society. Along with the centuries old Yi script, bimo are considered the Yi's most important carriers of identity and symbols of undiluted Yi cultural tradition (see Gaha Shizhe 1998; Wugashinuimo Louwu 1998: 38–39). Yi scholars nowadays view the bimo not only as "traditionalists" but also as

FIG. 3. A bimo *telling fortunes on the streets of Puge County*

intellectuals, philosophers, and persons with a "higher morality," which is in direct contrast to their state classification as "superstitious" figures and protagonists of a primitive religion. The Yi scholar Bamo Ayi argued at the Second International Conference on Yi Studies in Trier, Germany (June 1998), that bimo are characterized by their "love for their profession" and a belief in equality (since they are active on behalf of people from all classes and castes). They keep to all rules and laws, are hard working, love the truth, possess a high level of morality, and struggle against corruption (see Bamo 1997, 1998). She contrasted this ideal image with the decade-long state propaganda against the banned bimo; a Chinese participant at the conference commented in response that bimo would be "ideal candidates for the Communist Party."

According to the journal *Minzu*, the influence of traditional religion and religious sects among the Yi has also grown enormously in recent years. In the 1990s, in addition to the increase in traditional religious phenomena, chiliastic movements and sects organized by charismatic leaders (Ch: *mentuhui*) also gained popularity. While waiting for the end of the world, these sects were busy infiltrating party organizations and increasing their access to party and mass organizations in rural areas and their control of village-, township-, and county-level elections (Shen Jun 1997: 35; see also Baqie Rihuo 1998: 8–9). As we noted earlier, such movements surface during periods of rapid social change, when traditional norms and relationships are eroding. A utopian, eschatological, and egalitarian idealism is created to counter symptoms of social disintegration and decay and anxieties about social and ethnic threats, and such religious groups are a means to cope with widespread insecurity.

One evasive strategy against the threatening processes of social transformation is the migration of families, clans, and social groups into areas of retreat (mountains, forests) in order to continue their way of life undisturbed; the reemergence of traditional culture carriers and their training as bimo or shamans represents another strategy of resistance. Amongst the Nuosu, particularly in the core areas, where Yi constitute 60 percent or more of the population, increasing numbers of young men have chosen to be trained as suni (shamans) or bimo, the traditional scholars of the script, whose duties include healing and escorting souls (to the land of the ancestors). Although this is partly due to local unemployment, which particularly affects ethnic minorities, more importantly, pride and an unaffected intellectual interest play a major role in this trend. A smart, studious boy in Meigu has a much better chance of becoming a bimo than of passing the entrance exams for admission to Sichuan University. An apprenticeship as a bimo includes training in a number of practical skills in the medical, religious, and cultural domains, acquiring knowledge of Yi history and culture, and learning the Yi script. Bimo possess a high level of prestige in Nuosu society and bridge gaps in the official health and educational network. The return of this formerly persecuted profession to society can be interpreted as a sign of growing ethnicity and a reaction to modernization pressures perceived to be exerted by the Han.

Since the 1980s, bimo have been allowed to practice their activities as a paying profession. A training system now exists to connect young people from traditional bimo families with the experience of their forebears; bimo have once more become part of Nuosu everyday life and are respected by cadres and ordinary people alike. However, the reinstitution of bimo was not merely due to a friendly political climate; at the beginning of the 1980s, the collapse of the healthcare network had already led to a resurgence in bimo and suni activities and, according to local officials, by the late 1990s, there were more than 6,000 active bimo in Meigu County alone. Given the general lack of funds for increasingly expensive medical services, bimo and suni were the only trained professionals in a position to fill the healthcare gaps.

However, it would be a mistake to attribute the revitalization of the bimo tradition and bimos' renewed prestige solely to deficiencies in the health-care system or an increase in religious interest. In societies with high levels of illiteracy, magicians often function as guardians of knowledge and, within Nuosu society, bimo assume the function of intellectuals because of their knowledge and experience. Further, in a rapidly changing world, where change is often perceived as a threat, people cultivate a nostalgia for the past in order to protect and maintain their identity. Religion also assumes a central role in unpredictable social, economic, and cultural environments that call people's identity into question. Thus, the faster the processes of social change and the more unpredictable the environment, the stronger the need to hold on to traditions and religion. Turning to the bimo for guidance helps the Nuosu master the changing everyday world and preserve their ethnic identity.

CHALLENGING OFFICIAL CLASSIFICATIONS

The Communist Party's historical interpretation and classification of traditional Yi society as slave-owning and caste-defined have been challenged in recent years not only by Yi academics but also by Yi cadres and entrepreneurs. In the official state history, the Yi are recorded as the only slave-owner society in China that existed until the 1950s, which assigns the Yi to a relatively low status in the hierarchy of nationalities. This classification attempts to verify the Stalinist historical concept of social hierarchy[10] and promotes the perception of China as a nation of nationalities representing different stages of economic, social, cultural, and political development, with the Han at the pinnacle. This analysis, therefore, provides the Han with a justification for historical activities targeted at raising ethnic minority societies to the level of Han society. Thus, equality is brought to various ethnic groups in the name of modern socialist theory. He Baogang and Guo Yingjie argue that in China, history has become "a branch of ideology and a component of the new Chinese national identity" (2000: 95). In this context, the Yi scholar challenges not only the official historiography but also Han dominance and the view of history on which it is based, especially the concept of social hierarchy.

In its role as the guardian of all people living within China's borders, the Communist Party has taken over the role of "civilizing" the minorities, historically performed by China's rulers. The Party decides which customs are progressive and serve the interests of the people, and which customs to abolish. The minorities belonging to "lower" stages of development must strive to catch up with the Han who stand at the top of the social hierarchy, and the policies and means for catching up are determined by the Han. Needless to say, such determinations render impossible any notion of equality between the minorities and the Han.

A statement made by Yi scholars at the Second International Conference on Yi Studies is worth noting in this context. They argued that there was no unified Yi history, only differing historiographies. The official historiography, which casts traditional Yi society as cruel and slave-owning, is in stark contrast to numerous, unpublished Yi historiographies, which regard their traditional society as ordered and harmonious.[11] The Nuosu scholar Mgebbu Lunzy (Ma Erzi) fundamentally questioned the official view by pointing out that the term "slave" is unknown in the Nuosu language and that Nuosu terms take their meanings from the context. Moreover, Mgebbu argued, "slavery" was primarily a social institution intended to integrate non-Yi into Yi society and less of an economic institution. Both members of non-Han ethnic nations and Western scholars are now increasingly questioning the Stalinist conception of history as well as official Chinese State historiography. According to Ann Maxwell Hill, Yi society was a society *with slaves*, but not a *slave society*, as there is "not sufficient evidence that the economic and political mainstay of elite status was based on slave production." Nor was it a caste society in the strict sense of this term, as transitions into the upper or lower strata were possible (Hill 2001: 1040). Questioning the dominant discourse can be seen as minority members' resistance against the state and against the politics of hierarchizing ethnic minorities.

We could describe the development of state historiographies by using Paulo Freire's term "cultural invasions," which defines the phenomenon of a dominant group invading another culture, imposing its worldview on the invaded people, and blocking possibilities for that culture's expression and creativity. Cultural invasions, argues Freire, are always accompanied by force; the invaded people face the loss of their culture and individuality. In these processes, the invaders are the subjects and the invaded people the objects. The invaders form, select, and act; the invaded people are formed, and must follow or react while under the illusion of acting or being active (Freire 1971: 178–79).

The concept of a hierarchy of ethnic groups according to their historical development approves of and perpetuates inequality and state tutelage.

The philosopher Michael Walzer has pointed out that the idea of a cultural hierarchy always poses a threat for the people whose culture is being devalued. According to him, hierarchies are never "innocent" because they tend to be accompanied by a policy of discrimination (Walzer 1996: 186). The classification as inferior is an obstacle for autonomy or self-administration because "inferior" cultures are seen as incapable of handling their affairs and administering themselves.

DEVIANCE AS A FORM OF SOCIAL PROTEST

In the major southwestern cities of Chengdu and Kunming, unemployed Yi and Tibetan migrants have formed gangs and divided the cities into individual territories (Lai and Mujie 1996: 66–72). Poverty, unemployment, and lack of educational opportunities have driven many young Yi migrants into the cities, where they have ended up using or becoming addicted to drugs, including opiates, and many of these young people attempt to survive by stealing. Yi scholars maintain that members of Yi gangs feel that stealing from Han is an eminent or "glorious" (Ch: *guangrongde*) achievement.[12] In contrast, theft from Yi people is taboo. For example, if pickpockets on a train find out that they have stolen from Yi, they will sometimes return the stolen items and excuse themselves, or, on occasion, even pay compensation.

Increasing thefts by Yi have resulted in the Chengdu urban security authorities passing an "internal" order to the effect that Yi could no longer be accommodated in hotels and guesthouses in the city. According to numerous cadres and entrepreneurs, this impinges not only on migrants but also on travelers, cadres, entrepreneurs, artists, and scholars. While the security authorities dispute the existence of such a regulation, that it exists is confirmed by the fact that Yi are no longer able to find accommodation in hotels in Chengdu, and they have also been subject to open insults, discrimination, and even physical assault. Most of the Yi in Chengdu originate from Zhaojue County, the former capital of Liangshan Prefecture, and their migration is due to Zhaojue's economic and social problems, which will be further discussed in chapter 3.

Especially among young people, deviant behavior and criminal activity are on the rise, including crimes involving property and human trafficking as well as murder and robbery. There is a widespread phenomenon of theft that causes damage to water and energy infrastructure and to train tracks or electricity pylons. Organized crime is a separate issue altogether. Violent inter-ethnic and intra-ethnic clashes (clan feuds) have also increased over rights to land and water. The probable causes of criminal activity include lack of employment possibilities, lack of access to education, poverty, and backwardness in many counties. Crime also flourishes in environments characterized by processes of social disintegration, unemployment, and erosion of public values. An article published by the South-Central Institute for Nationalities calls the state's main defensive measure against these trends hard strike (Ch: *yan da*), i.e., the use of rigid police measures in a nation-wide campaign. As in the past, state authorities have not discussed prevention measures (Zhou Xinhua and Xia 1995: 30ff.).

The material causes of such criminal behavior are obvious. Disparities in income, standards of living, and quality of life between Han areas and rural minority areas continue to increase, and many traditional minority homeland areas are among the poorest regions in China. Ties within local ethnic communities are loosening, traditional values are decaying, and there is widespread dissatisfaction with the living conditions in rural minority areas. To many young people, criminal behavior appears to be the only opportunity to escape from the pervasive hopelessness and poverty. Thus, criminal behavior in traditional minority areas should be understood as a form of ethnic protest against this condition of hopelessness and the perception of being second-class citizens. Such behavior may also be the continuation of an anti-Han attitude, based on the former practice of "slave-raiding" and passed down through families and clans; young Yi may not be able to take Han as slaves anymore but they can steal from them and destroy their property. The rise of alcoholism and drug dependence among young people also appears to be a serious problem.[13] In Liangshan, Yi teachers have founded "voluntary information teams against drugs" in order to "save their nationality"[14] And Yi intellectuals and local and international NGOs have become active in the anti-drugs effort as well.

As I have indicated earlier, such anomie emerges when the collective consciousness of a society is weakened and traditional moral convictions erode. This is particularly the case in periods of rapid social and economic change, when moral safeguards do not keep pace with increasing social differentiation. Anomie is one consequence of the discrepancy between culture-specific goals and the socially determined distribution of legitimate means available for achieving those goals; the other consequence is conformity and acceptance (see Durkheim 1992: 500ff.; Merton 1957). Yi cadres, entrepreneurs, and intellectuals have formally and informally inserted themselves in the People's Congresses and People's Consultative Conferences in order to further local economic development and generate employment, as well as to maintain their culture. Members of different ethnic groups have strengthened their voices by forming coalitions within these institutions to promote their interests, such as improving the school system or obtaining subsidies and investments.

2

The Liangshan Economic Setting
and Private Entrepreneurs

Until the 1960s, there were few industrial companies and no Nuosu entrepreneurs in Liangshan. Except for opium production and trade in the first
half of the 20th century,[1] the economy was based on a subsistence (Ch: *zizu
zigei*) model. In the 1940s, the social anthropologist Lin Yaohua carried out
fieldwork in Liangshan and reached the conclusion that the Yi "are not interested in business dealings" (1961: 92). There were no predominantly Nuosu
markets in the core areas of Liangshan; instead, goods were exchanged among
individuals. Under the protection of Yi leaders, Han traders engaged in commerce, bringing in goods from outside and taking Yi wares back to Han areas.
Contrary to depictions in Chinese films, no slave market existed in the area
(see Long 1988: 86ff.).

Lin concluded that traditional Yi commercial thought had four characteristic features: one, placing a high value on meeting ethical and social obligations and a lower value on making a profit; two, ranking agriculture above
trade in importance; three, sharing and distributing goods through an egalitarian system; and four, juxtaposing frugality, abstention, and food storage
against feasting at festivals and on ritual occasions (Lin Yaohua 1961: 92).

Nuosu subsistence was based on farming and herding, and intensive cultivation and slash-and-burn methods predominated. The hilly terrain only
permitted the cultivation of grains like corn, buckwheat, and oats, in addition to potatoes. Because only simple cultivation tools were employed and
chemical fertilizer was unknown, the harvest yields were low, and there was
little interest in expanding agricultural production. The independent craft
and trade system was not well developed, and for the most part the economy was geared toward self-sufficiency.

Private industry and private trading existed only marginally (for exam-

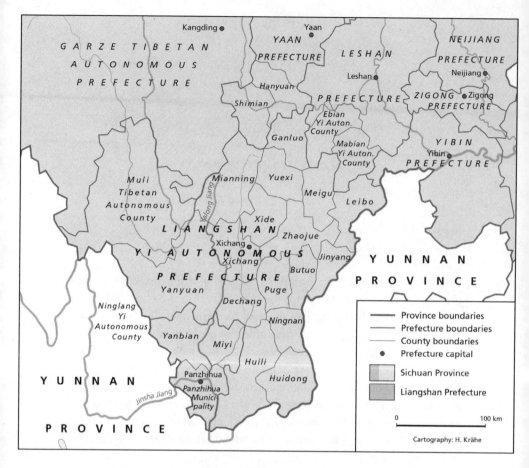

MAP 3. *Liangshan Yi Autonomous Prefecture*

ple, in salt). Clothing was manufactured on a household basis for family use only. A division of labor between agriculture, craft, and trade was largely absent,[2] and the trading system that had formed in the peripheral areas of Liangshan was limited to trade in everyday goods (Wang Luping 1992). However, there did exist a division of labor by class. As a rule, Black Nuosu (Nuoho) did not participate in cultivation; this was the task of Quho and the lower castes. While livestock rearing was also the domain of the lower castes, breeding livestock was Nuoho's work. But, as argued above—and this point needs to be emphasized—Quho were not slaves by any standard.

In the first half of the twentieth century, opium cultivation and trade generated increasing cash incomes and formed the most important branch of the Liangshan economy. In the eighteenth century, opium had reached the Liangshan area from Yunnan. Cultivation had been widespread since the end of the nineteenth century, but opium became an important cash crop mainly after it was forbidden by the Chinese authorities in 1906. Its economic significance also expanded in the Liangshan area, which at that time was almost completely outside the control of the Chinese authorities.

Opium developed into the single most important commodity for barter with the Han. In the Nuosu areas, it even became a type of currency. However, the income from opium cultivation and trading was not invested in production but used primarily to purchase modern weapons. The interest in purchasing weapons for clan fights, to defend Nuosu against the Chinese army, and, later, by the nationalists stimulated the opium industry and probably also led to more slave-raiding (Hill 2001), as serflike labor was needed for opium cultivation.[3] About 80 percent of the Nuosu households in Liangshan grew *Papaver somnerifum*, from which opium is derived, and a commodity economy emerged because the production was aimed at the market. A monetary economy developed in place of barter trading, with silver bars as the means of payment, and opium trading brought a certain degree of prosperity for some Nuosu. However, in the 1950s, the new Chinese government forbade both opium cultivation and its trade.[4]

Forced changes in the social system and integration into larger economic frameworks (state industrialization programs and collectivization of agriculture) brought with them economic reorganizations, but the backwardness of the agricultural sector handicapped the exchange between urban and rural areas. New local state enterprises established in the late 1950s by Han authorities required raw materials from state-owned companies outside the Liangshan area. For the most part, jobs in state enterprises were reserved for Han immigrants. The Great Leap Forward (1958–1960) and the political campaigns of the 1960s and 1970s destroyed large sections of the forests, the local agricultural structure, and organic geographic features of the region. The structure of the economy also changed partially as economic reforms began in the early 1980s. Most of the state- and collective-owned companies were closed down and the private sector gradually became the decisive economic force (Li Xingxing 2000; Lin Yaohua 1961: 93ff.).

However, "traditional economic thought" has remained very strong in the core agricultural areas of the Nuosu. Economic behavior continues to be primarily influenced by kinship, social obligations, moral norms, rituals, small-scale production, and the subsistence economy. A local functionary in Jinyang County described the current economic thought of many Nuosu: "With a small amount of wealth I am satisfied; without wealth I am satisfied; half hungry and half full I am also satisfied." Due to this widely held attitude, the Nuosu also have a saying: "Rather a hard life than hard work; rather inconvenience than too much drudgery."[5]

The evaluation of such thinking as "backward" and the Nuosu as an "uneconomic " people is out of place. Behind such negative assessments lie typical concepts of economics and modernization oriented toward the official state Weltanschauung. Sahlins has contradicted such perceptions, arguing against "business-like interpretations" of simple economies by demonstrating that such economies were not "economies of shortage," but, rather, "affluent" societies which were "easily satisfied either by producing much or desiring little" (Sahlins 1974: 1ff.)[6] The Nuosu sentiment that they had lived a good though modest life before the mid-1950s appears to confirm Sahlins's view.

Contrary to Han beliefs, Nuosu social structure was not based on a systematic exploitation of the lower castes for labor, particularly because the dominant stratum had slight interest in growing surplus produce. That stratum's modest degree of material wealth was described by the Nuosu scholar Mgebbu Lunzy: "In Europe the dominant and powerful strata had built for themselves magnificent palaces and splendid villas and lived a life of luxury. In Liangshan, by comparison, even the wealthiest of our upper stratum lived under relatively shabby and primitive conditions. This is probably related to traditional concepts of society."[7]

LIANGSHAN PREFECTURE

In the early 1950s, China's political leaders (including Mao himself) considered setting up an autonomous Yi region at the provincial level that would have included all areas inhabited by Nuosu. Part of the reason for not doing so was that the area was not contiguous and, furthermore, the Nuosu, due to their fragmentation along clan lines, pursued particularistic interests and did not pull together as a group. Today, many Nuosu regret this because the formation of an administrative unit at the provincial level would have meant a larger cash flow from the central government for their economic and social development, and would also have included areas of other non-Nuosu Yi in Yunnan and Guizhou.

A Yi autonomous prefecture was founded in 1952, with Zhaojue as its capital. The boundaries of the prefecture were revised a number of times over the years and in 1979, Xichang District, which was for the most part populated by Han, was integrated into Liangshan Prefecture. The administrative authorities and a section of the larger companies were transferred to the new capital city of Xichang. From then on, the Nuosu no longer constituted the majority of the population in the prefecture, and the new capital was almost exclusively populated by Han. The authorities responsible for the reorganization justified it on the grounds that the effects of economic growth in Xichang would spill over into the remaining counties of the prefecture, creating rapid development in these areas. The reality was that the counties mostly populated by Nuosu remained poor.

Panzhihua, nowadays a large steel-producing city near the Yunnan border, originally belonged to Xichang and Yi Yanbian Autonomous County. It was removed from the Yi territories after iron ore was discovered there. A large steel combine was founded in Panzhihua; however, the jobs created by the combine were not filled by local Yi or local Han, but by Han recruited from outside. When Panzhihua became a city, two counties, Yanbian and Miyi, were taken out of the Liangshan autonomous territory and incorporated into the new city (see map 3).[8] Although the combine represented the largest state investment in Nuosu areas, it brought no benefits to the Nuosu. Rights and considerations of autonomy played no role during the separation of Panzhihua.

After the provincial capital of Chengdu, Panzhihua has the second highest per capita GDP in Sichuan but, because it is not a part of Liangshan Prefecture, the taxes and income generated in Panzhihua cannot be used for the good of the Liangshan autonomous area. At the same time, the nine "*minzu* townships" (Ch: *minzu xiang*) of the Yi in Panzhihua are without exception "poverty townships."

Nevertheless, this modern city was, and continues to be, a magnet for Yi from the surrounding areas. Thousands settled at the edge of the city and hoped that they would be able to profit from the Panzhihua's prosperity. Han residents complained about their growing numbers because Yi migrants allegedly disturbed the public order. During the period 1997–1999, Yi were taken out of the city by force and abandoned in the countryside. Not a few are thought to have frozen or starved to death as a result.[9]

Ebian and Mabian Counties were likewise separated from Liangshan Prefecture in 1984 and put under the authority of Leshan (Han) Prefecture. The higher echelons of the provincial and central authorities argued that the distance from Xichang, the prefectural capital (200–250 km) was too large and was making administration and development too complicated. Moreover, there have been several attempts by Han officials in recent years to separate Xichang from Liangshan Prefecture or to completely break up the prefecture. For example, in 1998, 38 members of the prefectural People's

Consultative Conference made a motion to split the administrative territory into three parts, in all of which Han would constitute the majority. According to this motion, the more economically developed counties would have been incorporated into Xichang city and Huili Prefecture, and the eight poorest counties would have formed a truncated autonomous prefecture with Zhaojue as its capital. In 1999, delegates from Sichuan placed this motion before the National People's Congress in Beijing; however, last-minute interventions by outraged Yi defeated the draft resolution (Hou 2001: 127–28).

ECONOMIC DEVELOPMENT

As already mentioned in the introduction, economic conditions in Liangshan have made the development of the private sector and entrepreneurship essential for reducing poverty and unemployment. Hope exists among the prefectural leadership as well as among the population that economic and social problems will be solved by means of the development of the private sector. A majority of the private entrepreneurs we interviewed agreed fully (Yi: 60.5%, Han: 42.9%) or partially (Yi: 53.1%, Han: 52.4%) that the private sector was the most important sector for economic development in Liangshan. Not a single Han, and only four Nuosu entrepreneurs disagreed with this opinion.

Since the proportion of state and collective firms to private enterprises is continually decreasing, the private sector has become the central economic factor for development in Liangshan Prefecture. According to official statistics, by the end of 2000, only 964 (5.5%) of the 17,472 registered industrial companies were still state- or collective-owned (*Liangshan tongji nianjian* 2001: 68–69). These were mostly older firms that were significant outside the region or even nationally, or companies that provided basic local services such as electricity or waterworks. Of these, 627 (65.7%) were, however, concentrated in counties with a more than 60 percent Han population. Of the private enterprises listed in the Statistical Yearbook 2001, 794 private and 15,560 individually owned companies (78% and 76.3% of the respective total numbers) were likewise to be found in Han dominated counties. As in the rest of China, the tertiary sector in Liangshan Prefecture is also overwhelmingly in the hands of the private sector (84.4% non-state-owned) (*Liangshan tongji nianjian* 2001: 192–93).

As I mentioned above, the private sector in China is divided into the two spheres—individual businesses and private businesses with more than

TABLE 2.1 Businesses and Employees in the Individual Sector,
Liangshan Prefecture, 1999 and 2001

Sector	1999		2001	
	Businesses	*Employees*	*Businesses*	*Employees*
Agriculture, forestry, etc.	21	27	43	120
Construction	83	318	34	166
Mining	105	383	107	456
Manufacturing	4,582	6,173	3,530	5,470
Service	8,305	25,637	7,242	15,020
Transportation	10,581	10,735	6,033	10,560
Trade, food service	30,103	33,930	23,570	39,781
Other	389	486	279	413
Total	54,169	77,689	40,838	71,986

SOURCE: Bureau for the Administration of Industry and Commerce of Liangshan
Prefecture.

seven employees. The individual business sector plays an important role in our study for two reasons: one, in most of the counties we examined, the sector consisting of larger companies is relatively small and the border between larger individual and small private firms usually fluid, and, two, larger entrepreneurs often emerge from the individual sector, where they first gain experience and accumulate capital.

In the first half of 1999 in Liangshan Prefecture, the individual sector consisted of 54,169 businesses, with 77,689 employees, and the private sector had 888 businesses and 16,231 employees.[10] Thus, by the end of 1998, a significant portion of the population was already working in the private sector.

One feature of the private sector not evident from tables 2.1 and 2.2 is that many enterprises have more than one investor. In 1999, the 888 private businesses—primarily agriculture, forestry, and animal husbandry (4.65 investors per enterprise), the service sector (3.0 investors), and construction (2.86 investors)—had 2,185 investors (2.46 per enterprise). Two years later, statistics revealed that 2,976 individuals (2.98 per enterprise) invested in transport (5.9 investors per enterprise), construction (4.63 investors), and trade/catering (3.2 investors). Such businesses may have multiple investors because the peasants engaged in them lack the necessary funding and thus share the financial burden and risk with persons of the same clan or village.

TABLE 2.2 Businesses and Employees in the Private Sector,
Liangshan Prefecture, 1999 and 2001

	1999		2001	
Sector	Businesses	Employees	Businesses	Employees
Agriculture, forestry, etc.	20	455	41	531
Construction	28	808	43	890
Mining	181	4,871	167	4,322
Manufacturing	176	4,690	225	4,341
Service	33	510	41	827
Transportation	5	100	8	261
Trade, food service	428	4,604	441	4,503
Other	17	193	31	338
Total	888	16,231	997	16,013

SOURCE: Bureau for the Administration of Industry and Commerce of Liangshan Prefecture.

Two years later, by the first half of 2001, the number of individual businesses had decreased by 24.6 percent and the number of employees by 7.3 percent. The decrease was strongest greatest in construction (-59%), followed by transportation (-43%), manufacturing (-23%), and trade (-21.7%). Concurrently, the number of employees in trade increased (+17.2%), but decreased significantly in services (-41.4%). In the larger, private sector, the number of enterprises increased by 2001 (+12.3%) while the number of employees decreased slightly (-1.3%). Among the larger-scale private businesses, the number of mining businesses decreased slightly over the two years and manufacturing increased significantly (+27.8%), although the number of employees in manufacturing decreased (-7.4%).

Increase or decrease in numbers of businesses is strongly linked both to policy changes—new state regulations concerning industrial or traffic safety (affecting construction and transportation companies) or forest protection, as well as local policies (for promoting or curbing different types of businesses)—and to regional or global economic conditions. For instance, in the late 1990s, during the Asian financial crisis ("Asian Crisis"), the currencies of a number of Asian economies collapsed due to international speculation and domestic corruption, and businesses that depended on export, such as mining, were affected even in Liangshan. Furthermore, in 1999, a cholera epidemic in some counties affected catering businesses, and flood disasters in the same year affected other types of businesses.

In 2001, 53.5 percent of the businesses and 60.2 percent of the employees in the individual sector and 18.5 percent of the businesses and 26.5 percent of the employees in the private sector were located in "urban" areas.[11] Increasing numbers of entrepreneurs base themselves in urban areas with the goal of expanding their entrepreneurial activities. The slight increase in urban private economic activities in recent years may be a result of this phenomenon, which is fueled by better access to markets and, to some extent, to raw materials, better marketing prospects, and less binding bureaucratic controls. This is particularly true for Xichang, the prefectural capital.

The development of Liangshan, although much slower than in other parts of China, supports Yujiro Hayami's theory concerning East Asian rural entrepreneurs, according to which a productive upswing in agriculture (for example, as developed in the course of rural reforms and restructuring) creates entrepreneurs who make use of new agricultural potential in the industrial sphere (for example, firms that process agricultural products). In this way, the agricultural sector becomes linked to modern industry and urban markets (Hayami and Kawagoe 1993).

The development of industrial production potential in rural areas of Liangshan Prefecture depends upon traditional bonds within those communities (clan and/or village), which help keep costs to a minimum. At the same time, rural industrialization concentrates increases in incomes in the countryside; as a result, migration from the countryside to urban zones and the resulting urban poverty is restricted to a tolerable level.[12]

Rural entrepreneurs also link the rural private sector to urban areas. In Liangshan as in other parts of China, the transition from a planned economy to one based on market structures has fostered new opportunities for entrepreneurs not only in the market, but also in the spheres located between the market and those parts of the planned economy that continue to exist. Such links connect the market and the bureaucracy, and likewise private and state sectors.

Most of the private companies are small-scale individual enterprises in industry and crafts, transport, construction, catering (restaurants, hostels, etc.), trade, and other service industries (repair, computer services, entertainment). Private rural industries in particular have become the pillars of the industry, and larger companies are slowly but steadily emerging.

The proportion of businesses belonging to people of Yi ethnicity is small, particularly in the larger private sector. Table 2.3 summarizes data on mem-

TABLE 2.3 Ethnic Minority Entrepreneurs in the Private Sector,*
Liangshan Prefecture, 1999

Sector	Businesses		Employees	
Agriculture, forestry, etc.	1	(2.4%)	1	(0.2%)
Construction	1	(0.9%)	100	(8.9%)
Mining	7	(2.4%)	120	(2.3%)
Manufacturing	204	(4.3%)	370	(3.4%)
Service	1,044	(12.5%)	2,528	(9.7%)
Transportation	575	(5.4%)	785	(7.2%)
Trade, food service	3,259	(10.7%)	4,261	(11.1%)
Total entrepreneurs	55,057	(100%)	93,920	(100%)
Total ethnic minorities	5,091	(9.2%)	8,165	(8.7%)

SOURCE: Bureau for the Administration of Industry and Commerce of Liangshan Prefecture.
NOTE: Ethnic minority entrepreneurs are primarily Yi, but include a few members of other ethnic groups such as Tibetans.
*Individual and private businesses (with eight or more employees).

bers of ethnic minorities in Liangshan (almost entirely Yi) who were engaged in the private sector (individual and private economy) in 1999 (no data were available for other years).

In some cases the local authorities were not able to differentiate between the private and the individual sector. Including groups such as Tibetans, ethnic minorities in Liangshan Prefecture made up 47.1 percent of the population in 2001; 9.2 percent (5,091) of the private businesses were owned by ethnic minorities, and they constituted 8.7 percent (8,165) of employees in those businesses in 1999.[13] The figures in table 2.3 reveal that Yi-owned firms constitute only a tiny portion of the private sector. In larger businesses such as mining and manufacturing, their share was below 5 percent. Yi owned a significant percentage only in smaller lines of business such as trade and catering, or in services that did not need much professional knowledge and investment.

Further, the private sector is concentrated in more developed areas of Liangshan Prefecture, such as the cities of Xichang and Dechang and in counties that are primarily inhabited by Han, such as Huili and Huidong. As we shall demonstrate below, the reasons for this are not only historical but also strongly related to such factors as education, access to capital and credit,

TABLE 2.4 Income Disparities among Liangshan Counties, 2000

County/City	Per capita cash income (US$)	Han population (%)
Xichang	2,495	81.5
Huili	2,150	83.1
Huidong	1,545	91.8
Mianning*	1,545	66.1
Ningnan	1,512	77.4
Yuexi	1,195	29.7
Dechang	1,062	73.7
Ganluo*	988	27.9
Yanyuan*	951	45.3
Leibo*	921	52.3
Meigu*	917	1.9
Puge*	865	23.8
Xide*	685	14.7
Jinyang*	587	22.5
Butuo*	428	5.7
Zhaojue*	391	3.0
Muli**	365	22.7
Liangshan total	1,086	52.9
Sichuan Province	1,904	95.0
China	2,253	91.9

SOURCE: *Liangshan tongji nianjian* 2001: 2, 66.
*Counties surveyed for this volume.
**Tibetan autonomous county with about 30% Yi population.

the existence of a beneficial infrastructure, and specific patterns of official support. As we see from table 2.4, the differences in income between Han and Yi areas are considerable.

Table 2.4 suggests that in general, areas with a Han majority are economically better off than those with a Nuosu majority. This could be interpreted as a sign of economic segregation along ethnic lines but, in fact, access to railways, highways, and urban markets; the topography; and natural as opposed to cash economies all play a significant role in explaining why Yi areas have lagged in development. The Tibetan Autonomous County of

Muli, for example, does not suffer from the abject poverty and starvation of parts of Zhaojue and Butuo but it is so unconnected to the cash economy that people's cash incomes are low even though they have enough to eat. The development gap between Yi and Han areas has increased in spite of, or even because of, political reform.

Although they have received considerable financial support from the center of Liangshan Prefecture, Yi core counties are still classified as "poor" or "extremely poor." The government is not solely responsible for this, because some of these areas are remote regions of refuge into which Yi people have withdrawn in recent centuries. But it is clear that, since the founding of the People's Republic, there has been no development policy that is suited to these areas. Political reform has visibly diminished state control, but this has not benefited these counties. According to local reports, the national and provincial governments have not given enough credit, subsidies, foreign exchange, and materials to many Yi counties in Liangshan. In the next chapter I explore some of the forces that determine the development of the private sector by comparing data from different counties.

3

Private Sector Development
in Nine Liangshan Counties

....

The development of the private economic sector is affected by local factors such as geographic location, infrastructure, institutional corruption, and the extent to which local government is able to assist private enterprise. Despite innate county-to-county differences arising from these factors, as well as differences among counties in categorizing and recording business statistics, we can discern the overall forces working for and against entrepreneurship in Liangshan by comparing data from different counties.

THE COUNTIES SURVEYED

Jinyang County: An Example of Poverty

In many respects, the situation in Jinyang County is similar to that of other counties in Liangshan. By national standards in 2001–2002, a county with an average annual income of less than 1,000 yuan was classified as a "poverty county." Founded in 1952 and with an average annual income of 587 yuan per capita per year (Jinyang xianzhi 2000), Jinyang is one of the poorest counties in the prefecture. In 2002, more than three-quarters of the county's population were Yi (77.3%), and between 70 percent and 80 percent of the people live in the mountains, which rise to over 4,000 m.

Agriculture is the dominant economic sector in Jinyang, employing 95.7 percent of the population, but 90 percent of the land suitable for cultivation is in steep mountainous regions with poor soil quality, resulting in low crop yields. The mountainous areas lack adequate meadow pastures for animal husbandry and cattle stocks increase very slowly. Attempts at reforestation have proven difficult.

In 2001, 25 percent of the townships and 80 percent of the villages were not yet connected to the road network, and 30 percent of the townships and 65 percent of the villages did not have electricity. Very few townships (15%) and villages (only 5%) were connected to telecommunication networks. However, the county is rich in mineral resources; 54 mineral deposits have been discovered here and 20 of them are already being exploited. On the other hand, there is almost no industry. The majority of the rural work-force is illiterate and does not understand Han Chinese, which impedes the spread of technical knowledge.

Jinyang was classified as a poverty county at the provincial level in 1986 and at the national level in 1988. According to the county administration, both central and provincial governments have provided Jinyang with considerable resources under the auspices of a national program against poverty (1994–2000). In 1993, 85,220 people, or about 70 percent of the predominantly Nuosu population, lived below the subsistence level, i.e., in absolute poverty, with less than 500 yuan cash income and less than 400 kg grain per capita per year. This number was reduced to 23,600 (about 17% of the population) in 2000, but increased again to 38,000 in 2002 (28.5% of the rural population). In the late 1990s, crop failures caused by natural disasters or just bad weather con-ditions led to an increase in the number of people living below the subsis-tence level. In 2000, the poverty line was redefined by the central government to rest at an annual per capita income of less than 1,000 yuan; by these stan-dards, 93 percent of the population lived below the poverty line in 2000.

The state of the educational system reflects the conditions of poverty in Jinyang; in 2002, only a few of the county's 30 townships had a secondary school. The only senior secondary school was located in the county town, which meant that few children from the surrounding rural areas were able to attend. Children whose families live far away from school must pay room and board in addition to tuition fees, which is one cause of low attendance. According to the Party Secretary in Jinyang, 85 percent of the families can-not pay the school fees out of their own incomes. In rural areas, the school buildings are in such need of repairs that they are no longer usable for edu-cational purposes.

The healthcare system is hardly in a better condition. The cooperative medical service system, in which every village member pays a small sum into a healthcare fund, fell apart in the 1980s; since then, most trained med-ical personnel have left the county, and most of the township clinics have closed down. By 2002, there were no Normal University–certified physi-cians left in the entire county, and only a fifth of the villages had basic health-care provisions (injections, basic medicines, measuring blood pressure, etc.).

TABLE 3.1 Businesses in the Individual Sector, Jinyang County, 2002

Business	Households	
Agriculture, forestry, etc.	—	—
Construction	—	—
Mining	8	(0.8 %)
Manufacturing	58	(5.7 %)
Repair	31	(3.0 %)
Service	136	(13.4 %)
Transportation	12	(1.2 %)
Trade, food service	772	(75.9 %)
Other	—	—
Total	1,017	(100%)

SOURCE: Bureau for the Administration of Industry and Commerce, Jinyang County.

The costs of treatment and medication have become so high that few can afford to visit a doctor. As a result, bimo and suni have become the most important medical care providers, but they are unable to do much against commonly occurring epidemics such as cholera.[1]

A large-scale national program started in the 1990s to combat poverty intends to eliminate extreme poverty by the year 2010. Among other things, the program will implement measures to renew villages by providing new housing with access to electricity and drinking water, resettle residents from areas with very poor social conditions into better areas, and develop educational and healthcare systems. Jinyang is one of the 592 poverty counties nationwide and one of 11 in Liangshan Prefecture slated to receive additional funding from the central and provincial governments (see *Jinyang xian renmin zhengfu* 2001).

In 1980, there was only one registered individual company in Jinyang; however, by mid-2002, due to the campaign to facilitate the process of registering enterprises, there were 1,017 businesses, with a workforce of 1,765 people. Table 3.1 shows the distribution of businesses in Jinyang.

As in all counties, the tertiary sector (trade, service industries) dominates private entrepreneurship in Jinyang. Of the employees, 59 percent are Han and 41 percent are Yi. Table 3.2 contains the educational level of the individual company owners.

TABLE 3.2 Educational Level of Individual Entrepreneurs,
Jinyang County, 2001

Type of school	Persons	
None	27	2.35(%)
Primary	381	33.3(%)
Middle (junior)	487	42.5(%)
Middle (senior)	207	18.1(%)
Occupational middle	35	3.05(%)
Polytechnic	8	0.7(%)
University	—	—
Total	1,145	100(%)

SOURCE: Bureau for the Administration of Industry and Commerce, Jinyang County.

From table 3.2 we see that the majority of Yi individual company owners have attended only primary or junior secondary school, whereas Han typically attend junior or senior secondary school.

There were only three large companies in Jinyang County, with a total of 115 employees; a company for processing raw materials, a cement factory, and a large restaurant—the owners of all three were Han.

The Bureau for the Administration of Industry and Commerce in Jinyang stated that because many of them were not registered, the actual number of companies was higher than recorded, and our survey in Jinyang confirmed this. Moreover, we were informed that most of the rural firms registered as collectively owned were actually private companies. There were no state companies.

In 2001, the county revenue was 7.27 million yuan (about US$900,000)—the highest in county history—and 63.7 percent of it came from the private sector. Officially, the county administration has a preferential policy toward nonlocal investors, including tax reductions and/or exemptions as well as discretionary fee payments. The policy expressly prohibits imposing additional government charges on external (Han) investors,[2] but Han entrepreneurs in Jinyang complain about the authoritarian assessment of taxes and fees. We were told that Han from other areas have to pay significantly higher taxes and charges than local Yi. But even Yi, irrespective of where they come from, complain about taxes and charges; entrepreneurs we spoke to in Jinyang believe that the preferential policy is not operative.

Zhaojue County: The Social Impact of Poverty

Zhaojue became a county town in 1910, at the end of the Qing era.[3] It is located 2,143 m above sea level, and two-thirds of Zhaojue County lies at elevations above 2,500 m. Copper, iron ore, coal, and limestone are among the ten most important deposits of raw materials found here. The agricultural areas are mostly on steep slopes and extensive deforestation has brought about dramatic environmental and ecological damage, including soil erosion, flooding, and landslides.

In the 1990s, 34.9 percent of the county officials, 40 percent of company employees, and 97.7 percent of the teachers in Zhaojue were Han. The four most important companies also employed between 61.7 percent and 98 percent Han (Zhaojue xian Yizu quan 1999: 38).

In 1979, when Xichang District was merged into Liangshan Prefecture, the prefectural capital was relocated from Zhaojue to Xichang city, where the population is mainly Han. Since then, state investment has mainly focused on the catchment area of Xichang, which is also mostly populated by Han; Zhaojue County has seen little increase in state investment. In the 1980s and early 1990s alone, over a thousand trained personnel emigrated from Zhaojue. Although 95 percent of Zhaojue's population is Yi,[4] of the 80 people who passed the higher education entrance examination between 1992 and 1994 not one was Yi. Few Yi families can afford to pay the secondary school fees, and secondary school attendance is a prerequisite for the general university entrance exams. Also, jobs for school dropouts in this county are few and far between.

Zhaojue counts among the poorest counties in China. An exodus of companies and personnel accompanied the transfer of administrative functions to Xichang, which in turn led to a marked drop in accrued county income and a reduction in state subsidies. The number of jobs also dropped dramatically, and a stream of young people left Zhaojue to find work. In 1992, 2,000–3,000 Yi from Zhaojue, aged 18–30 years, were long-term residents in other places. Most had had no formal education, and 80 percent of them were drug-dependent. Many lived off street crime and train robbery (from loaded cargo trains or passenger trains) or from petty theft and robbery in the larger cities of Sichuan and Yunnan (Zhaojue xian Yizu quan 1999: 140–41).

To make matters worse, drug dependency and HIV infections (as well as full-blown AIDS) have increasingly spread in Zhaojue and elsewhere.[5] A 1995 study suggested that Zhaojue had become the largest center for narcotics traffic and drug dependency in Liangshan. At that time, 2,846 people in Zhaojue were thought to consume drugs (heroin and opium), including 1.4 percent of the population aged 20–30 years. Drug dependency was widespread even among the officials; 106 cadres, including 42 county-level officials, were heroin users.[6] In addition, many young women began to work in the sex industry.[7]

In Chengdu and Kunming, the provincial capitals of Sichuan and Yunnan respectively, criminal gangs from Zhaojue have become a problem for public safety.[8] As a result, Zhaojue County has acquired a bad reputation, and people from Zhaojue have difficulty finding jobs outside the county; this has also negatively influenced investment in Zhaojue.

Ma Linying, a Yi scholar researching the counties most affected by drug consumption, argues that only very few people are aware that they are breaking the law by growing, possessing, consuming, and selling illegal drugs. She suggests that in Zhaojue, people are unfamiliar with the state laws against drugs (Ma Linying 1999: 92). In fact, local people simply regard selling drugs a profitable business activity and argue that, after all, the state promotes individual business activities. Consequently, many illegal substances are openly offered and sold on the official market. Some of these substances are thought to be cure-all medications against "one hundred illnesses"; they are also attributed with the power to protect people against disasters. It has become a status symbol to give these substances as gifts, and they are highly valued for consumption on ritual occasions such as marriages and funeral wakes (ibid.; see also Ma Linying 2000). Widespread poverty and lack of employment are the primary reasons for these social problems. Agricultural activity is limited, and there are few jobs in industry or in the service sector.

Questions of ethnic identity are another cause of the social problems. Social research findings suggest that violent juvenile crime is caused by problems associated with social recognition. Both the victims' fear during the crime and the public attention generated by it create something akin to recognition or respect, even if it is in a negative sense, and this serves to acknowledge and define the perpetrator's identity. Although this method of searching for an identity is an unconscious process, the theory appears to be applicable in the case of juvenile crime in Zhaojue.

In the late 1990s, religious sects became particularly influential in Zhaojue County, a phenomenon that is also linked to the social problems in the area. In 1996, a chiliastic movement organized by a charismatic leader (Ch: *mentuhui*) spread quickly in Zhaojue; its followers were apparently waiting for the end of the world. The movement became active in 24 out of 47 townships in the county and infiltrated township and village leadership as well.

TABLE 3.3 Enterprises in the Individual Sector, Zhaojue County, 1991–1999

Year	Total Enterprises	Total Labor	Yi Enterprises	Yi Labor
1991	723	915	325 (45.0 %)	640 (69.9 %)
1992	1,062	1,349	498 (46.9 %)	593 (44.0 %)
1993	1,111	1,214	510 (45.9 %)	530 (43.7 %)
1994	1,163	1,580	518 (44.5 %)	770 (48.7 %)
1995	1,211	1,641	562 (46.4 %)	736 (44.9 %)
1996	1,373	1,845	603 (43.9 %)	825 (44.7 %)
1997	1,451	1,917	656 (45.2 %)	862 (45.0 %)
1998	1,133	2,109	516 (45.5 %)	849 (40.3 %)
1999	1,110	1,326	487 (43.9 %)	594 (44.8 %)

SOURCE: Bureau for the Administration of Industry and Commerce, Zhaojue County.

Although massive official state intervention appears to have been successful in combating the phenomenon, the underlying social causes have not been removed.

The private economic sector in Zhaojue is also underdeveloped; the private companies that *do* exist are mostly small and offer few jobs. According to the deputy chair of the Chamber of Commerce, only one out of the seven largest entrepreneurs in Zhaojue was Yi (the owner of a phosphate factory). Of the 1,483 individual firms, Yi owned slightly over 50 percent. The Chamber of Commerce places the blame for the poor investment climate and the county's poor reputation on the low number of private companies. One county-level cadre who preferred to remain anonymous remarked that "the only people who invest here are those who have evaded taxes elsewhere or have made themselves liable to prosecution in some other way." The few people who finish secondary school attempt to leave Zhaojue. The same local (Han) entrepreneur declared, "Hardly any Yi workers have a school education, and most of the local Han only have a primary school education."

The development of the private sector in Zhaojue is represented in tables 3.3 and 3.4. The tertiary sector dominates in Zhaojue as it does elsewhere. Entrepreneurs complain that while there are tax reductions and exemptions for investors from outside the county, many local government departments levy extremely high charges against locals (a problem that I shall address later in this work).

TABLE 3.4 Businesses in the Individual Sector, Zhaojue County, 2000

Business	Households and percentage	
Agriculture, forestry, etc.	—	—
Construction	—	—
Mining	—	—
Manufacturing	88	(7.5 %)
Repair	100	(8.5 %)
Service	136	(13.4 %)
Transportation	116	(9.9 %)
Trade, food service	739	(63.0 %)
Other	13	(1.1 %)
Total	1,173	(100%)

SOURCE: Bureau for the Administration of Industry and Commerce, Zhaojue County.

Butuo County: A Weak Private Sector

Butuo County was founded in 1955; the county town itself is situated at more than 2,000 m above sea level.[9] A leading Nuosu county official described Butuo by remarking that "the traces of a slave-owning society are still relatively strong here."[10] He was referring to the poverty, the low level of industrialization, and the major role of the clans in organizing social life as well as the common clashes among them. According to this functionary, the main problem for Yi in Butuo was finding sufficient nutrition and clothing. Market-oriented thinking amongst the Nuosu is considered to be low, as illustrated by the comment, "If a Han asked to buy a chicken from a Yi, the Yi wouldn't agree to sell it to him. After all, why would he sell something he owns?" As a peculiarity of the Nuosu in Butuo, the functionary mentioned that far more animals are slaughtered for funeral wakes in Butuo than in other counties (as a continuation of traditional behavior), and that the local Yi are still more "courageous" (i.e., traditionally minded) than elsewhere. Also, local Nuosu seem to possess large amounts of silver in the form of jewelry passed down through the generations, another sign of ongoing traditions.

Due to the mountainous terrain, agriculture is limited and animal husbandry (of sheep and goats) constitutes the dominant land use. The local businesses are mostly run by Han from outside the county; in 2001, 70–80 percent of the individual firms in Butuo were owned by non-local Han. In 2000, the average annual cash income per capita of the peasant population was 428 yuan (about US$52), which ranks Butuo's average income as the third lowest in the prefecture.

In 2000, the county's financial income was 10 million yuan (US$1.22 million), of which 30 percent came from the private sector. All the state industrial manufacturing firms (i.e., firms owned by the county), including leather processing, spirits, and sugar manufacturing firms, had closed down by 2000, and collective rural enterprises (Ch: *xiangzhen qiye*) had never existed. A former employee of the spirits factory told us that in the final days before the company closed down, they worked by candlelight because the company was no longer able to pay its electricity bills.

During our visit to the county town, we observed groups of Nuosu men sitting around on the streets all day, drinking and playing cards, probably as a consequence of the lack of jobs in the county. The morning street market is mostly staffed by well-dressed women who hike down from the mountains carrying baskets full of agricultural products on their backs. A Han entrepreneur declared that the Yi here were even "worse" than elsewhere, and the investment climate was "terrible"—"The local cadres do nothing but drink." He said his company was shortly going to relocate to Xichang.[11]

By the end of 2001, Butuo County officially had four private firms, with 59 employees, but it was locally believed that there were another three unregistered firms. In previous years, too, the number of registered firms had fluctuated between three and four. At the end of 2000, there were 586 individual laborers (owners of small businesses, 450 of them in the county town) and 838 employees (662 in the county town). These figures demonstrate that non-agrarian economic life was concentrated in the very small county town and there were still very few individual firms and no private companies in other parts of the county.

Table 3.5 shows an unmistakable drop in individual enterprises in Butuo after 1998 and slight increases in 2000 and 2001; the numbers dropped markedly especially in the manufacturing, transport, and trade sectors. There is no explicit explanation for these changes but 1998 was clearly a year of economic crisis more generally, because the average income fell in many other counties as well. Similar to Zhaojue, Butuo has become a center for intravenous drug use, drug trafficking, and HIV transmission. In 2001, officials estimated that up to 20 deaths each year were caused by heroin overdose and that hundreds of residents had HIV (Rosenthal 2001).

TABLE 3.5. Businesses (and Persons) in the Individual Sector,
Butuo County, 1998–2001

Sector	1998		1999		2000		2001	
Agriculture, forestry, etc.	—	—	—	—	—	—	—	—
Construction	1	(17)	—	—	—	—	—	—
Mining	3	(14)	3	(14)	3	(14)	2	(6)
Manufacturing	80	(119)	42	(81)	47	(87)	55	(120)
Service	46	(88)	47	(89)	51	(93)	51	(82)
Transportation	19	(22)	25	(30)	25	(30)	9	(11)
Trade, food service	507	(1124)	355	(407)	428	(553)	451	(603)
Other	—	—	—	—	—	—	—	—
Total	688	1445	579	846	586	838	589	843

SOURCE: Bureau for the Administration of Industry and Commerce, Butuo County.

Meigu County: The Rapid Development of a Private Economy

Meigu County was established in 1952 and the county town lies about 2,000 m above sea level.[12] Meigu is considered to be the center of Yi culture and some scholars call it the Mecca (Ch: *Maijia*) of the Yi or the "homeland of bimo culture" (Ch: *bimo wenhua zhixiang*). About 8,400 bimo live in Meigu and constitute approximately 4 percent of the population.[13] With an average per capita annual income of 917 yuan, Meigu is included among the poverty counties but the private sector here is relatively well developed. At the end of 2001, there were 920 registered individual firms, with 1,140 workers, and nine private companies, with 1,232 employees.

At the end of 2000, 14 firms, with 798 employees were registered at the Bureau for the Administration of Rural Enterprises in Meigu, but in September 2001, the Bureau for the Administration of Industry and Commerce recorded nine companies, with 1,232 employees. The Chamber of Commerce (Ch: *shanghui*) in Meigu provided a list of 23 firms, of which 17 were Yi-owned companies. It became clear during our survey that the number of existing firms was significantly higher than the number of registered firms, and this was due to a few different reasons. First, the differences among the statistics reported by different branches of the local government (tables 3.6 and 3.7) illustrate the difficulty of collecting and working with official data

TABLE 3.6 Individual and Private Enterprises, Meigu County, 1996–2001

Year	Individual Enterprises	Persons Employed	Private Enterprises	Persons Employed
1996	1,100	1,299	11	1,200
1997	1,195	1,420	11	1,200
1998	1,258	1,483	9	1,483
1999	1,150	1,340	5	1,340
2000	1,150	1,340	5	1,340
2001	920	1,140	9	1,232

SOURCE: Bureau for the Administration of Industry and Commerce, Meigu County.

TABLE 3.7 Individual and Private Enterprises, Meigu County, 1996–2000

Year	Individual Enterprises	Persons Employed	Private Enterprises	Persons Employed
1996	581	946	2	68
1997	673	1,163	5	190
1998	782	1,601	6	228
1999	843	1,860	10	430
2000	862	2,027	14	798

SOURCE: Bureau for the Administration of Rural Enterprises, Meigu County.

in China. For example, in table 3.6, the number of individual enterprises remains constant for 1999 and 2000, and the number of private enterprises remains constant for 1996 and 1997 as well as for 1999 and 2000; it is highly unlikely that the reported figures are precise.

Second, according to the Bureau for the Administration of Industry and Commerce, there was a sharp drop in the figures for the private sector in the first half of 2001. The Bureau explained this drop by saying that some entrepreneurs who were originally from outside Meigu had returned to their home counties. However, when more than a fifth of the entrepreneurs suddenly emigrate, there must be other factors at work. Our conversations with the entrepreneurs revealed that new forestry regulations forbidding private tree harvesting had caused a series of small private firms to close down, affecting timber trade and processing. The number of mines also dropped from 15 in the year 2000 to only one in September 2001. Mine closure was enforced after an official survey showed that numerous mines did not meet the new safety regulation standards. In addition, the number of firms in the manufacturing industry fell from 91 to 15, and in the trade and catering sector there was a decrease from 876 to 738 firms. Since the trade and service industries revolve around the dominant timber and mining sectors, decreases in trade and services are related to trends in timber and mining sectors. Shortages in electricity and capital also factor into the difficulties facing Meigu entrepreneurs.

Nevertheless, there is an alternative explanation for the decrease in the number of individual and private enterprises. In 1998, the Meigu Party Committee published a document on the development of "rural firms," giving only marginal attention to the private sector, which includes a portion of the rural firms (*Zhonggong Meigu xianwei wenjian* 1998). The document stated that it was necessary to strengthen the "cooperative system of shares with all possible force." Local government, companies, and individuals (including party and government cadres) were encouraged to acquire shares in such cooperatives, and shares could also be purchased in the form of real estate. The document declared that this would allow many firms to be classified as collectives rather than as private firms; and this would thereby have reduced the number of private firms.

The Nuosu chairman of the Federation of Industry and Commerce (the association for entrepreneurs) stated that he was aware of only six large private entrepreneurs in Meigu. Two of them, a phosphate fertilizer producer and a department store, had declared bankruptcy. The other entrepreneurs included owners of two construction firms with 54 and 65 employees each, a food factory with 20 staff, and a phosphate fertilizer factory employing 12. Five of the entrepreneurs were Han from outside the county; only one was a Yi from Meigu.

In contrast, the Bureau for the Administration of Rural Enterprises supplied us with the names and addresses of 23 private companies, 9 of which were owned by Han and 14 by Yi. However, only 13 of the 21 entrepreneurs we interviewed were on this list. Thus, the number of private companies actually in existence can safely be assumed to be significantly higher than the number reported; we may safely say that there are at least 30 of them.

While the Bureau for the Administration of Industry and Commerce reported 876 firms and 2,825 employees in the entire private sector, the Bureau for the Administration of Rural Enterprises reported 903 firms and 2,700 employees for the first half of 2001. The disparity is due to the fact that the latter only registers firms owned by entrepreneurs with rural residence permits (Ch: *hukou*). According to this office, no state or collective companies exist in the rural areas of Meigu. However, during the course of our conversation it became clear that the director of this office had difficulties separating the various forms of ownership from each other.

Furthermore, some private companies may be unregistered because the State Council permits entrepreneurs in ethnic minority areas to wait to apply for a business license until after a one- or two-year start-up and trial period. In contrast to other counties, Meigu County actually applies this policy. The county administration's flexible treatment of the private sector, especially the locals, may also be a reason why there were considerably more private entrepreneurs in Meigu than in other counties. Similar to other counties, Meigu grants investors advantages (lower charges for real estate and electricity, and tax reductions). In fact, the County Party Committee explicitly requires the county administration to provide concrete support and guidance to individuals with founding and running rural firms (*Zhonggong Meigu xianwei wenjian* 1998).

However, the chair of the Federation of Industry and Commerce complains that there are too few tax reductions for private entrepreneurs. The entrepreneurs also criticize the county administration, claiming that it is commonly not able to pay its bills. Apparently, the county administration supports and favors local Yi entrepreneurs over Han entrepreneurs from out of the county. If and when privileges such as tax advantages are granted, they go to Yi rather than to Han entrepreneurs. In Meigu as in other counties, most of the larger private entrepreneurs are Han from outside the county. According to the chairman of the Federation of Industry and Commerce, around 40 percent of individual firm owners were Han who were not born in Meigu. In the county town itself, 46 of the 220 (i.e., 20.9%) individual firm owners were Yi. In contrast, the Bureau for the Administration of Rural Enterprises stated that in 2000, 4 of the 14 private entrepreneurs were Yi (28.6%) and that in the rural areas, Yi made up 92.7 percent of individual firm owners. Han were concentrated in the county town and in larger townships, and Yi in rural areas. In 1999, the tax income from the private sector was 2.35 million yuan, which was 32.5 percent of Meigu's total tax revenue of about 7.24 million yuan.

All in all, policies regarding private entrepreneurship in Meigu are more positive than in most other counties. Despite many problems, Meigu apparently has understood how to promote the private sector in rural areas and how to utilize this sector for combating poverty. Accordingly, the business development plan for the county includes support for the "non-state," that is, the private, sector (*Minzu* October 2002: 47). The county government, for instance, granted private companies a series of fiscal advantages and advisory services; second, there was a specific county plan for the long-term development and consolidation of the private sector.

Is there a relationship between the strength of Meigu's traditional Nuosu culture—as evident in clan strength and religious traditions—and Meigu's success and relative prosperity compared to Zhaojue, Butuo, and Jinyang? According to the local people, drug addiction and crime are not as rampant in Meigu as in many other counties, and it is arguable that a comparatively intact culture contributes to the stability of local Nuosu communities. The locals in Meigu, including officials and entrepreneurs, appear to be more proud of traditional Nuosu culture than people in counties with a high percentage of Han, such as Ganluo or Mianning, or where local traditions have been eliminated by political movements, such as in Zhaojue, the former prefectural capital, where local traditions were strongly criticized and put under greater pressure than in other counties. The simultaneous influx of Han officials and experts into Zhaojue might have further contributed to a loss of pride in local Nuosu culture. In contrast, local culture is explicitly promoted in Meigu; for example, county government regulations require new buildings to be built in the Yi style (with specific paintings, roofs, and roof joist construction). The maintenance of traditions thus appears to create more stable communities and to foster more stable development processes.

Ganluo County: Mining and Exploitative Cadres

Ganluo County was first established in 1956. Because of its rich mineral deposits, mining plays an important role in the county's economy. Ganluo is also connected to the railway network via the line between Chengdu and Kunming.[14]

In Ganluo there were officially only "town and township enterprises" (Ch: *xiangzhen qiye*); no private companies were recorded at the time of our study. However, according to the Nuosu head of Ganluo's Chamber of Commerce (Ch: *shanghui*), all enterprises in the county were actually privately owned. There were two reasons for the classification of private companies as *xiangzhen* enterprises: the majority of the private firms operated in the mining sector, and the state prohibits private companies in the mining business whereas *xiangzhen* enterprises are permitted to mine. Since there were no more state companies in Ganluo and private firms represented the main source of income, the county administration allowed all private companies

TABLE 3.8 Businesses and Ethnicity of Entrepreneurs, Ganluo County, 1999

Business	Total	Yi	
Mining	141	24	(17.0 %)
Mining product processing	25	11	(44.0 %)
Smelting	16	4	(25.0 %)
Other (food processing, construction)	23	7	(30.4 %)
Total	205	46	(22.4 %)

SOURCE: Chamber of Commerce, Ganluo County.

to be classified as *xiangzhen* companies. This placed them under the administrative jurisdiction of the bureau for town and township enterprises (Ch: *xiangzhen qiye guanli ju*). Another reason for the change in classification was that Ganluo County policies promoted and gave preference to *xiangzhen* enterprises over private enterprises, and it was therefore advantageous for entrepreneurs to be classified as *xiangzhen* companies, even if they were then subject to stricter controls by the authorities.

The Ganluo Chamber of Commerce could only impart information about member companies, and apparently almost all large private companies were members. The smaller, individual laborers came under the jurisdiction of the Bureau for the Administration of Industry and Commerce.

According to the Ganluo Chamber of Commerce, there were 179 larger private firms, with 3,624 staff in Ganluo at the end of 1998. The Bureau for the Administration of Industry and Commerce claims that the number of firms and employees had increased continually since 1989. According to the Bureau for the Administration of Industry and Commerce, in 1999, the individual sector was said to comprise 3,387 self-employed people, with 3,620 staff, mostly in trade (60.4%), mining and manufacturing (13.3%), and catering (8.8%). Table 3.8 presents the 1999 distribution of entrepreneurs according to business types and ethnic groups.

Ganluo contains major deposits of lead, zinc, silver, fluorite, copper, iron ore, and bauxite, as well as various nonmetallic minerals such as gypsum, magnesium carbonate, sulfur, aluminum silicate, arsenic ore (a red pigment), and phosphorus. Mining and associated spheres are economically dominant here, while the proportion of other industries is relatively small. Ganluo thus has a very one-sided sector structure.

The Yi population of Ganluo county town possesses a markedly higher

FIG. 4. *Workers leaving a private lead mine, Ganluo County*

level of education compared to Yi in other county towns because Ganluo has had a school system since before the founding of the People's Republic. Thus, it was surprising to find that the percentage of companies owned by Yi entrepreneurs was smaller than the percentage of Yi within the population; although Yi made up 65 percent of the population, only 22 percent of the entrepreneurs were Yi.

The newspaper *Liangshan Daily* reported the closure of illegal mines in Ganluo County a few years ago (*Liangshan Ribao*, 20 August 2001); these mines usually did not follow the minimum safety regulations, leading to serious accidents. Some entrepreneurs will take over such mines in order to quickly accumulate capital, which they use to set up new companies in "safer" sectors. Such entrepreneurs follow a pattern similar to the "cut-and-run" entrepreneurism practiced elsewhere in China—after rapidly making short-term profits in one enterprise, they move on to new enterprises.

However, the costs of taking over these mines are very high, and to compensate the new owner for these costs, the county administration gives these companies a tax exemption for three years. Such mining serves only individual and short-term interests; it destroys the environment, ruins the landscape, and wastes resources. Quite a few of these factories pollute and even poison the environment and the nearby arable agricultural land. Moreover, some mines have unsatisfactory working conditions; for example, young workers in lead mines were found working only in swimming trunks without any form of protection.

In the Ganluo county town, there is an Office for the Development of the Non-State Economy, i.e., the private sector (CH: *fazhan feigong youzhi bangongshi*). This office was always closed. One look inside through the windows revealed that the development of this sector was not receiving much attention. Lying about on the desk inside were tiles used in *majiang*, the popular Chinese gambling game better known as Mah-jong in the West; the floor was covered with empty liquor bottles and cigarette packets.

The biggest private entrepreneur in the county was the brother of the director of the Bureau for the Administration of Rural Enterprises; the deputy director of this Bureau was also a major private entrepreneur. The direct connection between enterprises and the administrative authorities is unmistakable. Notwithstanding such relations, entrepreneurs have their own set of complaints against the administration.

The greatest complaint from entrepreneurs concerns the exploitative system of levying taxes (there are at least twenty types of charges), which has caused many to leave the county. Entrepreneurs have even been required to "donate" money to the county government to pay the wages of the local cadres. Also, the local government pays no attention to the private entrepreneurs' business concerns. A Han entrepreneur observed, "When my company is doing poorly, the government doesn't pay any attention. When it's doing well, they pay a great deal of attention!" If a company is prospering, payments and "gifts" must be made on a regular basis, and officials regularly borrow large sums of money from the entrepreneurs without paying them back. To take legal action is considered a waste of time. "If we did that," declared a Yi entrepreneur, "we would be finished; we would have to fear the revenge of the local cadres. Besides, the courts don't take on civil law cases."[15] A leading Han member of the Chamber of Commerce stated, "The only profitable sector here is mining. For entrepreneurs in other sectors, the circumstances are extremely difficult. The officials cause problems everywhere; there are too many taxes and charges. The bureaucracy interferes everywhere and skims off part of the profits for themselves. There are practically no possibilities for development."[16]

Entrepreneurs also develop strategies for circumventing some of these exploitative measures, for example, by evading taxes. One particular tax evasion tactic is conspicuously widespread in this county as well as in others— companies are declared to be "firms for the disabled" in order to exempt them from tax payments. Most of these firms, however, employ disabled people on a nominal basis and pay them wages without actually giving them any work to do.

Reports of criminal gangs who attack mines and rob their employees underscore the fact that public security is also a great problem. One newspaper report counted at least forty recorded cases of this kind in Ganluo County in recent years (*Minzu* August 2002: 22–23).

Mianning County: Successes and Burdens

Mianning County has existed since the first century BC and has been called Mianning since 1729 (*Mianning xianzhi* 1994). In 1998, there were 4,785 individual firm owners, with 5,395 registered employees. In contrast to the previous year, the number of small entrepreneurs decreased by 12.7 percent in 1998 (from 697 to 608), and the number of employees in small firms went down by 20 percent, from 6,735 to 5,388. As in most other counties, the Asian Crisis, a general economic lull, and a chronic shortage of capital forced countless small entrepreneurs to go out of business. In 1999, the number of small (individual) firms increased to 4,937, with 5,564 staff; they were divided among various businesses as shown in table 3.9.

The transportation sector in Mianning is particularly strong because of the relatively good links and proximity to the road and railway networks; the strong mining industry, which requires significant logistical infrastructure in the form of transportation; and Mianning's proximity to areas of sightseeing interest. China's major spaceflight center is located in Mianning County (though everyone refers to it as being located in Xichang), a fact that has led to the construction of modern roads connecting Mianning with Xichang, and one of Mianning's major townships is also directly connected to the newly constructed freeway between Mianning and Xichang. All these conditions provide a favorable climate and the required infra-

TABLE 3.9 Businesses in the Individual Sector, Mianning County, 1999

Business	Households		Persons	
Construction	8	(0.2 %)	107	(1.9 %)
Manufacturing	314	(6.3 %)	417	(7.5 %)
Mining	12	(0.2 %)	98	(1.8 %)
Service	1,164	(23.6 %)	1,432	(25.7 %)
Trade, food service	2,309	(46.8 %)	2,376	(42.7 %)
Transportation	1,117	(22.6 %)	1,117	(20.1 %)
Other	13	(0.3 %)	20	(0.3 %)
Total	4,937	(100 %)	5,564	(100 %)

SOURCE: Bureau for the Administration of Industry and Commerce, Mianning County.

TABLE 3.10 Yi Engagement in the Individual Economy, Mianning County, 1999

Business	Households	Yi (%)	Persons Yi	
Construction	—	—	—	
Manufacturing	69	22.0	83	(19.9 %)
Mining	4	33.3	32	(32.65 %)
Service	220	18.9	224	(15.6 %)
Trade, food service	689	29.8	698	(29.4 %)
Transportation	213	19.1	240	(21.5 %)
Total	1,195	24.2	1,277	(22.95 %)

SOURCE: Bureau for the Administration of Industry and Commerce, Mianning County.

structure for private entrepreneurs. And yet, in the individual sector in 1999, less than a quarter of the firms were owned by Yi.

In Mianning as in Ganluo, the Bureau for the Administration of Rural Enterprises produced different figures from those produced by the Bureau for the Administration of Industry and Commerce, reporting 5,414 rural individual and private firms, with 15,510 employees, in 1998. Also in 1998, the Bureau for the Administration of Rural Enterprises reported 59 registered private companies, with 2,039 employees. This figure grew to 77 firms, with 2,468 staff, by June 1999. Table 3.11 shows the breakdown according to lines of business.

TABLE 3.11 Businesses in the Private Sector, Mianning County, 1999

Business	Enterprises	Yi owners	Employees	Yi
Agriculture, forestry, etc.	2	—	15	—
Construction	6	1 (16.7%)	381	67 (17.6%)
Manufacturing	32	8 (25.0%)	779	176 (22.6%)
Mining	29	7 (24.1%)	1,056	250 (23.7%)
Service	3	—	37	—
Trade, food service	5	—	200	—
Total	77	16 (65.8%)	2,468	493 (63.9%)

SOURCE: Bureau for the Administration of Industry and Commerce, Mianning County.

In Mianning, as in other counties, mining and related lines of business predominate over the larger private sector, and Yi are proportionally underrepresented not only among entrepreneurs but also among the staff. As in Ganluo, entrepreneurs complain about excessive taxes and other charges, albeit to a lesser extent; here too, the authorities pay their bills either late or not at all.

Even officials complain that the investment climate and environment is poor, adding that they would not advise anyone to invest here. The county and township cadres' practice of forcefully charging fees has been copied at the village level, as was observed first-hand in a number of villages. In one village, the village population blocked the road and demanded a "transit toll" from every car traveling through. In another village, the street conditions were so poor (possibly created as such deliberately) that village residents waited at the roadside with shovels, hoes, and other tools and charged the travelers a fee for the service of getting cars out of the mud. This method of obtaining extra income is reminiscent of circumstances here up until the 1950s, when, on the way from Xichang to Zhaojue (a distance of about 100 km), Han had to pay "protection money" in order to travel without hindrance.

Puge County: An Emphasis on Tourism Development

Puge County was established in 1952 (Puge xianzhi 1992) and officially dubbed itself a "tourism county" (Ch: *lüyou xian*) in 2001, with a focus on developing the tourism industry in Puge. A large square was built above the county town, and plans were developed to build an adjacent modern hotel.

The idea was that tourists from other parts of China and abroad would come here every year to celebrate the annual torch festival. In addition, Luojing Mountain (Luojingshan) was to be developed for tourists by building an artificial temple, pagodas, and pavilions on it. A modern hotel not far from the county town was only sparsely filled during our stay.

These plans for expanding tourism were built on the hope that tourists could be attracted to Puge from nearby Mount Emei (Emeishan), which traditionally is one of Sichuan's main tourist attractions. However, Mount Emei has been progressively developed over a considerable period of time and is a well-known religious center with historic sights whereas in Puge, a brand-new tourist infrastructure needs to be built. A new tourist amusement park there consists of some benches, a restaurant, many colorful little flags, and a handful of shrubs, and is anything but attractive to tourists. The "focus on tourism" in the county's development plans had already led to the neglect of the private sector, which consequently is in a bleak state.

In an attempt to obtain information on entrepreneurism in Puge, we sought out the head of the Bureau for the Administration of Industry and Commerce, a Han. We encountered him in an inebriated state during working hours at a private restaurant in a township not far from the county town, where he was drinking with some of his colleagues. He promised to organize some information for our research, but nothing came of it. In the afternoon, we encountered him once again getting drunk in the amusement park, this time in the company of the local police chief and a young female colleague from Mianning County, with whom he flirted excitedly. He invited us to have dinner with him and, because he was drunk, he kept spilling alcohol on us and also demanding aggressively that we drink with him. We left, saying we were tired and not feeling well. He consequently excused himself for the following few days and let it be known that his department did not possess any data concerning the private sector. Thus, no statistics were obtained from the Bureau for the Administration of Industry and Commerce in Puge.

As in other counties, Puge's economy dropped dramatically in 1998 and had not recovered by the time we visited in 2001 (see table 3.12). The deputy director of the Bureau for the Administration of Rural Enterprises stated that of the 1,600 registered individual firms only 400 were actually still in business. Of the nine larger private firms, two had recently closed their doors, so that now there were only seven. Only one of the seven owners was Yi although, in 2001, 31.9 percent of the individual laborers were Yi. Here too, numerous entrepreneurs felt themselves to be disadvantaged and complained that officials and local governments did not pay their bills.

TABLE 3.12 Businesses and Employees in the Individual Sector,
Puge County, 1995–2001

Year	1995	1996	1997	1998	1999	2001
Businesses	1,894	2,403	2,500	1,227	1,436	1,603
Employees	2,323	2,877	2,980	1,388	1,636	2,403

SOURCE: Bureau for the Administration of Rural Enterprises, Puge County.

Yanyuan County: The Perils of Monoculture

Yanyuan has borne its current name since 1728 and is a county of very old standing (Yanyuan xianzhi 2000). Among other things, it is known for Lugu Lake, home to the Mosuo people, who are famed for their matriarchal society. Half of the lake belongs to Yanyuan County; the other half lies in Yunnan Province.

About one-half of Yanyuan's agricultural population is Han, and apple growing is the primary cash-earning agricultural activity, though there is more land in rice, buckwheat, and potatoes than in apple orchards. As a result of a fall in apple prices, the county tax revenue decreased dramatically in the late 1990s; the tax revenue in 1999 was 3 million yuan less than in 1998, and for months at a time, the civil servants' salaries could not be paid. The prohibition of private timber harvesting and a mining crisis resulting from the larger Asian economic crisis were also partly responsible for the drop in income.

A local Yi functionary reported that in 1937, Yanyuan employed 70 civil servants for 80,000 inhabitants, or one civil servant per 1,143 people. In the year 2000, the county employed 7,000 cadres for a population of 312,000, or one cadre for every 44.5 people. The cadres' pay swallows up practically the entire county's income! Consequently, the township schools are in a poor state and school attendance is extremely low (about 30%, though official statistics show over 96% enrolled), because many parents cannot afford to pay the high fees for schools.

In Yanyuan, both Yi and Han entrepreneurship are not well developed. There is a large gray area of statistically unrecorded but entrepreneurially active people, who, because of the favorable conditions for agriculture and unfavorable conditions for industry due to poor roads, primarily work in the agricultural sector. However, these occupations can certainly be classified within the scope of private entrepreneurship.

Many agricultural entrepreneurs complain about low market prices, high taxes and levies, as well as the chronic state of disrepair of the roads, which contributes to poor apple sales. Mines are among the county's main revenue sources, and the county administration has allocated a fixed tax rate for mining, which entrepreneurs have to pay even if, according to a county cadre, they have to take out a bank loan to do so. Many entrepreneurs also complain about the shortsightedness of local policies: as soon as a small company is founded, the local government pounces on the entrepreneur and demands high payments. A study carried out by the Bureau for the Administration of Industry and Commerce in 2000 confirmed this.

The structure of the economic sectors is extremely one-sided as it is primarily based on apple growing and mining. However, in 2000, even apple processing was underdeveloped. According to official figures, there were 16 private firms in 1999, with 475 employees, and 2,010 individual firms, with 2,661 staff. In 2000, due to the crisis in the apple market and in mining, and the closure of private timber firms, the number of private firms decreased to 12 (-25% change) and the number of employees decreased by 35.2 percent, while the number of individual firms decreased by 24 percent, to 1,528, and the number of employees fell by 18.9 percent.

Xide County

Xide County was founded in 1952 (Xide xianzhi 1992). The county retains 6,000 officials to administrate a population of 134,500 (1992: 2,209; and information received from the Statistical Bureau of Xide County on 18 August 2002), and at the time of our research, about 60 percent of the tax income came from the private sector. Additional data were not available for Xide.

COUNTY COMPARISONS

Because different counties have different ways of categorizing and recording business statistics, the data they provided on private enterprises are not easily comparable. Ganluo is a classic example: officially, no private enterprises exist here because they have been reclassified by the local authorities as township enterprises. Different county authorities, such as the Bureau for the Administration of Industry and Commerce and the Bureau for the Administration of Rural Enterprises, provide widely differing statistics. Despite such disparities, we have included the data in our analysis, not as an accurate representation of reality but as a depiction of general trends in the development of the private sector.

TABLE 3.13 Populations of Surveyed Liangshan Counties, 2001

County	Population	Yi (%)
Butuo	139,606	93.7
Ganluo	181,222	65.0
Jinyang	136,684	77.3
Meigu	177,573	98.1
Mianning	320,073	32.0
Puge	141,048	75.3
Xide	134,540	85.1
Yanyuan	318,647	46.0
Zhaojue	205,163	96.9

SOURCE: *Liangshan tongji nianjian* 2001: 2.

The number of private companies in Ganluo was greater than the number in Mianning, despite Ganluo County's significantly smaller population. This is because of Ganluo's superior transport connections via road and rail networks. However, the percentage of Nuosu-owned companies in both areas was less than the corresponding population percentage of Nuosu.

In Zhaojue, Yanyuan, Butuo, Puge, Xide, and Jinyang, the private sector is underdeveloped, and the majority of private business owners are Han from other counties inside or outside Liangshan. In 2001, the private sector was in a state of crisis in most counties. The number of private companies in Zhaojue had decreased fourfold compared to the year before, and in the first half of 2000, the tax revenue from the private sector had declined by 18.5 percent. By the end of 2000, the number of private and individual companies in Yanyuan had decreased as well. However, in Yanyuan, the uneven sector structure (with a concentration on growing fruit), the decline in fruit prices, and the poor transport connections may have been responsible for the decrease. Nuosu and Han entrepreneurship are also not well developed in this set of counties. In Yanyuan however, unlike in Zhaojue, Butuo, Jinyang, Xide, and Puge, there is a stratum of agricultural entrepreneurs.

The situation in Meigu is different from that in other counties. Until the 1990s, it was one of the poorest counties in Liangshan; however, what makes Meigu different is that, unlike in some other counties, the county government did not siphon off profits from the entrepreneurs in the form of taxes and financial contributions in the interest of developing the private sector.

As a result, entrepreneurism in Meigu developed astonishingly well although the local authorities acknowledge that many firms remain unregistered or are misregistered as township- or village-owned companies in order to more rapidly further local development. In Meigu, clan strength, pride in a strong traditional culture, and the stability of local communities may also be significant stimuli for local development.

Because there are few private companies in Zhaojue, there is no clear classification of different business areas within the private sector. In Yanyuan, where the economic focus is on growing apples, many companies are involved in apple cultivation or transport. The crisis in the apple market has apparently had a negative effect on the private sector there. Partly in order to mitigate the effects of the crisis, almost all companies involved in apple growing in Yanyuan are also linked with other sectors such as growing other types of fruit, cattle rearing, transport of people and cargo, and grain processing.

The situations in Ganluo and Mianning are also different from those in other counties, primarily because the business structure in these two counties is concentrated in one area. Because of the potential for rapidly making large profits, the majority of companies either process raw materials or mine. With the exception of mining, there are few processing industries in these counties that are adapted to local conditions, such as the processing of agricultural or animal products. In contrast, in Butuo, Puge, Xide, and Jinyang, due to the low numbers of enterprises, there is no discernible business structure. Puge is different from the others, however, because its government is focusing on developing tourism and appears to be fundamentally neglecting the development of the private sector. In Meigu, there is a broad spectrum of businesses, and the mining and manufacturing industries form one of several foci.

Many entrepreneurs in Ganluo wish to leave the county. The majority of Han and Nuosu company owners feels that the investment conditions are poor partly because of infrastructure weaknesses but mainly because of excessive taxes and necessary contributions to the government. In Ganluo, entrepreneurs in the mining sector report that they pay almost 50 percent of their turnover in taxes and contributions, and they are squeezed for more money by local cadres as well. There is both corruption (extorting "donations," protection money, or "credits") and crime (theft and robbery). In addition, especially in Ganluo, the companies are subject to fixed production rates and standards for each class of company size specified under the county plan. If the county government is unable to pay the (party) officials' salaries and bonuses, companies are required to make payments toward these salaries; in total, the firms make over 20 different types of payments. Companies with a greater profit margin purchase real estate or establish branches in Chengdu or, at least, in Xichang, in order to have an option for relocation if necessary.

Local entrepreneurs and officials stated that, given that the situation was otherwise advantageous in terms of available county resources, the inferior conditions of the administrative and social frameworks were the main reason for the lack of non-local and foreign investment. Their assessment was significantly more negative in Ganluo, Zhaojue, Yanyuan, Butuo, Puge, and Xide than in Mianning and Meigu. Another core problem in all counties is the entrepreneurs' inability to obtain local credit. The likelihood of being able to get credit from outside the region is higher, but only through social connections (Ch: *guanxi*), and it is generally obtained at exorbitant interest rates.

The private sector appears at present to be the only profitable sector. Because it is the primary source of revenue for some counties, the county administrations exert heavy pressure on private companies, especially as the few remaining state-owned companies are on the verge of bankruptcy. In counties where the private sector has not developed or is in crisis, there is a high level of poverty, and the county administration is sometimes not able to pay the cadres' salaries. In 1999, a considerable portion of the companies we visited had temporarily ceased production due to the Asian Crisis, the decline (both inland and abroad) in demand for raw materials, falling prices, and a lack of access to credit.

Problems Facing Private Sector Development

As I have pointed out, all the counties we surveyed faced similar problems. An official report discussed at the Zhaojue Political Consultative Conference in August 1998 listed six core issues facing the private sector in Zhaojue County.

Interference by local cadres. Local cadres, who think poorly of the private sector and do not understand the importance of the private sector to the "socialist market economy," implement policies designed to "frighten off capital" (Ch: *kongzizheng*) and otherwise try to hinder the development of the private sector because they perceive it as antisocialist. The local cadres insinuate that individual and private entrepreneurs are guilty of copyright violations, tax evasion, and fraud, as well as a slovenly lifestyle (excessive eating and drinking, visiting prostitutes, and gambling).

Arbitrary fees. The local authorities do not seriously fight against the phenomenon of "threefold arbitrariness" (Ch: *san luan*), i.e., officials arbitrarily demand fee, taxes, and donations from entrepreneurs. Arbitrary charges, fines, and compulsory payments are levied against private companies, including forced work, forced sharing of costs, and compulsory contributions to the government (Ch: *tanpai*). The Zhaojue report named 22 types of payment collected by the government that are not part of the state's fiscal and levy systems. For example, a watchmaker spent 399.52 yuan in official taxes and fees, and 586 yuan in illegal charges in one year, and the owner of a department store was forced to pay over 20 such charges. People are forced to subscribe to magazines and newspapers published by the Party or by a government office even if they are illiterate and cannot read them.

High taxes. Another core problem is that fiscal advantages granted to the private sector are cancelled out by the many fees. For example, citizens complain that Zhaojue's taxes and charges are higher than in other counties in the prefecture. The authorities borrow large sums of money from entrepreneurs without repaying them and often do not pay their bills. In addition, preferential policies toward the private sector are not being implemented; this is true generally but particularly as mentioned in the Zhaojue report. Many companies collapse because they do not receive the credit they were promised. Each of the 20 to 30 official departments in a county requires a number of permits for activities under its jurisdiction, and they continuously conduct so-called inspections and investigations. However, these authorities only extract income; not a single government department offers any kind of consultation or other services. There is no ultimate authority with the power to control and coordinate or discipline the different departments. The private sector entrepreneurs complain that they are being treated as "third-class citizens" (Ch: *sandeng gongmin*). The official preferential policy toward the private sector stipulates that investors from other areas may turn their rural residence permits (Ch: *hukou*) into urban *hukou* if they contribute at least 5,000 yuan annually to the county financial revenue, but at the time of the report, there had not been a single case of such a transaction.

Discrimination against outsiders. Over half of the individual and private entrepreneurs are from outside Liangshan and depend on local and regional infrastructure and an adequate supply of operating capital and other necessary materials. However, the infrastructure urgently needs improvement, which puts these entrepreneurs at risk. Their personal security is also at risk; they are frequently the victims of physical attacks, vandalism, or even of organized gangs involved in large-scale theft and fraud. They are also seri-

ously discriminated against in official dispute resolution processes and seldom receive fair treatment.

Need for education. The development of the private sector is also limited
by the low level of education among entrepreneurs. Over 40 percent of the
individual and private entrepreneurs in Zhaojue County, for example, are
either illiterate or only semi-literate. Because they do not understand state
and party policies toward the private sector, they worry about potentially
unfavorable political changes.[17] Officials and entrepreneurs from other counties confirmed that these same problems, discussed in the Zhaojue Political Consultative Conference report, exist in their counties as well, and that
in almost all the counties, preferential policies toward the private sector are
not being implemented.

Government exploitation. Entrepreneurs often state that government
officials and departments do not compensate them for their goods and services, and that it is difficult to collect outstanding debts because the cadres
respond with repressive measures or threats to boycott the companies. Government officials or departments borrow money and repay their debts either
very slowly or not at all, which, in some cases, has driven entrepreneurs into
financial ruin. For example, many Nuosu timber entrepreneurs in Meigu
County report that the local, state-owned timber harvesting company bor-
rowed 3.25 million yuan from them early in the 1990s, with the agreement to
repay the sum by 1995. Neither interest nor repayment had been made at the
time of our survey in September 2001. Although a number of complaints were
filed with the relevant prefectural and provincial offices and a joint letter was
written to the deputy governor of the prefecture, the problem was never
addressed. The deputy governor responded by referring the case back to Meigu
County with instructions to resolve the issue. Consequently, the entrepreneurs were no longer able to pay their employees' wages and the employees
reacted violently by taking away the entrepreneurs' cattle and other property.

In Ganluo, an entrepreneur who was in the business of processing mineral resources complained that a small conflict between his wife and the
county party secretary had resulted in his company being closed down in
retaliation, on the grounds that it was polluting the environment.

There is also ethnic discrimination against entrepreneurs. An investigative report in 2001 revealed that in the Han areas of Liangshan, Nuosu entrepreneurs were disadvantaged in relation to Han entrepreneurs when
competing for public sector contracts or for governmental leasing contracts.
In one case, a Nuosu entrepreneur subleased fallow land to grow fruit in a
township belonging to the city of Xichang and the lease was certified by a

notary; local Han officials intervened, however, and declared the contract invalid, saying, "Land can not be subleased to Yi."

In a different township, a Nuosu who had leased a pond for fish farming was harassed by local cadres for so long that he abandoned his farming plans. In Chuanxing township in Xichang District, the Nuosu Party Secretary was beaten to death in a brutal confrontation over land rights between Nuosu peasants who did not want to give up their land and Han who wanted to exploit the area commercially; another Nuosu was beaten to death afterwards at the local police station. In Leibo County, a Nuosu construction entrepreneur had already begun construction of a new bridge when, for no apparent reason, his contract was taken away and given to a Han entrepreneur from outside the county. Construction projects are generally granted to (Han) construction entrepreneurs from other areas, who bring in their own staff, and public companies in Han areas as a rule only employ Han. The Zhaojue Political Consultative Conference report also described numerous cases in which Han entrepreneurs overcharged Nuosu villages for their services or otherwise cheated them (Hou 2001: 128–29).

Han entrepreneurs, on the other hand, complain about discrimination against them by Nuosu cadres. In Jinyang County, for instance, despite the preferential policy for private entrepreneurs, one Han entrepreneur was forced to pay 50 percent higher taxes than the locals. He noted that many local cadres own their own businesses and/or firms and pay fewer taxes because of their connections within the bureaucracy.[18] Because stipulated tax quotas have to be met, higher taxes are demanded from non-locals who have no *guanxi* (connections) in the area, and these are mostly Han. The administrative fees normally charged by the local Bureau for the Administration of Industry and Commerce (50 yuan per month) are twice as much for people from outside the area (100 yuan). The Han entrepreneur cited above also told us that he had recently been obliged to contribute 300 yuan to rebuild a power plant. This charge was levied on every private shop owner, and those who refused to pay had their electricity cut off. Over 40 such arbitrary fees are collected in Jinyang, including the "administrative per capita fee" (Ch: *rentou guanlifei*) and the "residence fee for non-locals with a provisional residence"—most of these fees are illegally charged. The Han entrepreneur said that he had made these cases known to journalists from outside the area but so far there had been no measurable improvement.

Two significant trends should be noted here. First of all, the report issued by the Political Consultative Conference in Zhaojue reveals that official arbi-

trariness and attitudes are openly condemned in even smaller county towns
in which it was assumed that the political elite (the local leadership, consisting of primarily Nuosu but also some Han cadres) would attempt to pro-
hibit negative reporting. Such complaints should be understood as a direct
criticism of the failure of the county's political leadership to change such
intolerable circumstances. Also, a fragmentation of power has taken place
within the counties. This is apparently tolerated by the county leadership,
as is the direct criticism of the leadership.

The writer of the Political Consultative Conference report was not only
the chairperson of the Zhaojue Chamber of Commerce (Ch: *shanghui*) and
the director of the United Front Department of the county Party Committee,
he was also the deputy chair of the Political Consultative Conference. Without the approval of the local Party board, he could not have written such a
blunt report for a committee as important as the Political Consultative Conference. During an interview with us, he openly complained about the problems regarding the private sector and made it clear that, as chairman of the
Chamber of Commerce, he felt obliged to present the problems as they really
were and to try to find solutions. His endeavors were facilitated by the fact
that Zhaojue county leadership hoped that the private sector would be the
vehicle for developing the local economy, but had experienced difficulties
implementing the process. Some prefectural officials were fundamentally
sympathetic to such frank reporting and were able to exert pressure on the
counties to aid his efforts.

The Zhaojue Political Consultative Conference report also suggested concrete strategies for solving the core problems facing private entrepreneurs.
The United Front Department leadership should distribute a copy of the legal
provisions, the political guidelines, and the preferential measures in written
form to all government departments, officials, and private entrepreneurs in
the county. Training courses in implementing these guidelines should be held
to reinforce their effectiveness. Also, fees and cost sharing arrangements pro-
posed by higher government departments should be made publicly known.

Another solution was for people in the private sector to obtain registra-
tion cards on which all payments could be recorded and which would provide information on legitimate tax and levy payments; thus, entrepreneurs
could refuse demands for payment of fees not listed on the card and an
official receipt should be issued for every payment made. The report also
recommended opening a new center with exclusive jurisdiction over collecting fees and noted that justice and security organs should be required to
protect the entrepreneur's rights, and crimes against entrepreneurs should

be investigated without delay. The report called for implementing and expanding the scope of the preferential policies, as well as for enforcing their implementation. These measures were partially met within two years of drawing up the Political Consultative Conference report but local cadres were able to circumvent the stipulations regarding illegitimate charges by demanding "voluntary donations" in the form of money or material goods.

Some entrepreneurs have turned to higher authorities or to the press, and a few have even chosen to address their problems through the legal system. Entrepreneurs of both ethnic groups no longer simply accept unjust treatment; they are beginning to defend themselves publicly against injustices. They are not only willing to describe such issues in detail to foreign researchers such as ourselves, but they have also urged us to make their cases known in Beijing or even abroad.

This chapter has concentrated on factors that impair the development of the private sector. While some limitations are due to the corrupt institutional context, general geographic difficulties and infrastructural difficulties for enterprises in Liangshan also significantly hinder development.

The private sector in Liangshan is crucial for economic as well as social development. Although the development of this sector is different in each county, there is no alternative for developing Liangshan Prefecture as a whole. There is still a lot of potential for improvement: entrepreneurism among Nuosu is still underdeveloped, and more Nuosu entrepreneurs are undoubtedly necessary to create employment outside the agricultural sector, though this is less an economic issue than a social and political concern. Private sector development has proven to be the key to economic growth as well as a crucial factor for ethnic prosperity and harmonious ethnic relationships.

Thus, in summary, while county governments play a crucial role in providing the necessary context for development, entrepreneurship fosters a basic change in the role of the local state. Instead of operating county-owned state enterprises, the state becomes a developer that nurtures and assists private enterprises. Liangshan counties vary radically in the extent to which their entrepreneurial goals has been achieved. For example, the local government in Meigu has been much more focused on its role as a developer of private entrepreneurship than the government in Puge, where county authorities have remained stuck in the role of a local entrepreneur. Whether Liangshan as a whole can achieve economic success will depend on the ability of local government institutions to assist private local enterprises.

4

Comparative Profiles
of Nuosu and Han Entrepreneurs

Unlike Han, Nuosu are either native to the counties surveyed for this book or from other counties in Liangshan. As members of the indigenous population, they are tied into the local social structures (clans and lineages) and are therefore more capable than Han of mobilizing and using local relationships to their advantage. In their book *The Established and the Outsiders*, Norbert Elias and John L. Scotson point out that indigenous people who have lived in a local area for a longer time possess more power than do outsiders. This power stems from a greater degree of group cohesion and collective identity, more effective local channels of communication, and a feeling of superiority over those who have immigrated from outside the area (Elias and Scotson 1990; Brandstätter 2000).

The Han in these counties are either immigrants from Sichuan and other provinces who have settled more or less permanently in Liangshan for business reasons, or who are members of the families of cadres or skilled workers transferred to Liangshan Prefecture since the 1950s. This is especially true in counties where Nuosu are the majority of the population. Consequently, most Han are less integrated into local structures. Entrepreneurs who are recent immigrants do not perceive their lives to be centered on community structures in the counties in which they live; they are mainly interested in taking advantage of local opportunities for making a profit in a relatively short period of time. Interviews with such entrepreneurs revealed that they planned to move away afterwards, and that they would leave the area as quickly as possible if they experienced a downturn in profits. We interviewed a total of 81 Nuosu (65.3%) and 43 Han (34.7%) entrepreneurs (see table

TABLE 4.1 Age and Ethnicity of Liangshan Entrepreneurs

Age/Ethnicity	Han (%)		Nuosu (%)		Total (%)	
< 29	1	(2.3%)	5	(6.2%)	6	(4.9%)
30–45	25	(58.1%)	42	(51.8%)	66	(53.6%)
46–55	15	(34.9%)	29	(35.8%)	44	(35.8%)
< 55	2	(4.7%)	5	(6.2%)	7	(5.7%)
Total	43	(100%)	81	(100%)	123	(100%)

SOURCE: Author's survey, 1999–2002.

4.1) who were mainly between 30 and 55 years of age (Nuosu 87.6%, Han 93%). The distribution of business types among Nuosu and Han entrepreneurs is shown in table 4.2.

A majority of the entrepreneurs own different companies or are active in multiple economic sectors in order to insure themselves against economic crises and unpredictable circumstances. For example, a 43-year-old Nuosu entrepreneur in Ganluo County owned a road construction firm, with 11 Nuosu employees; an electric utility, with 17 Nuosu employees out of a total of 33; a tree farm, with 5 Nuosu employees; and a cattle ranch, with 3 Nuosu employees. He held a 50 percent share in a newly founded electric utility, a 25 percent share in the county electric utility company, and a 25 percent share in an employment company operated by the county bank. A 52-year-old Nuosu entrepreneur in Meigu was the owner of a distillery, an electrical appliances factory, a cattle feed factory, and had shares in an electric utility, a transport company (operating two trucks), two yak farms, with 700 yaks worth over 360,000 yuan, a 1,670-hectare cereal farm in Leibo County, and 15 hectares of leased land to be reforested. Economic insecurity drives this trend among entrepreneurs to be involved in multiple business activities as it provides a safeguard against potential losses due to poor performance in certain business sectors.

The majority of private enterprises were established prior to 1995 (Nuosu 70.4%, Han 69.1%), although a large percentage of these were established prior to 1989. Table 4.3 shows some continuity in the establishment of new businesses although the degree of year-to-year fluctuation is still very high.

TABLE 4.2 Types of Businesses of Nuosu and Han Entrepreneurs in Liangshan

Nuosu		Han	
Manufacturing			
Mining products	8	Mining	5
Building materials	8	Food	5
Distilled beverages	7	Rare metals	3
Mining	6	Building materials	3
Food	5	Distilled beverages	2
Nuosu clothes / arts and crafts	5	Agricultural equipment	2
Electricity supply	4	Metal products	1
Silver products	2	Furniture	1
Timber products	2	Packaging material	1
Water supply	2	Mining products	1
Agricultural equipment	2		
Rare metals	1		
Leather goods	1		
Traditional medicine	1		
Agriculture/Forestry/Husbandry			
Agriculture, orchardry, fish farming	10	Agriculture, orchardry	1
Animal husbandry	10	Animal husbandry	1
Afforestation	3	Medicinal herbs	2
Logging	1		

EDUCATIONAL BACKGROUNDS

More than one-fifth of the Nuosu entrepreneurs have not attended school. However, some of these entrepreneurs without formal schooling have a basic knowledge of the Nuosu script. Some declared with great pride that their knowledge of the Nuosu language and script corresponds to a senior secondary school level. In contrast, all interviewed Han entrepreneurs had at least attended primary school. Almost one-third of the Han and less than one-fifth of the Nuosu had formal education beyond junior secondary school.

TABLE 4.2 *(continued)*

Nuosu		Han	
		Construction	
Construction	7	Construction	3
		Transportation	
Of goods	2		
Of passengers	1		
		Trade/Food Service	
Restaurants	5	Restaurants	11
Wholesale and retail sales	4	Wholesale and retail sales	6
Petrol stations	2	Tea houses	2
Entertainment (karaoke/ disco, etc.)	1	Entertainment (karaoke/ disco)	1
Real estate	1		
		Services	
Hotels	5	Hotels	3
Parking garages	3	Photography studios	2
Repair shops (electric)	1	Post and telegraph offices	1
Hairdressers	1	Watch repair	1
Photography studios	1		
Hospitals	1		

SOURCE: Author's survey, 1999–2002.

The Nuosu entrepreneurs' lower level of education compared to Han entrepreneurs is an important reason why more Han than Nuosu are active in the private sector (see table 4.4). Most of the Nuosu entrepreneurs are thoroughly aware of the importance of education in upward social mobility and consequently deplore their deficit. A considerable number have sent their children to schools in Xichang or to elite boarding schools (Ch: *guizu xuexiao*) outside Liangshan Prefecture (for example, in Chengdu, the provincial capital) and are intent on sending them to university or enabling them to study abroad. A significant portion of the entrepreneurs, especially those with school-aged children—39.5 percent of the Nuosu and 30.9 per-

TABLE 4.3 Ages of Liangshan Companies

Year founded/Ethnicity of founder	Han	Nuosu	Total
Prior to 1989	17 (40.5%)	28 (34.6%)	45 (36.6%)
1989–1995	12 (28.6%)	29 (35.8%)	41 (33.3%)
1996–1999	12 (28.6%)	18 (22.2%)	30 (24.4%)
After 1999	1 (2.4%)	6 (7.4%)	7 (5.7%)
Total	42 (100%)	81 (100%)	123 (100%)

SOURCE: Author's survey, 1999–2002.

TABLE 4.4 Educational Level of Liangshan Entrepreneurs Interviewed

Level of Education/Ethnicity	Han	Nuosu	Total
None	0 —	17 (21.0%)	17 (13.8%)
Primary	11 (26.2%)	32 (39.5%)	43 (35.0%)
Middle (junior)	18 (42.9%)	19 (23.5%)	37 (30.1%)
Middle (senior)	4 (9.5%)	3 (3.7%)	7 (5.7%)
Occupational training	6 (14.3%)	6 (7.4%)	12 (9.8%)
Polytechnic	1 (2.4%)	3 (3.7%)	4 (3.2%)
University	2 (4.7%)	1 (1.2%)	3 (2.4%)
Total	42 (100%)	81 (100%)	123 (100%)

SOURCE: Author's survey, 1999–2002.

cent of the Han—declared without prompting that their goal was to enable their children to have a university education. For some, the goal of financing their children's university education was even their incentive for becoming self-employed.

REASONS FOR BECOMING AN ENTREPRENEUR

For Nuosu entrepreneurs, the possibilities of earning higher incomes and increasing their living standards are the most important reasons for becoming entrepreneurs. As table 4.5 shows, more than half of the Nuosu entrepreneurs stated that they had become entrepreneurs for this reason. This distinguishes Nuosu entrepreneurs from Han entrepreneurs, among whom the desires for economic independence and for self-fulfillment play the most

TABLE 4.5 Entrepreneurs' Primary Motivations for Founding Companies

Motivation/Ethnicity	Han		Nuosu	
Higher income	16	(38.1%)	45	(56.25%)
Job security	2	(4.8%)	12	(15.0%)
Desire for self-employment	21	(50.0%)	16	(20.0%)
No self-fulfillment in former job	3	(7.1%)	5	(6.25%)
Friction with superiors in former job	0	—	2	(2.5%)
Total	42	(100%)	80	(100%)

SOURCE: Author's survey, 1999–2002.

important role. Our qualitative interviews with Han and Yi entrepreneurs revealed that a greater share of Han conceived "interest in being self-employed" as a kind of self-fulfillment, whereas only a few Yi held such an interpretation of the phrase. In a survey conducted in Liangshan and in surveys of other regions of China,[1] an "interest in being self-employed" among Han was interpreted as the desire for self-fulfillment (Han 50%, Nuosu 20%, in the Liangshan survey alone). This is reflected in the survey results in table 4.5 as well.

Because they lack the necessary capital for founding a company, unemployed people only rarely become entrepreneurs; they become involved mostly in the individual sector. For many people, working as an individual laborer is a transitional stage of learning by doing, during which they acquire capital, learn management skills, and gain specialized knowledge.

PROFESSIONAL CAPITAL

In addition to educational opportunities and social resources for founding a company, entrepreneurs also need "professional capital," which includes previous business experience, professional skills, and personal qualities that facilitate business success (Mars and Ward 1984: 11). Before becoming entrepreneurs, many Han are active in the private sector—primarily in the individual economic sector—or they work as managers of county or town/township enterprises, technicians, or employees/workers. Whereas a significant number of Han entrepreneurs gain professional capital through previous technical training, many Nuosu entrepreneurs are former peasants, cadres, or employees/workers of other companies. Almost one-fourth

TABLE 4.6 Previous Occupations of Entrepreneurs

Occupation	Nuosu (%)	Han (%)
Peasant	35.8	16.7
Private sector employee	12.4	11.9
Manager of state- or collective-owned enterprise	3.7	23.8
Cadre (village, township, county)	19.8	7.1
Worker / public sector employee	18.5	14.3
Technician	1.2	14.3
Unemployed	4.9	7.1
Other	3.7	4.8
Total	100	100

SOURCE: Author's survey, 1999–2002.

of the Nuosu entrepreneurs (23.5%) had been cadres at the village, township, or county level, though mostly at the village level (see table 4.6). This explains the Nuosu dominance in many sectors of the bureaucracy in Liangshan. Due to their work and training within the Party, cadres possess better education, organizational skills, and knowledge, as well as access to different networks. This enables them to shift more easily into the private sector.

In contrast to Han entrepreneurs, many Nuosu entrepreneurs come from an agricultural background, and a small percentage are bimo. Han entrepreneurs have experience in state and collective enterprises as managers (16.7%), technicians (19.1%), and skilled workers (16.7%). For Nuosu, and to a lesser extent for Han, previous employment or training in a company, regardless of its form of ownership, is an important prerequisite for becoming an entrepreneur. While Han entrepreneurs are predominantly from peasant families (42.9%) or families of skilled manual workers, most of the surveyed Nuosu entrepreneurs are from peasant families (75.3%). For the surveyed Nuosu, entrepreneurship tended to represent social betterment. Many of them have gained experience in village and local businesses, or as employees in individual and private firms.

Most of the entrepreneurs' spouses had previously worked in the agricultural sector (Nuosu 56.3%, Han 38.1%). Almost a quarter of the Han entrepreneurs' spouses had been employed in companies in the state sector, compared to only 15 percent of the Nuosu spouses. Among the Nuosu spouses, the percentage of female officials (13.8%) was relatively high. It can be concluded that at least some of the spouses were able to assist their wives or husbands in their work, either through their work experience or through social capital (such as social connections with officials).

SOCIAL CAPITAL

More than half of the surveyed Han and Nuosu entrepreneurs found social connections (Ch: *guanxi*) to be an indispensable form of social capital, bringing significant advantages to their businesses. Most of the entrepreneurs (Han 90.2%, Nuosu 72.5%) had donated money to the authorities or for social purposes, for instance, for building schools, hospitals, and roads; these figures do not include donations to their clans. However, the goals of such gift giving vary, and it is necessary to differentiate between voluntary and forced donations. Whereas voluntary donations either raise the donor's prestige or improve *guanxi* with the local bureaucracy, involuntary donations prevent the loss of *guanxi* and circumvent administrative exploitation. Because most Han entrepreneurs do not have close social relationships with the local bureaucracy, they have to make more (forced) donations and invest more money to develop such relationships. Nuosu entrepreneurs are already embedded in local clan and other social networks and thus spend less money on developing *guanxi*. However, the clans also directly or indirectly place social obligations on Nuosu entrepreneurs to make donations. The Han do not feel this sense of obligation although a relatively high percentage complain about the authorities' "requests" for payment.

It is also important to keep in mind the difference between *altruistic* and *instrumental* motivation. People who are altruistically motivated donate to support people or communities in need or, according to Granovetter, "because of identification with in-group needs and goals." Instrumental motivations cause people to make donations in order to fulfill reciprocal obligations (returns of favors), gain higher social prestige or improve relationships with local authorities (see Portes 1995b: 15). For Nuosu, donations of financial support are based less on the calculated benefit to the individual than on an unquestioned social dictum: the common interest comes before individual interest, and all members of the community must support the common interest. This is particularly true for wealthy community members who are reminded of their community's contributions to their success and of the need to reciprocate. By making donations, the entrepreneurs demonstrate that they are not only pursuing their own interests but are also conforming to traditional social norms and obligations. Those who fulfill these obligations enjoy social respect and recognition. Bourdieu has termed this type of capital "symbolic capital" because the economic dimension of "naked interests" and "egoistic calculation" is diminished and the economic capital is transformed into symbolic capital in the form of social charity. The symbolism lies in the actions, interests, and considerations that are non-economic or even hostile to business (Bourdieu 1999: 215ff.). By means of donations, economic capital is thus converted into symbolic capital.

There is a high degree of social pressure to make donations and meet obligations to the community because most Nuosu found their companies in the same towns in which they were born and raised. The Han are mostly the descendents of people who were sent to Liangshan by the government or who migrated there after 1949 from other parts of China, which explains why Han are considerably less obliged to give money.

TYPES OF ENTREPRENEURS

In the introduction, we noted the difference between *push* and *pull* entrepreneurs. Pull entrepreneurs are attracted to social and financial business opportunities and give up their existing jobs to pursue entrepreneurial ventures; they find the adventure of economic independence exciting and actively make the choice to become self-employed. Push entrepreneurs, on the other hand, are driven into occupational independence by such factors as unemployment, conflicts within the companies where they are employed, and dissatisfaction with the working conditions of their existing positions (See table 4.7).

For both groups, the pull effect is much greater than the push effect although the employment situation of the Nuosu influences the pull factors as well. However, the two groups differ in terms of their entrepreneurial motivation. The Nuosu's primary motivation arises from material grounds— Nuosu entrepreneurs either want to increase their incomes (for example, managers of state sector companies who become self-employed, or individual laborers who expand their operations), or they see no other escape from a low standard of living than to take the initiative and start their own business. For some, the fact that their spouses do not have jobs or that they wish to provide a good education for their children also plays a role in their entrepreneurial initiative. Non-material factors play a greater role in Han entrepreneurs' decisions than amongst the Nuosu.

We could attempt to classify entrepreneurs according to their different reasons for choosing self-employment, which could include their ability

TABLE 4.7 Push and Pull Factors that Influence Entrepreneurship

	Nuosu (%)	Han (%)
Push factors		
Friction with superiors	2.5	—
No self-fulfillment in former job	6.2	7.1
Unemployed	15.0	4.8
Total	23.7	11.9
Pull factors		
Higher income	56.3	38.1
Desire for self-employment	20.0	50.0
Total	76.3	88.1

SOURCE: Author's survey, 1999–2002.

to make use of market opportunities and incentives (mostly in urban areas and more developed regions), blocked prospects for upward mobility, the acquired privileges and social connections of the political elite and sub-elite classes (particularly at the local level), and survival strategies (by the unemployed and pensioners). However, these individual factors cannot be separated from each other because the desire for independence and entrepreneurship is often created by a complicated mix of different needs and intents. Thus, it would not be possible to divide the entrepreneurs we interviewed into exclusive categories.

However, some general patterns do emerge among entrepreneurs in certain categories. The percentage of Han who make use of market opportunities and incentives is recognizably larger than that of Nuosu because they have emigrated from other areas for the express purpose of taking advantage of market opportunities. However, a percentage of the cadres' children also fall into this category, as do people with particular market skills or knowledge.

The Nuosu who become self-employed because of blocked upward mobility are mainly children of the former upper stratum who, until the 1980s, suffered through being labeled "class enemies." This category includes children whose fathers actively took part in the uprising against the "Democratic Reforms" in the 1950s and consequently were punished with compulsory labor.

Others become entrepreneurs because they find opportunities through their social connections with members of the political elite or because of certain advantages—for example, some entrepreneurs' parents were officials and some others acquired investment money. The children of cadres, of persons with social capital, or of people with other important social relationships (such as leading clan persons) are often among those with investment capital.

In some cases, people from other areas migrate specifically to a county in which they have relatives in high positions. In Butuo, we met an entrepreneur who had settled there because the county Party Secretary was his relative and this social capital provided him a significant economic advantage. A number of entrepreneurs found silver reserves buried by members of the upper class during the "Democratic Reforms" and used them as their starting capital. In other cases, entrepreneurism is a survival strategy for those who have no other options for making a living. It is also a survival strategy for people whose companies have gone bankrupt or for dependents of former slaves kidnapped by the Nuosu in Han territories (see examples later in this chapter).

The traditional crafts professions need some additional explanation, as the makers of traditional consumer objects out of leather and wood, clothing, silver jewelry, and saddles for horses, for example, cannot be put in any one of the four categories. Craftsmen earn a passable income less because of market demand than because of the traditional importance of their work. These people draw on their own clan traditions and pursue traditional crafts (making silver, lacquerware, etc.) through the support of their clans. They further the entrepreneurial legacy of their fathers and grandfathers who pursued the same craft within a different historical context. Although these firms extensively employ family members, the owners of such companies can certainly be classified as entrepreneurs. This type of entrepreneurial activity can be termed a "family handicraft tradition."

A small but certainly interesting group of people includes those who were previously self-employed or entrepreneurs and wish to regain that status. This group has been designated as occupying an intermediate stage toward entrepreneurship. Though we only met a few, we found that they understand themselves to be entrepreneurs even when they are temporarily still earning salaries and filling leading company positions. If they classified themselves as entrepreneurs, we included them in our survey, which amounted to two additional people.

Another specific group consisted of (mostly Han) entrepreneurs whose parents or grandparents had been kidnapped from Han territories and enslaved in Liangshan. Prior to the Democratic Reforms, they had belonged to the lowest Nuosu caste. We interviewed four members of this group who considered themselves to be assimilated and socialized Nuosu Yi and are registered as members of the Yi group. However, certain other people, such as the local cadres, treat this as a taboo subject, and we were asked by the locals not to discuss it any more. Some of the descendents of Han slaves we met were praised as model entrepreneurs because they had worked their way up the social scale from being beggars and illiterates to entrepreneurs with social prestige.

The following cases are individual examples and not intended to be representative. We provide these case studies in order to describe a wide range of situations, where each case represents one individual's particular story.

SIXTEEN ENTREPRENEURS

The following short biographies illustrate different categories of entrepreneurs and the effects of factors such as blocked prospects for upward mobility, the use of market opportunities and incentives, privilege, survival strategies, intermediate career stages, and family business on career development.

J. (Nuosu), Yanyuan

J. was born in 1948 as the single child of a so-called slave owner in Yanyuan County. He came from an old family of clan leaders; both his grandfather and great-grandfather had been clan leaders, and his father was the leader of one of the largest clans in Liangshan. His father actively took part in the uprising against the Democratic Reforms, and was sentenced to six years in a labor camp when J. was 12 years old. At that time, his parents passed him off as a girl so that their only son would not be forced to take part in the uprising against the Hans. His father died in 1962 in the labor camp in Dechang County, and his mother was sentenced to be re-educated through work on a state farm. J. was left completely on his own at home, so, an uncle took a little care of him now and then.

During the Great Leap Forward (1958–1960) and in the years following, there was almost nothing to eat; because J. was still very young, he was classified as only a supplementary laborer and received one potato per day for his nutrition. He did not own a complete set of clothes, and in the winter, he suffered terribly from the cold, trying to keep warm at night amongst the cattle. In 1959, he was sent to primary school, but the school was ten kilometers away, so, it was a long journey to get there, and after his father's death, he was no longer permitted to attend school because he was the son of a slave owner. He was forced to look after the village sheep and expressly forbidden from reading books. Though his books were confiscated, he read in secret and even taught himself to write. He was so successful in these endeavors that by 1965, when the political circumstances had become less tense, he was hired as a part-time teacher at a village school in spite of his youth. What this position actually entailed was that along with teaching, he also had to work in the fields for half the day. He received an allowance of three yuan per month for his teaching activities until 1969, when he became a regular teacher at a village school.

This was also a period of extreme difficulty for him because the Cultural Revolution was in full sway. Although no one in the village knew exactly what the revolution was for, Red Guards came to the village from outside and declared that the former slave owners had to be "criticized." In 1967, three members of J.'s clan, his grandfather, his grandfather's second wife, and his uncle, were beaten to death during a "public criticism session," and their entire property was confiscated. He and seven other members of his family were lined up in a row and, one after the other, were subjected to criticism and beaten mercilessly.

He felt that there was no future for him in society. Nevertheless, he sought a new path for himself and even strove for a bit of freedom, but at that time there was no concept or possibility of personal liberty for him. He immersed himself in learning quotes by Chairman Mao—some of which he remembers even to this day—and recited them repeatedly to protect himself. The village people said that if he had been born into another family he would have had a great future, because he was highly intelligent. By his own request, he was assigned a job with a group that installed water pipes. His production brigade (nowadays administratively classified as a village) permitted him to take on this work, which removed him from the harmful surroundings and improved his general situation. He became the director of the group's food department.

In 1972, he was transferred, again at his own request, to a newly constructed dam in Yanyuan County, where he worked for three years, acquired knowledge of hydrology, and even passed an exam to become a hydrologist. Consequently, he was transferred to a hydrological station in Baiwu Township, where he worked for another two years. While in Baiwu, he became involved in a dispute with the township Party Secretary, who was a former slave of a Black Yi family and had taken part in the armed insurrection in 1956 and fled into the mountains afterwards. In the heat of an argument the Party Secretary declared, "I'm going to shoot you, you damned slave-owner." J. bared his chest retorting, "Go on! Shoot!" Because

J. had not taken part in the uprising, he told the functionary that he had even dirtier hands than J. himself. This remark led to J.'s immediate dismissal. He returned to his home village, was sentenced to a year's forced labor, and from then on was sent to look after the cattle.

In 1977, beekeeping experts came to Yanyuan from Zhejiang Province in order to start businesses there. Since this subject interested him intensely, J. asked them to teach him the necessary skills. He proved to be such a quick learner that one of the experts called him "a great talent" and gave him a beehive. Since private economic activities were still forbidden at that time, J. began to keep bees in the name of the production brigade although in reality they were his own. In 1980, he became self-employed as a "special household" (Ch: *zhuanyehu*) and obtained 10,000 yuan in credit from the state with which he purchased 20 new beehives. He later expanded his range of products to include queen bee pollen. The Party Secretary in Xichang was so impressed by the quality of his products and by the expansion of his production activities that he granted him 50,000 yuan in credit. J. then expanded his operation to 12 employees and 400 beehives. By 1981, he had an annual income of 300,000 yuan. He purchased a small Japanese bus for 15,000 Yuan and became the first private entrepreneur in Liangshan Prefecture to own his own motor vehicle. In 1982, due to his economic success, he was offered a membership in the national beekeepers' association.

Nineteen-eighty-two was to be his most successful year. He took part in an international beekeeping congress in Beijing and became a member of the national committee of the beekeepers' association. He obtained a residence permit (Ch: *hukou*) for the urban area of Xichang, passed the driving test, and earned more money than ever before in his life.

In a group discussion at the beekeepers' congress, a deputy minister of agriculture was so impressed by J.'s remarks that he allocated him two motorized vehicles from the state. With this encouragement, J. founded the first private company in Liangshan Prefecture in 1983, though at that time it still had to be officially registered as a "collective company." Soon he was dubbed "the bee king," and he began processing honey and expanded both his marketing network and sales methods, including bartering. He was so successful that he became the youngest member of the Prefectural Political Consultative Conference and was distinguished by being the only large, private Yi entrepreneur. He was even nominated to become a member of the Standing Committee and thus a member of Liangshan Prefecture's political elite. In 1984, he was accepted into the Communist Party.

In 1985, while attending a foreign trade fair in Chengdu, J. learned that a Japanese businessman was interested in buying 10 tons of matsutake mush-rooms, which were very popular in Japan. He began to purchase matsutake wherever he could find them. With the profit he made from these transac-tions, he founded a taxi firm and purchased real estate in Xichang, where he set up business offices. In 1987, he made a total profit of 10 million yuan from the matsutake and was able to obtain 20 million yuan in credit. How-ever, he had to accept severe losses for the first time in 1988, selling his houses in Xichang when the price of mushrooms fell in the Japanese market.

Because of this experience, he lost the desire to continue his business activ-ities and decided to become a cadre in 1989. Developments after the Tianan-men massacre on June 4, 1989, also created problems for the private sector; from that point on, polemicists among the cadres called for private com-panies to be converted from capitalist to socialist enterprises and declared that private entrepreneurs were exploiters. This was the last straw for J. First, people had called him a slave owner, now a capitalist exploiter. He was fed up. In 1989, through clan *guanxi*, he became the director of the Bureau for the Administration of Rural Enterprises in Ninglang County, Yunnan. He transferred back to Xichang in 1992, where he worked as an assistant to the director of the Prefectural Bureau for the Administration of Rural Enter-prises, thus becoming an official "government cadre."[2]

J. then invested his entire capital and all the credit he could obtain (16 mil-lion yuan in total) in his native area, Baiwu Township in Yanyuan County. In the mid-1990s, he founded a forest recreation center with hotel accommo-dations, catering, opportunities for fishing, riding, swimming, boating, relax-ing, playing, and hiking. He addressed problems of poverty in the surrounding villages by building roads and donating money to build schools, clinics, and electric and water utilities. He organized the installation of drinking water pipes, electricity lines, and television connections for all the villages and, in this way, contributed to these villages' development and prosperity.

Relatives and friends had advised him that he should make further use of his business talents and abilities, and he had considered whether it would be wise to leave Xichang, where he was doing well, and return to Yanyuan. He had finally decided to return to his home county with the goal of con-tributing to eradicating poverty there. According to J., raising people's educa-tional level was the key to eliminating poverty; the Nuosu were discriminated against and looked down on not only because they were poor, but also because they were uneducated and considered lazy. Many Han associated the Nuosu with drug addiction and crime. That perception had to change. J. believed that the Nuosu had to develop themselves so that they could acquire economic, social, and political prestige. He noted that although he could invest his capital in Xichang, he would actually be able to do something for people in Yanyuan. He felt that although one day he would be gone, at least he would have done something useful for others.

At the time of our interview in 2000, J. owned apple orchards, timber firms, and fish hatcheries, as well as the forest recreation center mentioned above. He had also founded apple-processing plants, funded schools and healthcare centers in the villages, and financed the building of streets and bridges. He owned guesthouses and restaurants and was in the process of constructing a 1 million-yuan storage center with refrigerated storage rooms for fruit and meat. He told us that he was planning to build a "green" sales center with storage rooms, administrative buildings, guestrooms, and restaurants, and that all the food there would be produced using ecologically sound methods.

At the time of our visit, he was married to his third wife, who was in her early twenties. He had five children. His wives, he explained, had cost him a million yuan; after his divorces, he had settled incipient clan feuds with large sums of money.

In 2000, he was the most important entrepreneur in the county and a model prefectural level entrepreneur. J. told us that he had created jobs for both Nuosu and Han and had contributed to the prosperity of what had formerly been a very poor area. This had also brought about an improvement in the relations between the ethnic groups. Earlier, Han and Nuosu had stolen from each other; now, they were all prosperous and there were good relations between them.

According to J., there had been a lengthy dispute in 2000 among officials in Yanyuan about whether or not they should allow him to continue his business activities, but his success had settled the issue. J. said of the Party, "The Communist Party is a force which we entrepreneurs energize, nourish and keep alive."[3] Although he was an entrepreneur, he continued to function as the assistant to the director of the Bureau for the Administration of Rural Enterprises in the prefecture. He was also an acting member of the Standing Committee of the Political Consultative Conference, as well as the deputy chair of the Federation of Industry and Commerce of the prefecture.

S. (Nuosu), Meigu County

When interviewed in 2001, 52-year-old S.—who came from a well-respected Black Nuosu family—owned a liquor distillery, a variety of factories producing

FIG. 5. *Jize Ji Amu and his company organization chart, Yanyuan County*

FIG. 6. *Jize Ji Amu in his amusement park, Yanyuan County*

cattle feed, bricks, and electrical appliances, and four farms (one for agriculture, one for forestry, and two for yaks), and he also held shares in an electricity company. During the time of the armed insurrection in 1957–1958, his father received a long sentence in a labor camp. His mother died of grief in 1960 and his father in the labor camp in 1962. He was raised by a former slave of his parents and although he did not have any school education, he taught himself to read and write the Nuosu script as a child. He told us that he unfortunately only understood a little of the Han language. Somewhat regretfully, he added that if only he and other Nuosu entrepreneurs in the area could speak and write Chinese well, there would be no stopping their success.

During the Cultural Revolution, he spent some time in Chengdu as a vagrant in order to avoid the "criticism and struggle sessions." By 1977, word had spread that he was highly intelligent and a quick learner, and he was given a job as the deputy director of a cooperative brick factory in his township. In 1982, he founded his own brick factory and acquired two transport vehicles with which to run a small transport firm. In 1994, he leased a large area of forest from a state forest farm and, in 1997, he bought a large farm in Leibo County with 20-year land use rights. At times, he employed over 1,000 Nuosu as temporary workers.

The main motivation for his activities, he explained, was his desire to become rich. The clan was not able to help him; rather, he had actually helped them. He donated a large number of fruit trees and Sichuan peppercorn trees to his village and, in 1990, he was voted village head and has remained in that position ever since. He told us that the inhabitants correctly believed that he would be able to assist them in developing the village. He possessed good contacts outside the village, supported the villagers with money and advice when necessary, and financed the infrastructural connection of the village to water and electricity networks. As the de facto leader of the clan, he visited Beijing in 1989, when a court sentenced two of his clan members to death for stealing 90 yaks valued at approximately US$5,700 (about 50,000 yuan). Although he spoke no Chinese, he was able to prevent the death sentence from being carried out.

A. (Nuosu), Puge County

Forty-eight-year-old A. was an entrepreneur in the construction business from Puge County when we interviewed him in 2001. His brother was the county magistrate of a different county. A. attended primary school for only three years before the "Socialist Education Movement" in 1964 forced him and his brothers to leave school due to their parents' class status, and prevented them from returning. He was sent to a village to work in agriculture. After the fall of the "Gang of Four" he belonged to the last group permitted to attend a technical college without having passed an appropriate entrance exam. In 1979, A. completed a course in agriculture at the technical college in Zhaojue.

His first position after graduation was as an accountant in his native township. In 1983 he was transferred to the County Agricultural Bureau and, in 1988, to the Bureau for Land Administration, where he eventually became the director. He left in 1993 and founded a construction company because he believed that he would be able to fulfill his financial goals as an entrepreneur. By 2001, his company had 145 employees. He acquired 1,800 square meters of land in Xichang but lived in Chengdu, where he also owned a mid-sized restaurant, a hotel, and an amusement center. He stated that he would like to change his firm into a joint venture enterprise with a foreign partner because private sector companies are very vulnerable, still subject to major problems, and do not receive fair treatment by the government. The partner firm would not need to invest money; instead, he sought long-term political protection for his company through the partnership.

He told us that in the building and construction sector, a company would quickly collapse without good connections to the local authorities. The competition was tough and it was becoming increasingly difficult to obtain profitable commissions. He was considering moving into a new line of business, namely, setting up a company to act as guarantors to creditors. It would be the first of its kind in the prefecture—new and very promising, but with a high risk.

His future goals were to separate the company ownership from the management and to find a suitable successor, but this was proving to be very difficult. He confided that, as a rule, only four types of people were available: those who were potentially trustworthy as well as competent, those who were trustworthy but not competent, those who were competent but not trustworthy, and those who were neither trustworthy nor competent! None of these kinds of people were really suitable for his purposes. Although his own children had an excellent education, he did not consider any of them as his successor.

W. (Nuosu), Mianning County

At the time of our interview in 1999, 49-year-old W. was the owner of a tile factory in Mianning County. After completing secondary school, he had become a non-state-employed, community-supported teacher (Ch: *min-ban laoshi*) in a village school and, in 1970, he was accepted into government service as an official teacher. He sat on the 1972 Commission for the Revision of the Nuosu Script for the Prefecture. In 1975, he began researching Nuosu literature through a research institution, later becoming involved in popularizing the Yi script and in reforming the wedding and marriage system. However, in 1980, he was sentenced to six years in jail for his involvement in a drunken fight in which his opponent, the county magistrate, was beaten and heavily injured. He was also expelled from the Party. After his release, he once again became a secondary school teacher until founding his current company and becoming self-employed in 1992.

B. (Nuosu), Puge County

B., who has formally studied Chinese, owned a large, modern hotel complex with thermal baths, restaurants, a swimming pool, and shops at the time of our visit in September 2001; he was 26 years old. His father had been Wu Jinghua's bodyguard[4] and had later became the director of the United Front Department of the Puge County Party Committee. His father had once helped a poor, sick Han Chinese man who lived in Puge and had been labeled a "class enemy"; out of compassion for the man, he had paid for his medical treatment and for his medicines, which had saved his life. During the reforms, the man, who was originally from Chengdu, became a successful and prosperous entrepreneur. In the 1990s, out of gratitude for B.'s father's help, he built a hotel and donated it to B., who was then a cadre at the Bureau for Economic Administration.

At that time, it was still forbidden for an official to simultaneously hold office and be an entrepreneur. Thus, a new legal provision was devised: while remaining in office, B. was allowed to become the general manager of the hotel. In formal terms, he continued to receive a cadre salary while his work at the hotel was supposedly on a volunteer basis. Concurrently, B. was also the managing director of the county's Company for the Development of Tourism on Luojing Mountain.

Though the local officials were fully aware that B. was both an entrepreneur and an official, they did not consider him an entrepreneur. In those days, he told us, it was still too early for him to openly declare that he was self-employed, because it could have caused many difficulties for him. Since the hotel helped the county implement its tourism development strategy, B.'s double function was tolerated.

G. (Nuosu), Meigu County

When we interviewed him in 2001, G. was the 31-year-old owner of a Meigu department store (wholesale and retail). He owned nine subsidiaries in different townships in Meigu, which were leased to other managers and for which he was the sole supplier, as stipulated by the contract. G. had never been to school and was illiterate. He had not been allowed to attend school because his grandfather had been executed during the armed uprising and his father classified as a slave owner. One of his brothers was thrown into jail for several years during the Cultural Revolution but, by 2001, he had become an entrepreneur in the construction industry. Another brother was also an entrepreneur in the construction sector, and a third was the deputy director of the Meigu Party Committee's Propaganda Department and the head of the county trade union. Previously, his family had been very prosperous but had become impoverished due to Mao's policies. During the Great Leap Forward, his sister died of starvation.

Until 1990, G. had worked as a peasant and lived in poverty stricken conditions. Then he passed his driving test and obtained a job as a driver at the local Bureau for Animal Husbandry through clan connections. He was employed there only temporarily and did not obtain a permanent position. In 1992, the Construction Bank employed him as a chauffeur for a year. Because he often drove through the countryside, he came into contact with many businesspeople, and, in 1993, he set up his own firm. Subsequently, the development bank gave him a loan so that he could expand his business.

By 2001, the county's wholesale food sector was mostly under his direction. He purchased grain from markets in other areas and sold it to the local government; this freed the local government from the burden of growing grain and allowed it to make land available for afforestation projects.

A nephew assisted him with the administration of his company and he told us his next goal was to purchase a piece of property in Xichang and found additional companies there. He had no difficulty obtaining credit because he was achieving a turnover of up to 400,000 yuan per day. In the meantime, he had acquired a large number of rental houses; the income from these alone would suffice for him to make a living. He also traded in real estate and purchased realty, which was still officially forbidden. He told us that shortly before our interview, he had purchased a piece of land for 25,000 yuan and then sold it for 60,000 yuan.

G. regretted that he had never had the chance to get an education and wanted to give his five children, three sons and two daughters, the chance to pursue higher education. The three oldest attended an elite school (Ch: *guizu xuexiao*) in Meishan, Sichuan; though the two youngest were still in kindergarten, he wanted them to have the opportunity to go to university when they grew up. He and other entrepreneurs often invited educated people for lectures or to dinner to listen to their opinions and learn from them. He remarked that listening to others is also a method of learning.

H. (Nuosu), Mianning County

H. was 42 years old at the time of our interview in 1999. He attended a primary school for only three years but taught himself Chinese. He was from a well-known, traditional bimo family and, as a child, he was initiated into the knowledge, art, and techniques of the bimo. By the age of 13, he had carried out rituals by himself. Strictly speaking, this was forbidden but they lived high up in the mountains where nobody paid any attention to this prohibition. His clientele were mostly located in mountain villages and often sought him and his father out to ask for advice or to perform rituals. Even the county Party Secretary was amongst H.'s clientele and H. claimed to have healed a number of patients from illnesses that medical doctors had diagnosed as terminal.

To supplement the low income from his work as a bimo, he earned money through other activities after the Reforms. He worked as a logger and a cattle dealer, manufactured plant oils for export, and prospected for rare earth metals. In 1996, he purchased a hotel and, in 1998, set up an electric company, retaining 50 percent of the shares. He was the manager of the utility and a member of the board. At the time of our interview, he was still working as a bimo, not for financial reasons but because of the family tradition, his love for the work, and because he was in great demand. When he had earned enough money, he wanted to work only as a bimo again.

E. (Nuosu), Meigu County

E., born in 1945, breeds pigs and, although he is illiterate, owns a liquor distillery. In the 1960s, he was accepted into the Party and was active as a cadre at the village level, and later became the Party Secretary of a production brigade and of a township. In 1984, he was transferred to the Bureau for the

Administration of Rural Enterprises where he was the director until 1993. He left his functionary position, possibly because of the fact that he has eight children, and although he has no specific position, he still belongs to this work unit. In 2000, the year of our interview, he founded his own firm, mainly because his wife was unemployed, and he needed to be able to finance his children's education.

V. (Nuosu), Xide County

We interviewed 48-year-old V. in 2002. He is from a family with a centuries-old tradition of manufacturing lathes, hand-painted lacquered wooden containers, and other everyday wooden items commonly used by the Nuosu. He proudly told us that his family has been practicing this craft for seventeen generations, i.e., for 500 years. He attended primary school for only two years but can write the Nuosu script. While still a child, he learned the traditional handicraft from his father and he was skilled in all aspects of this handicraft, including selecting suitable wood and paintings, as early as when he was 12 years old.

During the Cultural Revolution, ethnic arts were criticized as "feudal"; his craft was forbidden and he was assigned a job in a company run by his production brigade. However, at home he continued to produce the traditional vessels. After the revival of ethnic arts in the early 1980s, he got a job as a designer in a state-owned ethnic art factory. In 1982, he was given the post of deputy director of this state company but due to poor product quality and limited markets, the company went out of business. In 1992, he founded his own private firm and resumed practicing his traditional work as a self-employed artisan. All of his twelve employees were members of his clan. His heartfelt desire was that one day his eldest son should continue the trade. The wares now being produced in his factory are actually not traditional wares but have been adapted and changed to suit new markets.

He was named a Sichuan Province Ethnic Folk Arts and Crafts Master in 1987, and since 1982 he has been a deputy of the Xide County Political Consultative Conference. This position is extremely important for his business because it helps to him advertise and sell his products. In addition, he has become recognized as a headman (Ch: *touren;* N: *suyy*) within his clan, which perceives the continuation of the lacquerware handicraft tradition not merely as a continuation of ethnic art but also as the continuation of the importance of the clan.[5]

C. (Nuosu, Son of Han Parents Formerly Enslaved by Nuosu), Meigu County

In 2001, we met 43-year-old C. who is a resident in the township of Hongqi, Meigu County. Though he is illiterate, he has become a mining entrepreneur. His parents were Han who were kidnapped in Yunnan and taken to Liangshan as slaves but he regards himself a Nuosu because he was born and raised in a Nuosu area. As a child, he survived by begging and collecting garbage. In 1979, he got a temporary job on a forest farm, which is still recorded as his official place of employment. In 1997, along with two other sons of former slaves, he purchased a large coal mine for 400,000 yuan. The county gave them considerable credit for this venture, partly because they were sons of former slaves and had no permanent jobs. All of the employees at the mine were Nuosu because, according to this entrepreneur, he had little to do with Han and because Nuosu were much cleverer than Han were.

K. (Nuosu), Ganluo County

K. was 43 when we interviewed him in 1999. He only attended school for three years and worked in a smithy and as a farmhand after leaving school. At the age of 18, he became a laborer in an explosives factory, and then he did a three-year stint with the railway police. He held a series of other jobs, too; he became a blacksmith and cattle breeder, a cook in a factory that produced non-military goods, the film projectionist for a local township government, and then a blue-collar worker in a liquor factory. When this factory went bankrupt, he purchased some horses and began a private, horse-drawn transport company. In 1983, he learned to drive, became a driver for the local government, advanced to driving trucks for the county's grain department, and eventually leased a truck from them. He became a chauffeur for a bank in 1987 and remained in this position until signing a contract to take over a mine in 1989. Out of his profits from the mine, he has donated a primary school to his native village.

In 1981, he began to get commissions to build roads, and he founded his own company in order to connect his native village to the road network. His intent was not only to make local resources such as metal and wood available to the market but also to enable the village inhabitants to take their agricultural produce to the local markets; he saw this venture as an opportunity to combat poverty. Between 1996 and 1998, he was also the deputy Party Secretary of Aga township, his native area. In 1999, K. was elected a deputy of the National People's Congress (the national parliament) as well as deputy director of the county's Bureau for Water and Electricity Supply.

His dream had always been to drive an automobile, which corresponded with his deeper desire to see, at least once in his life, the world outside of Liangshan Prefecture. This impulse to get to know the rest of the world was important in his becoming an entrepreneur. Most of all, he regretted that he had received no education. He supposed that this limited him in his development as an entrepreneur and commented that this was a great problem for both Nuosu and Han.

Y. (Han), Zhaojue County

Y., a 49-year-old owner of a brick factory when we interviewed him in 2000, was raised in poverty in a peasant family in Nantong, Sichuan. Because they were so poor, he became active in the shadow economy in the 1970s and founded a private "underground company" (private companies at that time were still illegal) and even trained apprentices. After that, he told us, he spent some years in a labor camp but did not say why. Some years afterwards, he claimed, he studied at the University of Industry in Wuhan. He did indeed show us a certificate but it became clear during the interview that he had only attended this institution for a short period of time and had paid a high price for a fake certificate of completion.

In 1984, he was transferred to Zhaojue County where he worked as a technician in a state company and rose to the position of deputy director. He then worked as an engineer in a rural company until it went bankrupt. After that, he became self-employed. He said that one of the main reasons for this decision was that enterprises founded in minority areas like Liangshan did not have to pay any taxes for three years. A third of his employees were his relatives and *laoxiang*, workers from his native village in Nantong. He stated with certainty that it was not possible to find any skilled workers in the Liangshan area.

However, his success depended on a man he had got to know during the Cultural Revolution and who later became minister for agriculture in Beijing. This man helped him obtain a large amount of credit as starting capital. He also helped him build up social capital; by the time of our visit, Y. had become a member of the Political Consultative Conference of the county and had been honored as an "outstanding manager." He was also the head of his company's trade union.

According to Y., although he was in fact the executive director of the enterprise, another man functioned as a figurehead. This arrangement had enabled Y. to get his hands on the property on which the factory stood. As a consequence, he had to pay part of his profits to the Nuosu clan who had leased this land, which actually belonged to the village. His company had also been registered as a "village-owned" collective firm until the tax department designated it a private company, which meant that it would have to pay higher taxes.

L. (Han), Zhaojue County

L., interviewed in August 2000, was born in 1950 in Zigong, Sichuan. He owns a copper mine and is a member of the Buddhist faith. In 1964, he finished primary school and worked first as a peasant and then as an individual laborer. In 1969, he was temporarily employed at a mine and then with the railroad. He migrated to Liangshan Prefecture as a railway worker in 1971 and, beginning in 1974, he labored in different mines in Zhaojue, always as a temporary worker (Ch: *linshigong*). He became a small entrepreneur on a subcontracting basis for a road-building project in 1981. In 1983, he officially took over a copper mine, which had previously belonged to the Zhaojue county government, but at the same time continued his work in road building. He owned houses in Zhaojue and Xichang. He had sent money to his clan and made donations to build and repair schools in his native area.

M. (Han), Butuo County

We interviewed 52-year-old M. from Anyuan, Sichuan, in August 2001. After serving in the military, he migrated to Butuo in 1975 because poor economic conditions in his native area prevented him from finding suitable work. An uncle from Butuo, a worker at a state electrical appliance factory, wrote to him that former members of the armed forces were generally considered competent employees and had good employment chances in Butuo; Han relatives of current factory employees were especially likely to find a job. M. became a temporary worker in the same factory as his uncle and worked there until 1978.

M. eventually got a permanent job in a collective company but was unsatisfied with his position. He told us that he had wanted to work in a state-owned company. As a former soldier, he had expected to get a better job offer, and he had been so frustrated that he had intended to return to his native village. Before he left, however, he was offered a job working in the grain department cafeteria where his aunt was an employee. His experience as a cook while in the army and the fact that he knew how to cook in the northern Chinese style worked in his favor. Because his employers were satisfied with his performance, he obtained an urban residence permit and was then able to invite his wife and children to Butuo.

M. had also been trained in making watches. After self-employment became legalized, he began a watch repair business in Butuo, where there was not a single watchmaker. His wife took over his job at the cafeteria in order to keep their apartment, which the local government grain department only rented out to their employees.

In 1996, M. opened his own restaurant using his profits from making watches. When his wife became ill, he gave up repairing watches and instead specialized in making noodle dishes at his restaurant. Through his work at the restaurant, he was exposed to the grain trade and finally became a grain trader. This trade brought in more income, which he needed to support his children—his daughter worked in a kindergarten and his oldest son had a diploma from the technical school and was a township cadre.

L. (Han), Butuo County

L. was 37 years old at the time of our interview in 2001 and he was the director of a feed processing plant. He had earned a degree in chemistry at the East China University for Technology in Shanghai and afterwards been employed in various feed processing plants in Sichuan. In 1992, he obtained a position in a Chinese-foreign joint venture company, where he gained two years of experience before deciding to become self-employed. He founded a company with two friends but when the partnership broke up due to differences in opinion, L. switched to working for a large, privately owned feed-processing manufacturer in Chengdu (a shareholder company). When this firm set up a subsidiary in Butuo, he was appointed as the director. However, he perceived this to be a transitional post because his goal was—as it had been before—to own his own company. Originally, the Butuo subsidiary plant was to have been situated in Yuexi County (also in Liangshan Prefecture), but the prefectural authorities convinced the company management that the raw materials and manufacturing conditions were optimal in Butuo and that special privileges were granted to private companies under the local preferential policy framework there. However, L. reported that not only were the promised conditions never realized, there were also no qualified local workers in Butuo; the local cadres had only alcohol on their minds and the county administration was incompetent as far as supporting the economy was concerned. Consequently, the feed-processing company was intent on moving its plant as soon as possible.

Z. (Han), Yanyuan County

Z. was 46 years old when we interviewed him in 2000. After attending primary school he had become an employee in Yanyuan County's Bureau for Goods and Materials and held temporary positions in various companies after that. Finally, he became a purchaser for a state-owned firm, from which he took an unpaid sabbatical in 1986 in order to lease an apple farm. With the resultant income, he purchased a truck and, in 1987, founded a private transport company for which he was the driver. He opened a small restaurant in Xichang but because it was so successful, the property owner terminated his lease and took the business away from him. He once again purchased a large truck and ran a long-distance transport business for three years until 1996, when he purchased a taxi and began working as a taxi driver, employing other drivers once he had the money. In 1998, one of his drivers was involved in a fatal accident and Z. had to pay 10,000 yuan for the costs of his funeral. He did not have enough money to purchase a new vehicle and opened a new restaurant in Xichang instead.

His main reason for starting another business was to pay for his children's education. During the day, he worked in his restaurant; in the evening, he ran a barbecue stand outside a hospital. This was an extremely difficult period for Z.; he worked until three in the morning and slept only four hours every night. When Z.'s father fell ill in 1998, Z.'s wife returned to Yanyuan to take care of him. Z. was unable to carry out all the restaurant work by himself and started buying and selling apples instead. However, he lost money in this endeavor, and when his father's condition deteriorated, Z. returned to Yanyuan, too.

After his father's death, Z. founded a new restaurant in Yanyuan where he earned more than 200,000 yuan per year. Again, the firm that had rented the property to him became envious of his success and took back the property. In January 2000, he moved to the island of Hainan, where he purchased a restaurant for 135,000 yuan and began to offer Sichuan-style cuisine. But because his wife wished to return to Yanyuan, he relented and bought a large building there in which they set up restaurants, massage salons, karaoke, and a dance hall. A relative now runs the restaurant on Hainan. Z.'s biggest problem, he declared, is that he did not drink or smoke, which continually creates difficulties between him and his guests.

CHARACTERISTICS AND MOTIVATIONS

These examples show that entrepreneurs seldom have one primary motivation for becoming self-employed. More often than not, different factors determine a person's motivation at different periods of his or her life. However, the examples illustrate three general characteristics that apply to either the Nuosu entrepreneurs or the Han entrepreneurs, or to both. Most of the Han depend on some form of education or technical experience, whereas most of the Nuosu do not. Except for those pursuing traditional family handicrafts, only a few entrepreneurs are interested in or even have a particular skill; they are primarily interested in business. The businesses themselves are often very short-lived. We thus get the strong impression that most of the entrepreneurs are simply interested in business in general, not in a particular kind of business.

Life Goals

Do Nuosu and Han entrepreneurs differ from each other in their life goals? In general, both ethnic groups are highly motivated by family and social considerations. Table 4.8 shows striking similarities, except in areas regarding improved living conditions for Nuosu (closely related to increased income and improved standard of living) and being a role model in society, which are privileged more by Nuosu than by Han. These exceptions are not surprising given that Nuosu are embedded in their local society whereas many Han have migrated from other areas. Although every single entrepreneur agreed that it was important to contribute to the development of society, this was less marked amongst Han entrepreneurs. To be "social role models" or to contribute to the prosperity of the local people was much less important to the Han. Compared to only 8.6 percent of the Yi, 21.4 percent of the Han claimed that being a social role model was not so important to them. There are a few reasons for this discrepancy. The Yi are far more embedded and involved in the local social relations than the Han, whose roots are not in the Liangshan area. Another hypothesis is that the socially oriented values of the Party correspond more closely to the traditional values of the Yi. To some extent Han entrepreneurs find themselves in surroundings in which they feel alien and isolated; it is not really *their* society.

TABLE 4.8 Life Goals of Nuosu and Han Entrepreneurs

Goals	Nuosu (%)	Han (%)
Good future for children	86.4	90.5
Improved living conditions for Nuosu	84.0	52.4
Development of society	80.3	76.2
Family happiness	77.8	83.3
Contribution to socialism	66.7	66.7
Social role model	66.7	42.9
Increased income/improved living standard	63.0	38.1
Economic liberty	53.9	40.5
Support of lineage	49.4	33.3
Higher social prestige	48.2	33.3
Individual happiness	43.2	38.1

SOURCE: Author's survey, 1999–2002.

Due to their life situations, they are perhaps more socially frustrated. On the other hand it may be that the combination of economic processes of development and their being outsiders among the local people causes the Han entrepreneurs to strive harder toward their individual life goals than the Yi.

Both Nuosu and Han entrepreneurs attach a similar significance to their children's future. However, the seriousness with which Nuosu entrepreneurs treat family and clan is decreasing (see table 4.9). For the time being, this change may be evident only in terms of a decrease in family or clan consciousness. However, at least 19.8 percent of the Nuosu were of the opinion that it was not very important to foster their clan.

On the other hand, social awareness was relatively high among both groups of entrepreneurs. Not a single entrepreneur said that it was *unimportant* to contribute to the development of society. Yet, in some respects, the desire to contribute to society was less marked amongst Han entrepreneurs. It was much less important to Han to be "social role models" or to contribute to the local people's prosperity. This is related to the fact that society in the form of the local community plays a less dominant role for the Han; Nuosu are far more embedded and involved in local, i.e., Nuosu societal relations than Han whose roots are not in the Liangshan area. This is reflected by the fact that 21.4 percent of the Han but only 8.6 percent of the Nuosu agreed with the statement that it was not very important to be a social role model.

Another hypothesis is that the socially oriented values of the Communist Party correspond more closely to Nuosu traditional values. In Liangshan, Han entrepreneurs find themselves in alien and isolated surroundings that are not directly part of "their" society and are perhaps more socially frustrated. On the other hand, it may be that the combination of being outsiders and the force of economic development processes causes the Han entrepreneurs to strive harder for their individual life goals than the Nuosu.

The emphasis on morality and on maintaining collective values and obligations within Nuosu society may also influence Nuosu personal goals, the means people choose to achieve these goals, and social reference. Prioritizing collective goals affects the individual Nuosu society members' targets and top priorities. Our survey responses reflect a preference for collective and social targets.

However, there is arguably another reason why Nuosu prefer collective goals: Communist Party membership. The percentage of Party members among the surveyed Nuosu entrepreneurs is much higher than among their Han counterparts (Nuosu 44.4%, Han 26.2%). It is not surprising to find a higher percentage of Party members among Nuosu entrepreneurs; Han immigrants only seldom become Party members, and a relatively large number of local Nuosu Party cadres are in a position to choose the path of self-employment.

More than two-thirds of the respondents in both groups expressed a desire to "contribute to socialism." This is considered an important life goal with a symbolic function; our inquiries established that socialism and China are synonymous for many people. One entrepreneur said that it was very important to him to contribute to the development of socialism "because I am Chinese." The Party's propagandistic attempts to identify the political system with the interests of the Chinese people appear to have had some impact. Criticism of the state, the Party, or the system is correspondingly evaluated as anti-national, and thus anti-Chinese. This propaganda has had an equal impact on Nuosu and Han.

Increasing income and improving living standards is of greater significance for Nuosu entrepreneurs (63%) than for their Han counterparts (38.1%). Similarly, higher social prestige was also more important for Nuosu (48.2%) than for Han (33.3%). For poorer Nuosu, entrepreneurship is a highly significant way to climb up the economic and the social ladder. Furthermore, given that Nuosu as a whole enjoy less social prestige than Han do, entrepreneurship might also assist them in improving their position within China's scale of ethnic hierarchy.

Interestingly, more than 40 percent of the Nuosu and almost 40 percent of the Han interviewed believed individual happiness to be an important goal in life, and only between 14 percent and 15 percent (Nuosu and Han, respectively) stated that it was not important to them. This is a significant indication of a certain individualism among both Nuosu and Han.

In a survey of spending priorities, both Nuosu and Han at first glance appear to have similar goals (table 4.9). Individual lifestyle-related desires are not very important. Instead, the responses show that family, company, and social factors are more significant. However, for Han, the wish to invest a larger sum of money in their own companies was at the top of the list, whereas Nuosu would rather put money into financing their children's education. The second most important goal for Nuosu entrepreneurs was to invest in their own companies whereas for Han, the second most important goal was to provide for their children's education.

The groups' responses were similar regarding social purposes, but more than twice as many Nuosu as Han would invest their money to improve the living conditions of local Nuosu and Han, respectively. Almost a quarter of the Han would put money into their own ongoing education, which could also be justified as serving the interests of their own firms. Overall, for both groups the preferred choices are those that benefit their immediate families and their own companies.

Attitudes toward the Market Economy

The vast majority of the entrepreneurs support the market economy and its principles. Only one entrepreneur disagreed with the statement, "a market economy fosters economic development." This is a clear indication that entrepreneurs have a positive attitude toward the market economy. One expression of this attitude is that only 2.4 percent of the surveyed Han and 7.4 percent of the Nuosu were dissatisfied with the market economy. In addition, a large percentage of both entrepreneur groups defined "economic freedom" as a "very important" life goal (Nuosu 53.1%, Han 40.5%). Only a very small percentage defined economic freedom as less important (Nuosu 7.4%, Han 7.1%).

A thoroughly positive attitude toward the market economy is apparent in table 4.10, which examines the entrepreneurs' economic beliefs.

Large majorities within both entrepreneur groups believed that dispar-

TABLE 4.9 Economic Priorities of Nuosu and Han Entrepreneurs

Priorities	Nuosu (%)		Han (%)	
Children's education	72	(88.9%)	35	(83.3%)
Investment in one's own firm	65	(80.3%)	40	(95.2%)
Donations for social purposes	45	(55.6%)	23	(54.8%)
Improvement of local living conditions	35	(43.2%)	9	(21.4%)
House purchase	14	(17.3%)	6	(14.3%)
Enhancing social connections	13	(16.1%)	5	(11.9%)
Travel	11	(13.6%)	5	(11.9%)
Own education	8	(9.9%)	10	(23.8%)
Retirement savings	5	(6.2%)	5	(11.9%)
Car purchase	5	(6.2%)	7	(16.7%)
Savings/investments	2	(2.5%)	2	(4.8%)
Retiring, enjoy one's life	1	(1.2%)	0	
Money-lending	0		0	

SOURCE: Author's survey, 1999–2002.

TABLE 4.10 Economic Beliefs of Nuosu and Han Entrepreneurs

Beliefs	Nuosu (%)	Han (%)
Naturalness of wealth and poverty	73 (90.1%)	34 (81.0%)
Income according to personal achievement	72 (88.9%)	33 (78.6%)
Unequal income distribution as a temporary result of economic development	40 (49.4%)	17 (40.5%)
Necessity of government regulation to lessen income disparities	25 (30.9%)	7 (16.7%)
Responsibility of market economy for many social problems (e.g., criminality, unemployment, corruption, moral decay)	17 (21.0%)	2 (4.8%)
Dependence of wealth accumulation upon illegitimate methods	15 (18.5%)	4 (9.5%)
Lack of difference between socialist and capitalist market economies	12 (14.8%)	1 (2.4%)

SOURCE: Author's survey, 1999–2002.

ities in income are a naturally occurring phenomenon, and they would like these disparities to be tied to their achievement, performance, and success. At the same time, almost half of the respondents perceived such disparities as transitional phenomena and not as characteristics of a market economy. In addition, more than four-fifths of the Nuosu and more than two-thirds of the Han did not see income disparities as a source of social envy; almost all rejected the view that there is a connection between wealth and illegitimate behavior. However, a larger percentage of the Han negatively evaluated some aspects of the market economy.

The increasing income gap was seen as a problem that could potentially cause social and political instability. A third of the Han respondents stated that differences in income can cause envy and resentment, and almost a third of the respondents (Nuosu 29.6%, Han 31%) were basically dissatisfied with the income disparities in society and with how these were continuing to become worse. Accordingly, a significant number in both ethnic groups (Han 73.8% (a majority), Nuosu 49.4%) differentiated between a "socialist," more equal and stable economy and a "capitalist," more unequal and unstable market economy. The higher percentage of Han agreeing with this statement is probably because of their higher educational level.

Although only 5 percent of Han "strongly" agreed with the statement that market economies lead to many social problems, as many as 40.5 percent found it partially true. The respective percentages among Nuosu were much higher for the first statement and comparable for the second (21.2% and 42.0%). Nearly two-thirds of the Nuosu and almost half of the Han recognized that the market economy can cause many social problems. Nevertheless, their assessment of the market economy was ambivalent; many entrepreneurs indeed wished for a market economy but not for a market society at the mercy of the free play of market forces, which could create social problems and lead to instability. Thus, it might be understandable that at least a third (Nuosu 32.1%, Han 21.4%) favored a certain degree of state control of the market economy. In fact, awareness of market economy problems appeared to be widespread.

That Nuosu seem to trust the market economy less than Han can be expected due to the clan society's different value system and the crucial role the clan plays in social security and the moral economy. The market is understood to have potentially negative affects on personal and clan relationships, and on Nuosu culture and values because it erodes and changes organizational structures and damages the natural and social environment through migration, industrialization, and environmental destruction.

TABLE 4.11 Relative Importance of Different Factors on Commercial Success, according to Nuosu and Han Entrepreneurs

Success Factors	Nuosu (%)	Han (%)
1. Individual abilities	85.2	53.3
2. Knowledge of market	30.9	35.7
3. Sufficient capital	21.0	38.1
4. Clan support	14.8	2.4
5. Good relations with cadres	13.6	7.1
6. Good infrastructure	9.9	14.3
7. Frugality	8.6	19.1
8. Relatives in high positions	2.5	4.8
9. Other	4.9	2.4

SOURCE: Author's survey, 1999–2002.

Nearly all Nuosu and 90.5 percent of the Han agreed "very strongly" or "quite strongly" that the Party should provide a model for the market economy. This attitude has two implications: on the one hand, quite a few entrepreneurs see the Party as an instrument to control and curb the market economy's negative impacts; on the other, many entrepreneurs interpret the Party providing a "model" to mean that it accepts, promotes, and develops the market economy and private entrepreneurship.

Neither the Party and its policies nor the market alone are the most important factors for commercial success; entrepreneurs consider individual skills central in determining entrepreneurial ability and social success. More Nuosu entrepreneurs than Han feel that individuals play a decisive role in their economic development, whereas Han believe much more strongly that economic parameters such as knowledge of the market, investment capital, frugality, and good infrastructure are key. These factors also play a role for Nuosu entrepreneurs but their lower educational level and confidence in their own courage, bravery, and heroism— central values in Nuosu society—may be reasons for their emphasis on individual skills and abilities.

Interestingly, table 4.11 shows that the clan is not regarded as a central factor for commercial success, by either Nuosu or Han. Instead, even though the Nuosu are strongly embedded in clan networks, they find that individual strengths and abilities have a greater influence on commercial success; the Han barely consider clan support as a factor at all. In this case, Nuosu

TABLE 4.12 Relative Economic Prestige of Professions,
according to Private Nuosu and Han Entrepreneurs

Progression	Han	Nuosu
Private entrepreneurs	2.50	2.71
Cadres, central	2.77	3.25
Managers, state firm	3.59	3.61
Managers, rural firm	3.83	4.33
Individual entrepreneurs	4.15	4.55
Intellectuals	4.18	4.49
Technicians	4.34	4.27
Cadres, local	5.03	5.00
Workers, private sector	5.88	6.33
Workers, state firm	7.03	7.14
Peasants	8.20	7.99

SOURCE: Author's survey, 1999–2002.

may not consider the clan to be highly important for commercial success because entrepreneurs actually need to break through their clan bonds in some senses in order to pursue individual economic advantage. This relates back to the entrepreneur's dilemma discussed in the introduction.

Assessment of Economic, Social, and Political Prestige

Both entrepreneur groups rated their own economic, social, and political position on a scale from 1 (high) to 10 (low) against eleven listed status groups (see tables 4.12, 4.13, and 4.14). There were only small variations in their assessment of their own economic prestige; with an average score of 2.64, both groups accorded entrepreneurs the highest prestige, followed by leading cadres in Beijing and managers of state-owned enterprises. They generally believed that cadres could not keep up with entrepreneurs in terms of income.

In social terms, the entrepreneurs placed themselves in an upper middle position: Han ranked themselves fourth and Nuosu ranked themselves fifth—this would suggest that they want to rise socially. Chinese surveys taken in the 1980s consistently show private entrepreneurs to occupy the lower third of the social stratum. They have apparently achieved upward social mobility since then, whereas small entrepreneurs (individual laborers) are

TABLE 4.13 Relative Social Prestige of Professions,
according to Private Nuosu and Han Entrepreneurs

Profession	Han	Nuosu
Cadres, central	2.16	1.75
Cadres, local	4.08	3.17
Intellectuals	4.18	3.30
Managers, state firm	3.97	3.89
Private entrepreneurs	3.88	4.13
Technicians	4.66	4.27
Managers, rural firm	4.10	4.50
Individual entrepreneurs	4.93	5.65
Workers, private sector	6.09	6.67
Workers, state firm	6.45	6.93
Peasants	7.69	7.45

SOURCE: Author's survey, 1999–2002.

TABLE 4.14 Relative Political Prestige of Professions,
according to Private Nuosu and Han Entrepreneurs

Profession	Han	Nuosu
Cadres, central	1.55	1.75
Cadres, local	3.20	2.93
Intellectuals	3.68	3.30
Managers, state firm	3.55	4.15
Managers, rural firm	4.00	4.89
Private entrepreneurs	5.62	5.21
Technicians	5.53	5.34
Workers, state firm	6.41	6.55
Individual entrepreneurs	6.63	6.79
Workers, private sector	6.66	7.20
Peasants	7.98	7.79

SOURCE: Author's survey, 1999–2002.

still not particularly socially respected (ranked eighth in this survey). It is also interesting that Nuosu rank cadres slightly higher than Han rank them. This may be because most local cadres, other than at the central level, of course, are Nuosu, or because Nuosu generally accord government officials a higher social status.

The highest social and political prestige was attributed to cadres at the central and local levels but there were differences in the ranking of local cadres' social prestige. Han ranked them fourth (at 4.08) and Nuosu ranked them second (3.17). As most of the local cadres were Nuosu, Han may have had reservations about them, considering them crude and poorly educated. Politically, the entrepreneurs ranked themselves in the lower middle stratum, which underscores their increasing prestige; Chinese surveys in the early 1990s placed entrepreneurs at the bottom of the scale for political prestige.

Economically and socially, workers in state enterprises enjoy less prestige than workers in private enterprises do. Because state companies have uncertain futures and because some parts of the private sector offer higher wages, workers in private sector firms have higher status than workers in state sector companies. The state workers who were privileged in the past are now ranked at the bottom economically, along with the peasantry. In contrast, workers in state companies ranked highly in their political prestige, even above individual entrepreneurs. Here, the former political role of workers as the "forerunners of all classes" may still have a lingering effect.

There were marked differences in the ranking of intellectuals. Socially, both groups ranked them in the middle, but Nuosu entrepreneurs ranked them third while Han ranked them sixth. Intellectuals were accorded a relatively high political rating (Nuosu ranked them third, Han fourth). Political prestige is the expression of authority, power, and control over decision making, which is concentrated in the hands of both central and local officials. Entrepreneurs perceived intellectuals as being more competent in rational decision making than other people because of their educational level and knowledge. One factor that plays a role here is that Han businessmen have always disdained intellectuals, probably because intellectuals disdained them. In addition, education has become more generally accessible throughout China, so, the prestige associated with scarcity has diminished. However, in core Nuosu areas of Liangshan, education is still a rarity and may still carry some mystique.

To summarize, entrepreneurs have gained enough self-confidence to view themselves as occupying the top socioeconomic stratum. However, both

Nuosu and Han entrepreneurs perceive their own economic capital and corresponding economic position as superior to that of the other. That this phenomenon was consistent across all the surveyed counties indicates that a relatively homogenous consciousness of economic position exists among Liangshan's entrepreneurs. Private entrepreneurs also classified themselves relatively highly in social terms. Politically, however, entrepreneurs perceived themselves as having only an average or marginal influence, at least in terms of their visible participation in political life and in their ability to shape political events and circumstances.

Chinese surveys have also suggested that the prestige of private entrepreneurs is growing. A 1999 survey of 2,599 people in Han areas throughout China evaluated the prestige of 69 professions and ranked private entrepreneurs twenty-fifth on the list, with 78.6 points (where 20 was the lowest and 100 was the highest attainable score). In 1987, private entrepreneurs had received 67.6 points in an identical survey. In each case, respondents between the ages of 16 and 35 years ranked entrepreneurs the highest. In addition, in response to a question on desired careers, entrepreneurship ranked third in the 16-to-45 age group and fourth among those over 46 (Xu Xinxin 2000).

5

The Effect of Entrepreneurs
on Local Politics

The degree to which entrepreneurs are satisfied or dissatisfied with local politics reflects on the market situation, local government, and the state of local entrepreneurship. "Local government" here refers to county and town or township governments; local politics in China involve Communist Party organizations as well. When asked whether they believed their interests were adequately taken into account by the local government, 24.7 percent of Nuosu entrepreneurs answered "yes," 51.8 percent said they were only partially taken into account, and 23.5 percent answered "no." Among Han entrepreneurs, the corresponding figures reported in our survey were 9.5 percent, 54.7 percent, and 35.7 percent. About one-third of both Nuosu and Han entrepreneurs (Nuosu 35%, Han 36.6%) were satisfied with their current business situation. More than 50 percent were more satisfied than dissatisfied, and only one Nuosu out of 81 and two out of 43 Han entrepreneurs declared themselves to be dissatisfied. Dissatisfaction with government policies, on the other hand, was much more obvious, albeit with notable differences between Han and Nuosu responses. Almost a quarter of the Nuosu stated that the local administration took their interests into account, compared to only 10 percent of the Han. More Han than Nuosu also negatively evaluated the work done by their local governments.

Only a small number from each group (less than 10%) found their local government's performance adequate, indicating a significant degree of dissatisfaction. Their discontent arises from the problems outlined in chapters 3 and 4, namely, discrimination against private entrepreneurs, excessive taxes and fees, and inadequate assistance for entrepreneurs. The frustration also has an ethnic component; as we have noted, ethnic networks and relationships are critical to carrying out business activities, and creating and

TABLE 5.1 Opinions of Nuosu and Han Entrepreneurs
on Government Economic Policy

	Nuosu (%)			Han (%)		
	Believe	Partially believe	Do not believe	Believe	Partially believe	Do not believe
Government's policy for the private sector is good, its implementation is problematic	62.8	34.6	2.6	85.4	14.6	–
Currently limitations on private enterprises are detrimental to the development of the private economy	42.1	43.4	14.5	61.0	24.4	14.6

SOURCE: Author's survey, 1999–2002.

maintaining relationships with local Nuosu officials is more difficult for Han entrepreneurs than for Nuosu. There is a widespread feeling within the Han community that they are at a disadvantage compared to Nuosu entrepreneurs and some Han have even considered leaving the county for this reason. This lack of satisfaction is represented in table 5.1.

More than four-fifths of the Han and nearly two-thirds of the Nuosu have reservations regarding government policies, revealing problems with implementation in various areas. But here, too, as shown by the responses in table 5.1, the percentage of dissatisfied or skeptical Han entrepreneurs is significantly larger than of Nuosu entrepreneurs. A majority of the entrepreneurs also held the opinion that local cadres were insufficiently prepared for the introduction of a socialist market economy; only a small number disagreed (Han 16.7%, Nuosu 24.7%).

When asked what they would do when confronted with a local department or government decision that was unfavorable to the development of their company, 27.2 percent of Nuosu entrepreneurs said they would accept the decision, 53.1 percent would provisionally accept it and also try to alter it, and 19.7 percent said they would not accept it and would work to change it; on the other hand, 25.6 percent of Han entrepreneurs said they would accept such a decision, 46.5 percent would both accept and try to alter it, and 27.9 percent would try to alter it.[1] Thus, about a quarter of both groups of entrepreneurs were willing to accept unsatisfactory decisions made by the local authorities. However, the overwhelming majority said they would try to oppose such decisions. Han said that they would work through the official channels ("I would try to alter [the decision]") while Nuosu indicated that they would use more informal channels ("I would accept it but. . . .") such as local networks and ethnic resources. These findings reveal that entrepreneurs, therefore, do not passively experience policymaking—they feel they can actively shape it and they use various means to try to influence local politics and combat unfavorable decisions through informal mechanisms or through active resistance.

The majority of entrepreneurs also believe that, in principle, the state should be less interventionist, that it should concern itself with creating adequate infrastructure for the entrepreneurs and not with company matters. Clear majorities (Nuosu 75.6%, Han 68.3%) prefer the state to be responsible for macroeconomic direction and to leave company management processes up to the entrepreneurs. Only a small percentage (Nuosu 1.3%, Han 9.8%) contradicted this opinion; the remainder agreed somewhat.

LOCAL POLITICAL PARTICIPATION AND POLITICAL INFLUENCE

Political participation and political influence can follow formal and informal patterns. The formal system is characterized by external rules and institutions determined by the state. The informal system is defined by "interpersonal activities in support of a tacitly accepted, but unofficial matrix of political intent, which exist outside of legal, institutional frameworks, such as government, constitutional and bureaucratic constructs"(Fukui 2000: 3). The use of non-legitimate means to pursue public goals is explicit in such arrangements. The concept of formal systems refers to planned organizational commitments in contrast to informal, unplanned, and spontaneous ones. Formal systems can be characterized as state institutionalized and codified; informal systems are characterized by social self-organization or collective action by social groups. Formal political structures primarily exercise power; informal political structures influence politics.

Nonetheless, formal and informal political spheres are not entirely separable; they complement each other and are indispensable to the entrepreneurs who seek to run their companies without friction with the government. Informal politics are frequently a reaction to challenges posed by the formal system. Life is not shaped solely by the relationship between state and society but also by social obligations and networks. Informal, local political influence is exerted through networks of clans, lineages, social relationships (Ch: *guanxi*), or through political corruption in the form of bribes. In societies with underdeveloped formal institutions, such as China, informal institutions are an important and necessary supplement to the policy-making process.

In China, direct intervention in political matters and formal attempts to exert direct political pressure tend to be politically explosive. Informal and indirect operations, behind-the-scenes negotiation, and informal power structures (relationships and networks) may often be more successful in influencing political outcomes. Formal, organized forms of political participation and influence include Party membership, use of deputy positions in People's Congresses and Political Consultative Conferences, or membership in representative associations for entrepreneurs.

Entrepreneurs are not fundamentally interested in politics; rather, political involvement is a necessary component of entrepreneurial activity. They try to influence local politics through membership in political institutions and interest organizations and through personal connections with Party officials. However, it is impossible to entirely separate formal and informal patterns of influence. Entrepreneurs (or their institutional representatives) are strongly influenced by their clan or affinal connections, which are, in fact, informal networks.

POLITICAL INFLUENCE THROUGH MEMBERSHIP IN POLITICAL INSTITUTIONS AND INTEREST ORGANIZATIONS

In addition to Party membership, becoming a deputy of the local People's Congress or the Political Consultative Conference is an important political instrument for developing and asserting entrepreneurial interests. Members of the People's Congresses represent a cross-section of society. As deputies to these organizations, entrepreneurs thus come in contact not only with the local political elite but also with other influential local personalities. Almost all of the entrepreneurs interviewed expressed an interest in becoming a deputy of either the People's Congress or of the Political Consultative Conferences.

For some years now, the People's Congress has been undergoing a process of institutional change. The intent is to grant increased rights to entrepreneurs, giving them greater control over decisions and allowing them to have a greater say in political matters, which has attracted many entrepreneurs. Interestingly, a much higher percentage of Nuosu entrepreneurs

TABLE 5.2 Organization Membership of Nuosu and Han Entrepreneurs

Organization	Nuosu (%)	Han (%)
Federation of Industry and Commerce	21 (25.9%)	25 (59.5%)
Association for Private Enterprises	12 (14.8%)	11 (26.2%)
Other entrepreneur or professional associations	3 (3.7%)	5 (11.9%)
Communist Party	36 (44.4%)	11 (26.2%)
Communist Youth League	15 (18.5%)	1 (2.4%)
Other	4 (4.9%)	7 (16.7%)

SOURCE: Author's survey, 1999–2002.

rather than Han are interested in playing a role in politics. Our interviews revealed that because of the ethnic environment, Han felt that they had a smaller chance of attaining political positions and that the dominance of the Nuosu would limit their ability to participate. Given the problematic local conditions, they thought it best not to be active in political institutions. Accordingly, less than half of the Han entrepreneurs (41.5%), as compared to more than two-thirds of the Nuosu (70.5%), responded that they would "very gladly" become deputies of the local People's Congress; 56.1 percent of the Han and 23.1 percent of the Nuosu said they would "quite gladly" become deputies, and 2.4 percent of the Han and 6.4 percent of the Nuosu said that they would "not very gladly" do so.

Both Han and Nuosu entrepreneurs are highly involved in their communities and are interested in politics and political participation. Only 9.5 percent of the Han and 16.1 percent of the Nuosu supported the opinion that entrepreneurs should concern themselves only with company matters and leave politics to the Party and government. More than half of the entrepreneurs rejected this opinion entirely (Nuosu 53.1%, Han 52.4%). In addition to the standard political organizations (parties, mass organizations), since the mid-1980s, entrepreneurial and occupational associations have also emerged in Liangshan. The entrepreneurs we interviewed were members of the associations listed in table 5.2.

Party Organizations

A 1999 Chinese survey sampled 1 percent of all private entrepreneurs and found 19.8 percent of the sample to be Party members.[2] As table 5.2 reveals,

the percentage of Communist Party members within our sample of entrepreneurs was far greater. Membership in occupational and specialist associations is also an important political resource, as is membership in official,
non-Communist organizations; entrepreneurs gain some measure of political influence by being highly involved in different organizations.

Private entrepreneurs were not officially permitted to join the Communist Party or the Communist Youth League until the 16th Party Congress
of the CCP in 2002. However, the local Party branches in all of the counties we researched had accepted private entrepreneurs prior to this date.
Many private businessmen hoped their Party membership would bring them
greater local influence. The local Party leaders, on the other hand, expected
that accepting entrepreneurs into the Party would better integrate and control the private sector and hoped to effectively utilize the entrepreneurs' economic and financial potential in the Party's interest. Some entrepreneurs
even had leading positions as directors or deputy directors of county
bureaus, Party secretaries of townships or villages, or village heads. Such
positions as well as membership in general gave entrepreneurs the ability
to protect their own interests and to make important political *guanxi* with
which to influence local politics.

Of the Nuosu enterprises surveyed in 1999–2002, 8.6 percent had Party
committees, 13.6 percent had trade unions, and 6.2 percent had Communist Youth Leagues; of the Han enterprises, 9.5 percent had Party committees, 38.1 percent had trade unions, and 2.4 percent had Youth Leagues. These
figures show that private enterprises are not embedded in the organizational
structures of the Communist Party and are therefore important pathways
for increasing social liberty. However, because the private sector is an economically important segment of its membership, Party leadership tries to
control it by extending the reach of the Party organizations into the private
firms.[3] But Party or mass organizations existed in relatively few of the private companies we surveyed; the majority of the firms were not bound into
Party organizational structures.

Party organizations in private sector firms are different from those in
public sector companies: they are more strongly subjected to market requirements and to private entrepreneurs' interests and decisions. The entrepreneurs themselves are often members of the Party, or at least would like to
be. Conversations with entrepreneurs show that in spite of their reservations toward the Party, Party organizations are understood to be part of an
important network of Party institutions, which may be used in the com-

pany's interest. Entrepreneurs also believe that they can shape Party organizations to suit their own interests.

As we see from the data above, a significant number of Han companies and a smaller number of Nuosu companies have trade union committees. This is because of a Sichuan Trade Union Umbrella Organization mandate requiring that trade union organizations be founded in all individual companies and small private firms in all counties. The mandate also imposed compulsory membership, and in 2002 the organization exacted six yuan in monthly dues. Part of these proceeds went directly to the provincial trade union organization. Through our interviews, it became clear that this was simply a new way of acquiring income for the organization and not a way to fund assistance programs for entrepreneurs. For example, the chairperson of the Jinyang County trade union organization, a Han hotel and construction company owner, was unable to name either the duties of his organization, apart from "mutual assistance," or how it differed from existing lobby associations.

The trade unions actually represent the interests of the employers rather than the employees; the entrepreneurs themselves are the heads of their companies' trade unions and are able to request union intervention or support in cases of conflict with their employees. The majority of the trade union committees are found in Han-owned companies; it is difficult to persuade Nuosu entrepreneurs to become trade union members, and local Nuosu entrepreneurs need less protection than Han do. The trade union organizations actually see themselves as interest groups protecting the interests of Han entrepreneurs, at least in those counties where the majority of the population is Nuosu and the Party organizations are dominated by Nuosu. Many Han feel that the local Party organizations are special interest groups representing the Nuosu.

The number of Party and Communist Youth League committees in private companies is still low. For the most part, the entrepreneurs themselves establish and direct (nominal) Party or Youth League committees within their own companies. To some extent, they are anticipating the wishes of superior Party organizations that mandate establishing such committees in private firms. By voluntarily setting up such Party organizations, entrepreneurs are thus in a position to demonstrate their pioneering spirit and loyalty to the Party.

In general, private company organizational structures and functions have subverted the Party's organizational structures and functions. Party organizations exist in only a minority of companies and where they do exist, the entrepreneurs exercise control over them.

Interest Associations

In the late 1980s, the central government permitted the creation of professional, entrepreneurial, and other associations. As far as the private entrepreneurs are concerned, there are no official, *non-state* associations that represent their interests. However, there are two semi-governmental associations that officially act on their behalf: the Federation of Industry and Commerce and the Association for Private Enterprises. Both of these associations have branches in the majority of the counties we surveyed.

The Federation of Industry and Commerce (Ch: *Gongshanglian*) is a semi-governmental organization that primarily accepts large entrepreneurs and is financed partly from the state budget and partly through membership dues. When it was founded in 1953, the Federation's goal was to link private entrepreneur representatives with the Communist Party. The current official primary function is to promote the private sector, support state regulations for administrating the private sector, and form a bridge between the CCP and private entrepreneurs. Federation branches exist from the national to the county level. Lower level branches are not subject to oversight from the national headquarters; they are overseen by the United Front Departments at each respective administrative level. In contrast to the Association for Private Enterprises, membership in the Federation is voluntary. Federation of Industry and Commerce representatives advertise that their organization prioritizes entrepreneurs while the Association for Private Enterprises pays more attention to companies.

Currently, the Federation's main task is to influence private entrepreneurs and ensure that they are covered by government policies. However, concerning its role in the larger social process of economization, the Federation's intent is to expand economic activity and represent the larger entrepreneurs' interests. In contrast, the Association for Private Enterprises is merely somewhat of an appendage to the Bureau for the Administration of Industry and Commerce. The Federation works more independently of the state administration and in a more interest-oriented way. Its autonomy is strengthened by the formation of local chambers of commerce (Ch: *shanghui*), which do not fall under governmental jurisdiction. However, in poorer regions, such as Liangshan Prefecture, financial shortages limit the chamber's sphere of influence. The president of the Federation of Industry and Commerce in Zhaojue County said his organization had charged no membership fees until the year 2000, which limited the local federation to a very small budget.

Organizational and operational differences between branches and their degree of influence depend on a number of factors: the strength of local entrepreneurship, financial power and independence, the local political structure (level of autonomy permitted by the Party committee), the local authorities' interest in developing the private sector (influencing, for instance, the amount of taxation), and the branch leadership's personal prestige and its connections to the local political elite. As a rule, the president of the local Federation of Industry and Commerce is also the vice president of the Political Consultative Conference in his or her respective area. The vice president of the Federation is frequently a well-known and important entrepreneur.

In order to entice new members, the local Federations of Industry and Commerce have increased their efforts to represent private entrepreneurs in dealing with the government and with other authorities. For example, the president of the Federation of Industry and Commerce in Zhaojue wrote a letter to the National Federation in which he described problems in market organization and administrative discrimination and complained about the Bureau for the Administration of Industry and Commerce. The Federation of Industry and Commerce followed up with an investigation and presented the results to the county mayor. The mayor personally looked into the issues and tried to find solutions to the problems. Resolving conflicts thus still depends on the leading local officials' attitudes, but the Federation of Industry and Commerce is able to bring problems out into the open and help solve them.

Our interviews did not reveal an ethnic aspect to membership or activities in these organizations. In industrially more developed counties like Ganluo or Mianning, the organizations created ties between ethnic groups. In other counties, entrepreneurs of both ethnic groups felt that the organizations were weak and not adequately able to represent their interests. In such cases, Nuosu entrepreneurs turned to other methods for promoting their interests, such as via clan networks and *guanxi* to officials.

The Association for Private Enterprises (Ch: *Siying qiye xiehui*), established under the direction of the Bureau for the Administration of Industry and Commerce in the early 1980s, started out as an association for small individual firm owners (Ch: *getihu xiehui*) and started to take its present form in 1993. Even at the local level, this semi-official organization is directly run by the Bureau for the Administration of Industry and Commerce. Membership is compulsory; private companies automatically become members when granted their business licenses. An assistant director of the Bureau for the Administration of Industry and Commerce generally chairs the Association for Private Enterprises, and larger private entrepreneurs serve as the vice chairs. At the time of our study, the Association's budget was partly derived from administrative fees paid by private entrepreneurs and partly from membership dues.

Although their duties are similar, the Association for Private Enterprises and the Federation of Industry and Commerce function differently. One major difference lies in their membership. The Association for Private Enterprises represents private entrepreneurs and private sector employees and consists of juridical members (firms), not natural persons (entrepreneurs). The Federation of Industry and Commerce only accepts entrepreneurs as members. The Federation also primarily performs a political function; it contacts large, influential private entrepreneurs and convinces them to become delegates to People's Congresses or Political Consultative Conferences. In contrast, the Association for Private Enterprises addresses internal company processes, as well as political socialization and control. Another difference is in hierarchical structure. The Association is subordinate to the Bureau for the Administration of Industry and Commerce and this hierarchy facilitates contact and cooperation between its members and other official departments. Entrepreneurs use their connection with the Bureau for the Administration of Industry and Commerce to put administrative force behind their entrepreneurial interests. On the other hand, the Federations for Industry and Commerce are subordinate to the local United Front Departments of the Party, which are hierarchically superior to the local Bureaus for the Administration of Industry and Commerce. Consequently, the Federations for Industry and Commerce possess a hierarchical and institutional advantage over Associations for Private Enterprises during negotiations.

However, the two organizations are in a permanent conflict of interests. On one hand, they represent CCP and government interests, and, on the other hand, they represent the entrepreneurs' interests. Since the two spheres of interest seldom overlap, there are not only internal confrontations between the members of these organizations and their leadership, but also external conflicts between the organizations and the government. Private sector employees, who are a significant part of the Party membership, thus threaten to elude the Party's organizational control. This could mean a loss of members and possibly of political control. To maintain and ensure political control, Party branches have been set up within private sector firms;

it was felt that the control exercised by the Bureau for the Administration of Industry and Commerce alone would be insufficient.

The organizational situation of the Federation for Industry and Commerce and the Association for Private Enterprises varied among the surveyed counties. In Ganluo, for instance, an Association for Private Enterprises did not exist because private companies were classified as "town- and township-owned enterprises." Private entrepreneurs were members of the Federation of Industry and Commerce instead. Both the Association for Individual Laborers (Ch: *gexie*) and the Association for Private Enterprises (Ch: *sixie*) had branches in Mianning under the supervision of the Bureau for the Administration of Industry and Commerce. The Bureau argued, however, that the two associations were actually "one organization with two signs," in other words, two nominally separate organizations that functioned as one organization.

In Zhaojue, Yanyuan, Meigu, and Puge, branches of both the Association for Private Enterprises and of the Association for Individual Laborers actually existed. In Butuo, there was a branch of the Association for Individual Laborers and of the Federation for Industry and Commerce. Because membership in the Association for Private Enterprises was compulsory, it was surprising that a significant number of entrepreneurs denied that they were members. Some stated that they did not know anything about it or that they ignored their membership. Many others indicated that this association simply did not represent their interests. In Yanyuan alone, nine entrepreneurs said they were non-members, three said they were members of both associations, and a few entrepreneurs said they were members of just one. For many business people, membership in an association seemed to be unimportant.

In Ganluo, a branch of the Federation of Industry and Commerce was established in 1994, and it had 428 voluntary members by 1999. The Chamber of Commerce was subdivided into associations for three sectors: mining, mining products, and the manufacturing industry. The chairperson, a Nuosu, was also the deputy director of the United Front Department, which was overseen by the County Party Committee. He had studied law and had previously been the director of the Bureau for the Administration of Rural Enterprises. His biggest ambition was to become an entrepreneur himself. However, he was unable to explain to us the difference between the Federation of Industry and Commerce and the Chamber of Commerce. The former is an administrative organ assigned to the County Party Committee and the Chamber of Commerce is a "non-governmental" (Ch: *minjiande*) organization that does not receive state subsidies; it finances itself through donations and membership dues. In Butuo as well, the head of the Federation (a Nuosu) was not able to articulate the duties of his organization and stated that it possessed "a bridging function between government and entrepreneurs."[4]

In the Ganluo People's Congress, there were three deputies from the ranks of the entrepreneurs; in the Political Consultative Conference, they made up 23 out of the 144 deputies. At one time, three different entrepreneurs were said to have been deputies of the Prefectural Political Consultative Conference, and one had been a deputy of the Prefectural People's Congress. There was only one deputy in each of those institutions at the provincial level. The vice chairperson of the Federation of Industry and Commerce was also the vice director of the Bureau for the Administration of Industry and Commerce and the vice president of the Chamber of Commerce. In our interviews, we learned that the Associations possess a certain degree of leverage in bargaining with the county leadership, which will yield to their pressure and insert their proposals into the local development plan.

In Zhaojue, a branch of the Federation was founded in 1995. Their chairperson's report to the "Third conference of the Zhaojue County Federation for Industry and Commerce delegates" in 2000 clearly and openly described Zhaojue's existing problems (see chapter 3). The county leadership's interest in combating poverty through the development of the private sector was the key for promoting this kind of discussion. The director of the Zhaojue County Party Committee's United Front Department (a Nuosu) was also chair of the Federation of Industry and Commerce, chair of the Chamber of Commerce, and deputy chair of the County Political Consultative Conference. Consequently, he was an important figure in the political hierarchy and wielded a certain degree of bargaining power. The county political elite appreciated his position because he was able to use his power to benefit the Federation. The two deputy directors were both entrepreneurs and not members of the Party.

In Mianning, the Bureau for the Administration of Industry and Commerce oversaw the Association for Individual Laborers and the Association for Private Enterprises. The administration of both associations and their members stated that the two organizations basically had little significance. Officials informed us that the associations "organized basketball competitions and other sports events" and organized various excursions.[5] There was little available information on the Mianning Federation of Industry and Commerce. The associations, according to the interviewees, were still relatively new.

In Meigu, the deputy director of the County Party Committee's United Front Department (a Nuosu) was the vice president of the Federation of Industry and Commerce. The branch was established in 1995 and had 220 members at the time of the interview, including all of the larger private and individual entrepreneurs. The organization still had no chairperson and only two officers, a deputy director and a secretary. There was neither a described position nor a salary available for a chairperson, who would have to have been a state official, and a lack of funding prevented the Federation from actively taking on projects. The county government only paid 900 yuan per year. The Federation did not charge membership dues because Meigu was classified as a poverty-ridden county. If they had charged membership fees, nobody would have joined. The Associations for Individual Laborers and for Private Enterprises were also inactive.

From the examples in the different counties, we can see that the Association for Private Enterprises and the Federation of Industry and Commerce are not autonomous interest organizations. In some places, they are almost entirely an extension of the bureaucracy, and private entrepreneurs do not feel that the organizations represent their interests. A Chinese research survey found that over 80 percent of the entrepreneurs desired strong, i.e., independent representative associations (Qin 2000: 109); only a small percentage rejected the idea of forming nonofficial representative organizations.

Of the entrepreneurs surveyed, more than four-fifths (85.4%) of the Han and almost two-thirds (65.4%) of the Nuosu were in favor of setting up a nonofficial association on behalf of private entrepreneurs. The difference between the ethnic groups can be explained by a difference in representation: Han entrepreneurs view an independent organization acting on their behalf as very important in order to balance out the discrimination they experience locally. For Nuosu entrepreneurs, such an association is less significant because they have other means of asserting their interests. More than a quarter of entrepreneurs in both ethnic groups wished for separate associations for Nuosu and Han.

Entrepreneurs feel that the most important function of an independent association is to facilitate cooperation between private companies and the government (see table 5.3). Although highly important in Western countries, an organization functioning either as a lobby group or as an industrial representative for bargaining with employees plays only a minor role in China. A lobby group would have no place in the present-day authoritarian system in China. Entrepreneurs would prefer an organization that achieves their goals

TABLE 5.3 Most Important Functions of Non-Official Associations, according to Nuosu and Han Entrepreneurs

Function	Nuosu (%)		Han (%)	
1. Cooperation with the government	33	(40.7%)	34	(81.0%)
2. Improvement of management and market knowledge of Nuosu entrepreneurs	28	(34.6%)	6	(14.3%)
3. Assistance with business contacts and advertisement	23	(28.4%)	17	(40.5%)
4. Support in raising social prestige	20	(24.7%)	23	(54.8%)
5. Provision of information	12	(14.8%)	15	(35.1%)
6. Representation of entrepreneurs' interests against the authorities	10	(12.4%)	7	(16.7%)
7. Representation of entrepreneurs' interests against employees	8	(9.9%)	5	(11.9%)
8. Training	7	(8.6%)	2	(4.8%)
9. Other	0	(—)	0	(—)

SOURCE: Author's survey, 1999–2002.

in the negotiating process with the state by representing and asserting their interests in a non-confrontational, informal, behind-the-scenes way.

While 81 percent of the Han felt such an association's most important task would be to cooperate with the government, only 40.7 percent of the Nuosu felt this way. Again, this reflects Nuosu entrepreneurs' closer contacts with the local authorities and their attempts to promote their interests at an informal level. The Nuosu would like to see practical services provided by a representative association; over a third of the Nuosu (34.6%) expect outreach and assistance in improving their knowledge of management and markets. More than a quarter of the Nuosu expected help in setting up commercial contacts, advertising, and increasing the social prestige of being an entrepreneur.

For over 50 percent of the Han, assistance in increasing prestige is the second most important service that could potentially be provided by an autonomous association. This is followed by assistance in making business contacts, advertising, and serving as an information center. The existing associations and organizations did not provide such services. The idea of providing further training was not well received because, as we discovered in our interviews, "further training" is a loaded term implying all kinds of political or ideological "studies" greatly removed from business or company interests.

In general, the Federations of Industry and Commerce and the Chambers of Commerce have a limited ability to represent entrepreneurs because they are subject to the control of the local Party committees. However, they do contribute proposals to local discussion on how better to organize the work of private companies and entrepreneurs. Their degree of influence should not be underestimated, but it depends on the openness of the county leadership—in most counties, money shortages exacerbate the Federation's dependence on the county bureaucracy. In contrast, rather than acting as a representative organization, the Associations for Private Entrepreneurs act as organs for control exercised by the Bureaus for the Administration of Industry and Commerce; they focus on the firms, not on the entrepreneurs as persons.

Because both the Federation of Industry and Commerce and the Association of Private Entrepreneurs depend on the local bureaucracy, the majority of entrepreneurs hope for a new independent organization to represent their interests, even if their primary wish is for this organization to try to cooperate with the state. The wish for an independent lobby association can be interpreted as showing a consciousness among entrepreneurs of their commonly shared interests.[6] This is shown by the number of entrepreneurs who believe that in order for the private sector to develop, private entrepreneurs need to stand together to support their interests: of the 78 Nuosu and the 42 Han entrepreneurs we surveyed, 72.8 percent of Nuosu and 78.6 percent of Han fully believed this, 23.5 percent of Nuosu and 19.1 percent of Han partially believed it, and no Nuosu and only 1.2 percent of Han did not believe it. The overwhelming majority recognized shared interests and the need to assert themselves proactively in shared activities. This is a basic precondition for political participation and for developing political influence. The common sentiment is emphasized by the fact that only a single entrepreneur spoke against this statement.

PERSONAL AND SOCIAL CONNECTIONS (CH: *GUANXI*)

Social relationships and networks are not only important for developing business contacts and for reducing uncertainty and risk, they are also important for raising social prestige and exerting political influence. Politically, *guanxi* forms an important link between communities and social groups such as different clans and lineages, villages, associations, and occupational groups as well as among individuals and between individuals and the government and/or Party. Moreover, it facilitates interactive negotiation processes and enables decision making, which are often either impossible or difficult to achieve in other ways. Formal options for political participation are lacking and institutional mechanisms for implementing or encouraging political participation are marginally developed. Thus, *guanxi* becomes a means with which to influence politics and political decisions and serves as a link between the government or Party and society. However, using *guanxi* favors corruption and, in some ways, is indistinguishable from corruption. This is because some individuals and groups use *guanxi* to acquire influence, power, or advantages in order to set themselves above governmental, legal, ethical-moral, social, or political standards; in their use of *guanxi*, they consciously breach norms, seeking to obtain advantages only for those involved.

A Chinese study found that private entrepreneurs develop local political influence by using their financial potential to create personal relationships with highly placed officials. In this way, the entrepreneurs influence state institutions and local policies according to their own political interests (Li Peilin and Wang 1993: 49ff.). Since the entrepreneurs had informal personal connections to cadres, they did not want to speak about them during interviews with us. However, all the entrepreneurs (Nuosu and Han) we interviewed admitted that they attempt to build up close personal bonds with local officials.[7]

Guanxi plays a crucial role primarily among persons of the same ethnic group, i.e., between Nuosu entrepreneurs and Nuosu cadres or between Han entrepreneurs and Han cadres. However, in individual cases, particularly with larger entrepreneurs and in counties with a mixed Nuosu and Han population, *guanxi* transcends ethnic lines. As far as members of the same clan are concerned, Nuosu entrepreneurs, in contrast to the Han, do not perceive their relations with Nuosu cadres as *guanxi* and therefore do not perceive relations with local cadres as a problem. They argue that it is only natural to have connections to their kin (clan members). However, there is still an ethnic aspect to what we call *guanxi*. A prominent Nuosu entrepreneur noted,

> We all know that nothing gets done in China without social connections. Han are the masters of *guanxi*; the Nuosu are not as well versed in this art. This is why Nuosu influence ends at the prefectural level [of government].[8]

Though *guanxi* as a type of social relationship exists all over China, it is ethnically perceived in different ways. The above statement indicates that Nuosu perceive *guanxi* as a Han institution. They feel that Nuosu must adapt to it in order to handle certain types of situations. This is particularly true for entrepreneurs who have to establish *guanxi* with Han officials or with Nuosu officials with whom they have no kinship. Historically, clan relationships were more important to Nuosu than social connections to officials, as there were few officials in Liangshan. Thus, *guanxi* is perceived as historically alien to the Nuosu people.

Today, clan associations are another form of kin network (Ch: *jiazhi xiehui*). An example of a kin network would be an association founded by a Nuosu entrepreneur including people from the same clan, amongst them leading county, prefectural, and provincial officials. An example of a business established for the purpose of making *guanxi* is an amusement park built by an entrepreneur from Yanyuan. The primary purpose of his establishment is to have a place to invite county and prefectural officials to relax and have work related conversations. According to our observations, the park made no profit; it served simply to establish and maintain *guanxi*.

It is also relatively common to find family relationships among people in administrative positions. We met one important entrepreneur whose brother was the mayor of a neighboring county, his sister was a member of the local Party committee, one of his sons was a township mayor in the same county, and another son was the director of the County Bureau for the Administration of Rural Enterprises.

Guanxi and networks can be differentiated into strong ties, which are based on shared social identities (kinship and *tong* relationships; see chapter 6), and weak ties, which are not based on a shared social background. The strength or weakness of these ties depends on four factors: duration of the relationship, emotional intensity, ease in getting along or social comfort, and reciprocal services that characterize the bond (Granovetter 1973). A strong-ties relationship refers more or less to "broken-in" relations with people and groups with whom a person is associated through "natural" bonds. Weak ties refer to looser relationships with people outside of such natural bonds; Bourdieu calls these ties "practical relationships" (1998: 205ff).

Weak ties bring an actor into new relationship networks, exposing him or her to new ideas and new information and providing access to new resources. Strong ties go deeper and are easier to mobilize. People with few relationships outside of their immediate surroundings (family, clan, village) have to rely on a multiplicity of weak-ties relationships in order to survive as entrepreneurs. Li Fang has pointed out that both types of relationships are important: strong ties are more helpful when there is institutional uncertainty; weak ties are important when there is market uncertainty (Li Fang 1998: 180).

Both strong and weak ties can be found in bureaucracy and business. Business processes and access to markets as well as acquiring market information and resources require an expansion of relationships to include new groups, persons, and institutions, and, thus, an increase in weak ties. Whether entrepreneurs rely on weak or strong relationships depends to a great extent on whether the political, institutional, and legal preconditions for fair and equal access to markets are in place. This also applies to reducing bureaucratic interference in the market, in competition and in companies. Further promoting local incentive structures may help define normal relationships between enterprises and local authorities, but this also depends on access to markets.

Weak Ties at the Bureaucratic Level

Relationships with officials and government institutions are an important prerequisite for successful business activity. From the entrepreneurial point of view, these relationships are necessary because the local authorities have extensive power over important economic, financial, social, and political resources. David Wank names three methods that entrepreneurs use to influence officials: making financial or other contributions (in the form of gifts or privileges granted), offering real or fictional employment in their companies in high-salaried positions as consultants or managers, and by means of partnerships (patronage). For example, one Nuosu entrepreneur gained a former county Party leader's support by employing him as a consultant. Due to this man's high reputation among local cadres, his support enabled the entrepreneur to solve difficult problems quickly and efficiently. A partnership consists of giving the official a stake in the company, not in the form of capital shares but by sharing power or by giving him or her a post on the advisory board.

Direct financial contributions to government officials are illegal and could, without a doubt, be used against an entrepreneur, for example, in legal cases uncovering corruption amongst local cadres who protect a certain entrepreneur or in cases of conflict between local cadres. The larger entrepreneurs, especially in commercially developed regions, thus seek to transition from independent patron–client relationships with individual officials to a relationship of mutual patronage between the company and the institution (see Wank 1995: 166ff.). Independent patron–client relationships can be uncertain because every change of cadres requires building a new relationship, which costs a lot of time and money. Mutual patronage builds *guanxi* between the company and an institution, which is profitable for both parties. Such institutional relationships are generally of longer duration and not so strongly based on personal relationships. However, in Liangshan, the dependent patron–client relationship predominates in most fields of activity. For example, in our interviews, private entrepreneurs expressed themselves relatively openly about credit which they, as clients, had access to because of their individual personal relationships with local officials.

Numerous company activities require clearance from the local authorities, such as large investment projects, real estate purchases, certification of product quality, and environmental or production clearances. This is where *guanxi* can be especially important. Officials often expect a service or some privilege to be granted in exchange for their stamp of approval. Legal uncertainties and significant elbow room in decision making give civil servants the power to grant authorization quickly or to delay the process. Our interviews revealed that particularly Han entrepreneurs use gifts and donations or "gastro-politics" (invitations to dining and drinking, karaoke, or bars) to influence local officials. Yet, it is more difficult for Han than for Nuosu entrepreneurs to gain access to Nuosu officials. Nuosu entrepreneurs use local connections and networks to gain access to the officials and to influence them. One Nuosu entrepreneur commented,

> I used to be a township official. Then I became a county cadre and worked in several different counties. Through county and prefectural Party schools, I met many other officials, particularly Nuosu. Nuosu officials generally know each other rather well. These connections are indispensable for me as an entrepreneur; I can use them for company purposes. 'Comrade X, remember the wonderful time we shared in the Party school? Comrade Y, didn't we share hardships in township Z, without any light on those dark and cold nights where we drank together to forget our difficulties?' Who could refuse to provide some benefit to an old friend and comrade? To decline support to an old friend would be a moral offence.[9]

In addition, legal insecurity and unpredictable officials also make *guanxi* indispensable. The state has worked for years to improve legal conditions for companies but the private sector still suffers from legal insecurity. As a result, more than 60 percent of the Han and Nuosu survey respondents were either not satisfied or only partially satisfied with the legal situation.

Without a doubt, cadres possess an especially large amount of social capital, particularly when they are part of cadre networks and Party structures and are able to make use of their relationships for entrepreneurial activities. Many entrepreneurs stated that the extent and level of their of social relationships had played a central role in their decision to become self-employed. Relationships to officials in public office and companies are decisive for establishing and developing their companies. The entrepreneurs thus make great attempts to create relationships and to ensure adequate *guanxi*. Clan members, relatives, and friends are also very important in this respect. According to a Chinese study, 17.2 percent of private entrepreneurs believed they were proficient in making *guanxi*, as opposed to 10.5 percent of company heads who directed companies under other forms of ownership (state, township, etc.) (Zhongguo qiyejia diaocha xitong 1998a: 16).

However, the greater the distance between the entrepreneur and his or her relatives, the greater the degree of his or her contacts with cadres. In this scenario, the entrepreneur's connection to important networks is not through family members, kinship, and friendship, but through choosing leading company figures who can bring important social relationships into the firm. Some people obtain their positions in a company only because of their outside connections. Links to cadres maximize the entrepreneur's political maneuvering room and minimize his or her political risk. The relationships between cadres and entrepreneurs are not usually based on friendship but rather on considerations of economic usefulness and which networks are useful for the company's development.

The relationship between power and money is as well explored in Chinese social science literature as it is in the media. Bribery is apparently an effective and widely used means of building social relationships, even though the Communist Party and the government have officially declared a war on corruption.[10] Bribes take many forms: monetary transactions, material goods or gifts, services and favors, grand hospitality, travel both within China and abroad, and the use of luxury cars provided by entrepreneurs.

Weak Ties at the Direct Business Level

In all societies, it is vitally necessary for companies to build and maintain a network of relationships with customers, suppliers, banks, and authorities. In China, however, networks also serve as a means for learning new production methods and for expanding sales. Networking can occur during regular meetings, information exchanges, or working dinners.

Of the entrepreneurs we surveyed, 41.7 percent of Nuosu and 33.3 percent of Han seldom talked with other entrepreneurs about business experiences, 45.8 percent of Nuosu and 42.9 percent of Han talked with other entrepreneurs two or three times per month, and 12.5 percent of Nuosu and 23.8 percent of Han talked once per week. Over half of the Nuosu and Han entrepreneurs regularly exchanged views with other entrepreneurs. However, the frequency of such exchanges, especially for Nuosu, was relatively low. This is both because of distance between places of operation and business people's chronic lack of time. Nuosu entrepreneurs are spread out across their counties whereas Han entrepreneurs are concentrated in the county administrative centers. Still, it should be noted that entrepreneurs come into contact with each other not only through business interactions; since almost half the Nuosu entrepreneurs are also Party members, we can assume that contacts are made in official capacities as well.

CHARITABLE CONTRIBUTIONS

Financial donations are an important element of building social capital and political influence. Although the size of a company is generally the most important indicator of an entrepreneur's success, this "positive image" factor is not independent of other variables, especially donations. Regular donations contribute to a positive company image among the local authorities and population. Donations may be made to social causes, such as building roads, and educational and social institutions for the needy, for "political" purposes, such as bonuses or salaries for officials, or in the form of contributions to the local Party organizations.

Strategies involving institutional presence, such as joining the Party or assuming local office, are apparently less effective than donations in raising social prestige. However, entrepreneurs feel parliamentary membership is still a good way to increase their prestige. The People's Congresses require less work than a job with the local bureaucracy, do not involve entanglement in everyday politics, and nevertheless ensure a high level of contacts. Involvement in the People's Congress also involves greater freedom because deputies are not as strictly controlled by direct supervisory organs as are members of the local government. For this reason alone, being a deputy of the People's Congress or of the Political Consultative Conference carries more prestige. At the same time, good contacts with the local bureaucracy and participation in government tasks, such as submitting proposals, also increase prestige.

Almost three-quarters of the Nuosu entrepreneurs and more than 90 percent of the Han stated that they had made donations for social and public interest purposes. Their donations were in the form of public acts, done with a view toward an audience, in the sense of "Look at how generous I am!" Of course, donations presuppose the company owner's financial ability to make them. Larger entrepreneurs with greater financial resources could donate more often than smaller ones. More Han than Nuosu had made donations, again illustrating that Han are under greater pressure to develop *guanxi* than Nuosu entrepreneurs are. On the other hand, Han entrepreneurs also hoped the donations would give them a better public image. Over a third (35.7%) of the Han interviewed and 22.2 percent of the Nuosu stated that they hoped the donations would increase their prestige in the area. The fact that Han make more direct donations to officials and that Nuosu make more donations to community causes, while making sure that officials know about them, is a peculiarity of Nuosu and Han donating behavior.

Social obligations are the dominant motivation for making donations. Over 56 percent of the Nuosu and 80 percent of the Han believe that donations are key to social development. Survey respondents cited other motivations much less frequently. Some had obligations either to their native communities (Nuosu 34.6%, Han 31%) or to the local government, or felt the need to express "thankfulness" (Nuosu 24.7%, Han 21.4%). Others, as we have seen, wished to increase their social prestige (Han 35.7%). Whereas the entrepreneurs' obligations toward their native communities are based on traditional duties, the donations to the local governments serve a dual purpose of creating and/or maintaining *guanxi*. A large percentage of the entrepreneurs complained about government "requests" for donations that were actually demands, as we saw earlier in this chapter. Because entrepreneurs tended not to make such comments when local officials were present, the actual percentage of involuntary donations may be much higher than we determined.

Donor behavior is not only determined by the calculated benefit to the company, it is also based on internalized social obligations, according to which public interest has priority over the interests of individuals. This applies particularly to the wealthy, who are expected to remember their community's contributions to their success. Successful entrepreneurs are expected to give something back to their communities. Through their donations, entrepreneurs demonstrate that they are not simply pursuing their own interests but also abiding by social norms and fulfilling obligations. People who comply with these requirements enjoy respect and social recog

TABLE 5.4 Most Interesting Topics in the Media,
according to Nuosu and Han Entrepreneurs

Topic	Nuosu (%)		Han (%)	
Ethnic policy	64	(79.0%)	17	(40.5%)
Market information	62	(76.6%)	37	(88.1%)
Economic policy	57	(70.4%)	35	(83.3%)
Social problems	53	(65.4%)	28	(66.7%)
Legal system	51	(63.0%)	22	(52.4%)
Reform policy	51	(63.0%)	33	(78.6%)
Politics	48	(59.3%)	16	(38.1%)
Culture, sports	38	(46.9%)	6	(14.3%)
Everyday life	21	(25.9%)	6	(14.3%)

SOURCE: Author's survey, 1999–2002.

nition. Donations also serve as a kind of social capital. By demonstrating the donor's financial superiority and success, donations can increase an entrepreneur's social prestige and social position.

INTEREST IN SOCIAL AND POLITICAL ISSUES

Political participation includes joining and supporting social or political organizations, helping to shape policy, and exerting influence on decision making. However, effective political participation depends on access to relevant and interesting information. In our survey, we asked Nuosu and Han entrepreneurs what kinds of information were of the greatest interest to them (see table 5.4).

Nuosu interest in government policies regarding minority ethnic groups requires no great explanation, because it affects their everyday life, their very identity and existence. Business-related information (market information, government economic policies) was important to both groups, although Han entrepreneurs showed a markedly greater interest. This reflects a higher level of education and stronger market orientation among the Han.

Nuosu entrepreneurs showed a surprisingly high level of interest in the development of a legal system. Han entrepreneurs foresaw little improvement in their situation through changes in laws and legal institutions, whereas Nuosu hoped for stronger protection through entrepreneurial laws and eth-

TABLE 5.5 Sociopolitical Conditions with which Nuosu and Han
Entrepreneurs Are Dissatisfied

	Dissatisfied		Partially Dissatisfied	
Conditions	Nuosu	Han	Nuosu	Han
Efficiency of local authorities	21.0	26.2	45.7	61.9
Party work	34.6	35.7	51.9	81.0
Public security	50.6	28.6	82.7	71.4
Legal system	32.1	23.8	63.0	61.9
Social morality	17.3	9.5	45.7	61.9
Relations between nationalities	13.6	4.8	39.5	38.1

SOURCE: Author's survey, 1999–2002.

nic rights. Nuosu also had more interest in everyday issues, and because the news was generally local, this was less interesting to the Han. One explanation for this phenomenon is that Han are not as included in local political frameworks and thus have less of an interest in local developments. Oddly enough, these results indicate that Nuosu are less cynical than Han about the possibility of having good government, despite the fact that many Nuosu perceive the state as a Han state.

DIFFERENCES BETWEEN NUOSU AND HAN

Table 5.5 reveals that dissatisfaction with the Party and the government is relatively high among entrepreneurs in both ethnic groups. We should note that a feature of doing surveys in China is that those interviewed do not always state their opinions openly. Because of this, although our survey reveals a relatively high level of dissatisfaction overall, many respondents qualified their statements and did not clearly answer whether they were "dissatisfied" or "satisfied."

Table 5.5 reveals that apparently many more Han than Nuosu are dissatisfied with the Party and the government. This reflects the fact that Nuosu can achieve more results on an informal level than can Han, who are not as strongly integrated into local networks. It may also indicate that Nuosu are less cynical about government, perhaps because they are less familiar with it. A higher level of education among Han may also help them to recognize problems.

TABLE 5.6 Entrepreneurs' Level of Satisfaction
with Local Government and Party

Satisfaction	With Local Government		With Party Work	
Satisfied	16	(35.6%)	21	(45.7%)
Not fully satisfied	18	(40.0%)	10	(21.7%)
Dissatisfied	11	(24.4%)	15	(32.6%)
Total	45	(100%)	46	(100%)

SOURCE: Author's survey, 1999–2002.

Table 5.6 combines answers that ranged from "somewhat satisfied" to "somewhat dissatisfied" to create the category "not fully satisfied." This emphasizes that there is a range of critical viewpoints among the entrepreneurs.

Interestingly, the responses of entrepreneurs who were Party members did not differ significantly from those of non-members. The majority of the party members were also not fully satisfied with the work and the policies of the local government and the Party. Entrepreneurs are dissatisfied with the local officials' policies regarding the private sector, as well as with corrupt behavior and official arbitrariness.

Disparities in our research prevent us from fully describing attitudes toward Party and government in each county. The number of respondents in Butuo, Puge, and Xide was statistically too small to demonstrate a significant difference in responses. Also, the survey we gave in Ganluo and Mianning (the first phase of the survey) only allowed "satisfied" and "dissatisfied" as responses. Because some of the respondents would have liked to respond somewhere in between the two possible answers, we changed the survey for the second phase of our fieldwork to include "relatively satisfied" as a third possible response. Thus, the results from Ganluo and Mianning are not entirely comparable to those from other counties. Also, the number of Han entrepreneurs in each individual county was too low to allow us to make general statements about them on a countywide basis. The following descriptions of the situation in individual counties pertains only to Nuosu entrepreneurs.

The degree of satisfaction and dissatisfaction with the work of the local government and the Party differed sometimes widely between counties. The results in table 5.7 to some extent reflect our own experiences. In some counties both the local government and the Party take care of the private sector and actively work on solving problems, such as discrimination against the

TABLE 5.7 Satisfaction of Nuosu Entrepreneurs
with Local Government and Party, by County

County	Local Government		Party	
	Contented (%)	Discontented(%)	Contented (%)	Discontented (%)
Zhaojue	75.0	12.5	78.6	14.3
Mianning	70.0	30.0	50.0	50.0
Jinyang	50.0	16.7	66.7	16.7
Meigu	42.8	7.2	64.3	21.4
Ganluo	41.7	58.2	33.3	66.7
Yanyuan	7.7	23.1	54.5	27.3

SOURCE: Author's survey, 1999–2002.

private sector or excessive taxes and fees, and attempt to increase public
scrutiny. In these counties, the entrepreneurs' assessments were generally
more favorable. However, there was a lesser degree of satisfaction among
Han respondents who evaluated all areas, with the exception of "public security," more negatively than their Nuosu counterparts. In Meigu, where the
private sector was more successfully developed than anywhere else, the degree
of dissatisfaction with the local government was the lowest by a significant
margin.

Dissatisfaction with developments in the legal system was highest in the
counties where entrepreneurs were also the most critical of the work done
by the Party and the government; widespread political and administrative
arbitrariness signaled low legal standards. The entrepreneurs' evaluations
of their government and of the party were influenced by the level of legal
security provided to them as well as by the effectiveness of public security.
Problems with public security were an expression of government and Party
negligence in law enforcement. More Nuosu entrepreneurs than Han were
dissatisfied with the state of public security—only 17.3 percent of the
Nuosu and 28.6 percent of the Han said they were satisfied.

Table 5.9 shows that, apart from Meigu entrepreneurs, more than 50 percent of the entrepreneurs were dissatisfied with public security. This leads
to the conclusion that there is a lack of public security in almost all counties
and a high level of crime. The reason why Meigu is the exception may be that
clan control helps preserve order and security. The most glaring contrasts
between Nuosu and Han evaluations were in Ganluo, Zhaojue, and Mian-

TABLE 5.8 Satisfaction of Nuosu Entrepreneurs
with the Legal System, by County

County	Contented (%)	Discontented (%)
Mianning	80.0	20.0
Jinyang	60.0	40.0
Meigu	50.0	21.4
Zhaojue	25.0	25.0
Yanyuan	22.2	11.1
Ganluo	18.2	72.7

SOURCE: Author's survey, 1999–2002.

TABLE 5.9 Satisfaction of Nuosu Entrepreneurs
with Public Security Situation, by County

County	Contented (%)	Discontented (%)
Meigu	35.7	14.3
Mianning	20.0	80.0
Jinyang	14.3	57.1
Zhaojue	13.3	83.4
Ganluo	8.3	83.4
Yanyuan	0.0	50.0

SOURCE: Author's survey, 1999–2002.

ning. In these counties, more than 80 percent of the Nuosu, but only 25 percent (Ganluo), 40 percent (Zhaojue), and 60 percent (Mianning) of the Han entrepreneurs were dissatisfied with the state of public security. Evidently the Nuosu entrepreneurs felt themselves to be more threatened by criminal behavior than did the Han. Han seem to be less affected by criminality because they reside in county towns, where they experience fewer of the inter- and intra-clan conflicts that occur in rural areas. Rural areas are more prone to lawlessness than urban areas, which are more tightly policed. Nuosu feel strongly about the menacing growth of violent juvenile crime and the legal system's failure to solve these problems. The Han, on the other hand, respond more strongly to what they see as the downfall of traditional morality.

With regard to interethnic relations, more than four-fifths of the surveyed Nuosu entrepreneurs (81.3%, compared to 65.9% of the Han) felt that greater support for Nuosu entrepreneurs was a priority. Almost all the Nuosu, or 95 percent, and 56.1 percent of the Han maintained that Nuosu entrepreneurs face greater difficulties than their Han counterparts do. Nuosu felt their main difficulties were a lower level of education (82.7%), acquiring capital (66.7%), a lack of market knowledge (51.9%), and too little state assistance (49.4%). Han thought the Nuosu's main problems were their low level of education and lack of market knowledge (each 42.9%). Only a few Han named acquiring capital (23.8%) or too little government assistance (14.3%) as important problems for the Nuosu.

Han and Nuosu entrepreneurs perceive local politics differently and assess local institutions and influences differently. Particularly in counties with strong Nuosu majorities, Nuosu entrepreneurs are perceived as locals. They are embedded in networks of relationships with members of their respective clan or ethnic communities. As a result, Han entrepreneurs feel they are treated as outsiders, excluded from decision-making processes, and thus prevented from accessing economic and political resources. This is why Han entrepreneurs are more disappointed in local policies and less interested in local political participation than Nuosu entrepreneurs. Many Han have developed a sense of isolation and have difficulty gaining access to local networks or to unofficial channels of political influence, such as making *guanxi* or making donations. In contrast, Nuosu are somewhat more satisfied with local policies and show a greater interest in engaging in formal and informal organizations.

Entrepreneurial organizations are useful to entrepreneurs, but only where the local government leadership gives them room to represent their members' interests and where their chairpersons have standing among the local elite. As the local impact of these organizations appears to be rather weak, clans are less interested in dominating them. The majority of entrepreneurs in both ethnic groups would like there to be autonomous, nonstate interest organizations, and a large percentage would even prefer to establish such organizations along ethnic boundaries.

Relationships between Nuosu entrepreneurs and Nuosu cadres are complex. They are fed by ethnic feelings of solidarity in the form of strong ties (kinship) as well as by weak ties (relationships with officials). Nuosu entrepreneurs use these relationships to obtain advantages in the market and economic and political resources. One side effect of these relationships is that Han entrepreneurs feel like outsiders. In counties where the Nuosu entrepreneurs and Nuosu cadres are most connected, the majority of the Han entrepreneurs intend to leave as soon as possible. Nuosu entrepreneurs are thus able to use ethnic ties to improve their position in competition with Han entrepreneurs. The reform process has given more weight to local space, in terms of local ties and local knowledge that can be utilized by the locally established Nuosu entrepreneurs, vis-à-vis the outsiders (Han), as the former now constitute the dominant ethnic group in Nuosu areas.

6

Entrepreneurs
and Social Change

....

Nuosu entrepreneurs are embedded not only in local political structures but in social structures as well, and frequently serve as agents of social change. Opportunities for social influence are often found in such ethnic resources as family ties, moral obligations toward a clan or lineage, and the assumption of clan or lineage leadership, and increasingly are evident also in non-kin relations and processes of individualization.

ETHNIC RESOURCES

Nuosu ethnic resources include clan and lineage networks, connections to Nuosu cadres from the same clan, and resources within the ethnic group or within the same clan. Membership in a clan is one of the most important ethnic resources for Nuosu. The clan represents cultural and economic capital as well as political, social, and cognitive capital. It functions as an inside network with myriad connections. The clan can become a primary economic resource for entrepreneurs; the clan as a whole or some of the clan members may possess financial resources for founding companies or organizing economic activities based on a division of labor. Clan membership is gaining significance as an ethnic resource and its growing significance finds expression in the shared language of clan members.

The clan can also be classified as social or ethnic capital. The term "social capital" refers to the relationship structures that connect individuals with their families and communities. Portes and Sensenbrenner divide economically related social capital into four major types: value introjection, reciprocity transactions, bounded solidarity, and enforceable trust. The moral aspects of economic transactions can be described as a process of value introjection. Value imperatives accumulated through the process of socialization become consensual beliefs, which then determine moral considerations in economic situations. Reciprocity transactions are a package of mutual social duties and obligations. Bounded solidarity is defined by norm-oriented behavior, moral obligations, and individuals' situational reactive sentiments within their group. The fourth aspect is enforceable trust in which norm-driven obligations generate confidence within a group, where rewards and sanctions are linked to group trust (Portes and Sensenbrenner 2001: 114).

These four factors are generally embedded in social relationships and can be transferred to an ethnic context. However, within the Nuosu ethnic context, *ethnic capital* refers specifically to the clans, not to the larger Nuosu ethnic community. The definitive attribute of clan social relationships is that each individual knows how he or she has to behave toward other clan members. But since these values (patterns of reciprocity, norms, solidarity, and behavior) are equally binding for all Nuosu clans, they can also be perceived as markers of ethnicity. They have been internalized by every member of the group and can be fundamentally distinguished from Han relationship patterns. These values are a clear marker of separation between Nuosu and Han; they generate symbolic and cultural capital, which, in turn, maintain their identity and protect the group.

Under institutionally and legally uncertain conditions, entrepreneurs often recruit workforce and administrative personnel from their own families or clans, and for external processes, too, they count on family members who have access to the needed resources. The main reasons for including family or clan members in an enterprise are that family or clan members are seen as more trustworthy, loyal, and hardworking. Reasons for avoiding family hire have to do with conflict resolution and the danger of becoming unprofessional. To borrow Niklas Luhmann's term, depending on the clan enables people to be "resistant to being disappointed" (*enttäuschungsfest*) by their employees, because their expectations of other clan members' behavior are based on shared norms of trust and mutual assistance (Luhmann 1999: 56). In general, lineage or clan relationships still play a paramount role in Nuosu society and are based primarily on trust. Clan members feel that a sense of collective responsibility, bounded solidarity, trust, shared identity, and loyalty exists between them. This extends to economic considerations, for example, when a fellow clan member is given a job in which a high degree of responsibility and loyalty is expected. Such relationships of trust can be used to gain access to labor, credit and loans, customers, and suppliers.

Kinship relationships figure in internal and external functions. Inside a company, this refers to employing and cooperating with members of the family or kin (clan members).[1] Kin relations played an important role in almost all of the Nuosu companies we surveyed; in some companies, all the leading company positions were in the hands of kin. Many rural enterprises in Liangshan can be classified as "clan enterprises" (Ch: *jiazu qiye*), which refers to enterprises owned or operated by a clan and/or run in the interest of the clan (Yao and Wang 2002: 10, 56). Clan enterprises can also be enterprises in which a significant number of the employees are members of the entrepreneur's clan, however; or at least the primary company functions are in the hands of the entrepreneur's clan members. In our survey, more than one-quarter of the investigated Nuosu enterprises (25.9%) could be classified as clan companies. Respondents had different opinions about employing and otherwise allowing the participation of lineage and kin members in their own companies. Many entrepreneurs welcomed such involvement and argued that it was risky and even dangerous to trust people who were not family members. In difficult times, kin would work without payment if necessary; they were reliable, obedient, and, above all, a relationship of trust existed with them.[2] One entrepreneur argued that outsiders were seldom truly reliable even when paid at the best rates.

Other Nuosu entrepreneurs were of the opinion that, with increasing company size and modernization, the benefit of employing kin gradually diminished in favor of employing non-kin. Family bonds and obligations often impaired company management procedures; and criticism or laying off employees due to poor or inefficient work could lead to massive, intrafamilial confrontations. Family members were often less easily controlled or guided, and irrational behavior patterns could lead to conflicts.[3] These entrepreneurs argued that their family and kin's work performance could not be measured in the same way as the performance of other employees. There were behavioral expectations embedded in their working relationships, and it was difficult to criticize or to transfer them. For this reason, some entrepreneurs paid off their clan members and kin, providing them with capital for founding their own companies, and were thus able to separate their professional relations in a harmonious manner.[4]

However, the benefits of employing kin or lineage members must be decided on a case-by-case basis. In highly insecure political, legal, or social environments, it may be that a family company based on trust is able to operate more flexibly and securely than others. Wong has argued that a lack of trust in the system is a major reason why entrepreneurs prefer family or clan enterprises (Yu 2001: 54; Wong 1991: 15). Moreover, employees whose familial obligations tie them into a close relationship with an entrepreneur are more prepared to continue working when a company finds itself in economic difficulty. A lack of confidence in the government also contributes to the success of family companies (Bowen and Rose 1998: 443). Because local institutional development is still weak, building trust is extremely necessary as a strong force of local development.

In some companies, the transaction costs of employing kin and clan members are too high, for example, in sectors with fixed specifications concerning work times, such as the construction industry, or in mining, where frequent accidents may lead to internal clan conflicts. Entrepreneurs in these industries thus develop evasive strategies, employing people from outside of the clan or sometimes Han. If the transaction costs of not employing clan members are too high, for instance when companies are within clan territory or when clan resources are required (for cheap labor, capital, and raw materials, for example), entrepreneurs generally hire clan members. At the same time, trusting relationships with kin may compensate for economic difficulties and legal uncertainties.

The issue of company employment on the basis of clan membership is a topic of frequent and controversial discussion in China. Generally speaking and in communist China in particular, employment relationships based on social or familial relationships have been regarded as disadvantageous for company development. However, recent reassessments in China have shown that there are specific advantages to this employment strategy. In cases of an economic crisis or a downturn in business, clan employees reduce company difficulties by making interest-free credit available, temporarily working without pay, or engaging themselves more strongly for company interests due to greater loyalty and trust.[5]

The field of New Institutional Economics argues that existing economic structures should be evaluated as intelligent strategies for solving problems rather than in comparison to "traditional" economic structures. Transaction costs can be lowered through existing economic structures and, in times of economic and political insecurity, trusting relationships are more important than rational, impersonal relationships (see Granovetter 1995: 129–30; Yu 2001: 58–59). However, our findings show that this hypothesis is only partially true. The advantages of employing kin or clan members, such as loyalty, trust, self-exploitation, selfless commitment to the required work, and more effective social control, have to be economically balanced against numerous disadvantages, which potentially have very high social costs. These costs include the danger of conflict with kin and clan members, tolerating unsatisfactory work in order to avoid conflict, and tolerating a discrepancy between existing and required worker capabilities.[6]

On the other hand, kin or clan relationships play an important role in acquiring investment capital for founding a company. Since private entrepreneurs as a rule have hardly any access to bank credit, clan or lineage members are an important source of (interest-free) credit; clan members who are entrepreneurs may provide credit or members who enjoy good relations with banks and credit institutions may support entrepreneurs in acquiring credit. If the clan has any solvent entrepreneurs, there may also be an existing system of mutual support, and clans or lineages themselves may also act as guarantors. This is not only the case for bank credit but also for private credit. In the case of the latter, the honor of the clan is the basis for trust and determining credit worthiness. One entrepreneur told us, should a German company provide his enterprise with investment capital, his clan would act as the guarantor! Familial or clan relationships also play an important role outside the company, especially when family members and kin are leading functionaries in state or party organizations; these relationships facilitate access to resources, investment capital, markets, and information.

Networks of entrepreneurs within individual clans assist with the sale of the goods produced by their clan members and with acquiring supplies, credit, subsidies, or customers. Clan networks can also support the creation of paired production and marketing companies. In one case, a group of clan members jointly founded a production firm in Ganluo County, while another group founded a transport company to carry manufactured goods to cities like Xichang and Chengdu, where other clan members opened retail shops in which to sell the products. The clan can also be a political resource. Legal problems with the police or with other authorities can be dealt with through clan networks. This takes place informally, however, because the government does not view the clan as an acceptable form of organization. The clan thus functions as a bridge between individual members and the state, taking on tasks such as mediation and social control.

New clan networks appear to be developing in addition to the above mentioned clan associations. In one case, an entrepreneur organized a clan association including clan members who were county, prefectural, or provincial officials. He argued that obligations to the clan were more binding than Party obligations. Above all, he emphasized that these relationships were based on equality, since all clan members had equal rights. At the annual torch festival there was a "small gathering" of all the association members and every three years there was a "large gathering" of members, and the costs were shared by all participants. This example shows that clan associations make up a classic ethnic network.

Migration processes and a growing degree of social mobility have led to the formation of such associations in order to protect the clan and its functions. Clan members have begun to organize according to location; for example, in Xichang, the Loho clan has a branch association consisting of 32 families. The association has a "managing director" who is responsible for organization, group cohesion or team spirit, contacts, information, and finances, and business costs are shared through levies. These groups represent a way of resisting the weakening of the clan and its members' reciprocal obligations due to geographical and/or social distances between them.

Especially because the Nuosu have no other representative organizations, the clan associations can be seen as a type of interest organization. Other forms of organization are currently not viable because of rigid state control. Yet, the existence of clan organizations (Ch: *jiazhi xiehui*) shows that informal organizations will emerge, filling the vacuum created by the absence of autonomous interest associations. Such formalized, quasi-modern institutions further serve to strengthen clan ties.

Non-clan social relationships and networks are two other important ethnic resources. These networks consist of informal relationships between essentially equal social actors; unequal actors have a relationship of patronage. Network relationships are based on cooperation and loyalty, and successful networks are maintained by building confidence and preserving mutual trust (Frances et al. 1991: 14ff.; Reese and Aldrich 1995: 124ff.). Networks connect individuals and groups of individuals, institutions, and smaller clusters in which the network members are active. Because each individual is a member of multiple networks, each member serves to connect networks with each other. Thus, a network extends far beyond simply a collection of individuals.

For the entrepreneurs we interviewed, such relationships and networks function in the following three ways. In economics terms, networks facilitate resource preservation and exchange, the exchange of goods and services, as well as cooperation in production. Social connections to important decision makers assist members in obtaining economic advantages when setting up their companies, such as easier access to markets, credits, information, raw materials, state sector commissions, tax remission, or reductions, and networks also facilitate information exchange. On the political level, networks increase the influence of business-oriented interests by assisting members in gaining political advantages (obtaining public positions, party membership, getting around political restrictions) and defending them against disadvantages (by influencing local officials and preventing excessive restrictions). On the cognitive level, networks help strengthen identities. Members provide cognitive and affective support for each other and ensure their recognition inside and outside the group. Networks also foster specific expectations and norms on the basis of members' various commonalities.

Again, these network functions contain the four economically related attributes of social capital described earlier this chapter, i.e., value introjection, reciprocity transactions, bounded solidarity, and enforceable trust. Ethnic networks presuppose these markers of social capital in order to be able to operate with any degree of success in the economic sphere. However, Portes and Sensenbrenner argue that compliance with group norms involving enforceable trust is stronger in the face of external discrimination than under more pluralistic and equal conditions. Ethnic networks (for instance, clan associations and networks between entrepreneurs and local officials) therefore play a crucial role in Liangshan. However, if access to economic resources and to social and/or professional advancement outside an individual's own group is more promising, or if the group is not able to fulfill the expectations of group members, the cohesion of that community and the observance of community norms will be weakened (Portes and Sensenbrenner 2001: 124).

Ethnic resources also include Nuosu labor and connections to Nuosu cadres. Nuosu labor is less costly than Han labor, as long as the workers are either members of the same clan as the entrepreneurs are or have other highly trusting and loyal personal relationships with them. Entrepreneurs use their personal, ethnic, and kinship affiliations with local cadres to create clientele-like ties with the local bureaucracy. In turn, indigenous cadres use their positions to create ethnic political machines. Because of the considerable ethnic resources available to Nuosu, many Han entrepreneurs feel that they are disadvantaged and that the local authorities confer privileges on the Nuosu enterprises. Some Han said that this was an important reason why they would like to leave the Liangshan area.

MORAL OBLIGATIONS

Despite the economization of Chinese and Nuosu society, entrepreneurs have enabled the clans and lineages to maintain and even increase and diversify their economic functions. The Nuosu use clan networks to optimize their business opportunities and secure competitive advantages over Han entrepreneurs. New entrepreneurs make use of the economic division of labor within their clan and reciprocate by providing social services for the clan. As mentioned above in the discussion of social capital and financial support, our study confirms James Scott's hypothesis that clan members who become well off will be expected to share their wealth with other clan or village members, or support and assist them in some other way. This moral obligation, which Scott (1976) calls "the moral economy of the peasants," has changed very little in Nuosu society. However, as the market grows, Scott expects this principle to be challenged by personal profit maximization, causing the principle of mutual help to decline in value.

Is Scott's hypothesis also true for Nuosu entrepreneurship? The interviewed Nuosu entrepreneurs had very different opinions regarding their clans, ranging from considering the clan a burden to thinking of it as an indispensable support system. Although Nuosu entrepreneurs complained about their considerable obligations to their clans, the majority could not shirk these duties. As a result, some decided to hire only non-local Nuosu and to give monetary support to the clan and/or to individual clan members. This choice represents the trader's dilemma. When the clans are poor and a single or a few entrepreneurs are obliged to subsidize them, the clan quickly becomes a strain.

Financial obligations toward the clan can be more or less burdensome, depending on the business situation. In the difficult founding and/or the initial phases of a firm or during business crises, such obligations are a heavy load to bear. In times of prosperity, on the other hand, giving behavior can be tailored specifically to contribute to the entrepreneur's acceptance and his or her social prestige within the community. Marin Trenk notes, "Many entrepreneurs feel 'their wealth is their ruin.' Their kin's demands are their undoing. But at the same time, entrepreneurs feel the challenge of becoming the 'big man', both within and outside kinship circles, is socially more important" (Trenk 1991: 514).

Economically successful clans that have produced a number of entrepreneurs play a strong economic role in society and enjoy great prestige. Clan entrepreneurs support each other financially and in the search for markets. Some entrepreneurs organize worker training sessions, or build roads and schools for the villages in their clans. Cadres provide advantages to Party members and/or entrepreneurs from their own clans.

Nuosu entrepreneurs assist their clans in a number of ways: by providing family support during illness, poverty, and debt; helping to pay school fees and other educational expenses, as well as expenses such as dowries; financing ritual festivities such as weddings and funerals, the construction of new houses, the purchase of vehicles and appliances, water and electrical projects, television stations and satellite dishes, schools, reforestation programs, and road construction; providing employment in their companies; and providing start-up capital for new companies.[7]

Annual financial support or donations to the clan vary between a thousand and tens of thousands of yuan, or even greater than one hundred thousand yuan, depending on the entrepreneur's financial capacity. In total, hundreds of thousands of yuan are spent on community services every year. However, monetary contributions are not the only investment in community solidarity; people constantly try to secure jobs and loans from their kin who are entrepreneurs. In his research in Bali, Clifford Geertz points out that entrepreneurial success "will lead to a higher level of welfare for the organic community as a whole," even when massive obstacles impede the expansion of entrepreneurial activity (Geertz 1963: 123). The obligation to employ clan members can be one such obstacle. Many Nuosu entrepreneurs evade their social obligation to employ clan members by seeking Nuosu personnel from outside their clan and/or the county. One entrepreneur argued, "If I hire workers from elsewhere, I can choose the most able and competent people, but if I hire from within the clan, I have to take on the laziest and most incompetent."[8] However, employing and training clan and family members may create a snowball effect, which supports Geertz's concept of increasing overall community welfare. Acquiring technical knowledge prepares able staff members to become self-employed, sometimes with financial support from another entrepreneur.

Financing schools is a particularly significant community service that entrepreneurs may provide for their communities. In counties where entrepreneurs have funded schools, official publicity increases the impact of their achievement, which then stimulates emulation. In Ganluo County, an entrepreneur from the Jjike clan constructed a large clan school, Jjike School, in his native village, which was exclusively populated by members of his lineage. Members of the Jjike clan from other counties traveled there to view the school, which inspired them to construct schools in other areas.

In general, there are two types of donors—those who fund productive activities and those who make donations to meet personal goals or for nonproductive, ritual purposes. Productive donations are a form of symbolic capital that can be used to develop social capital. Social recognition is generated within and outside the clan, especially amongst the local political elite. These donors are often designated "model workers" and obtain positions as deputies of the various People's Congresses or People's Consultative Conferences. One of these donors, a successful entrepreneur in the construction industry in Ganluo, distinguished himself by building a school and by financing road construction, reforestation programs, and programs to combat poverty. As a result, he was named deputy director of the county office for water and electricity supply and given a deputy position in the National People's Congress. His success was rewarded commercially as well; he was able to employ four retired cadres who had connections throughout the county and the prefecture as managers and "advisers" in his business. They included a former Ganluo County deputy Party leader, the former county head of finance, a former bank director, and a highly placed engineer from eastern China. This is one example of how symbolic capital can be transformed into social capital and then into economic capital.

The second group of donors gives money, goods, and services not for productive use but to meet their basic needs, overcome everyday problems, or for ritual purposes. Such donations fulfill social obligations, and meeting these obligations generates social capital within the clan or the village. Payments for ritual purposes are especially important in determining a per-

FIG. 7. *School funded by a Nuosu entrepreneur, Ganluo County*

son's position within his or her clan. In addition, spending on rituals can demonstrate a clan's power to outsiders. For example, one entrepreneur told us that he had had 110 cows slaughtered at his mother's funeral, which promoted his prestige within the clan and promoted the clan's prestige externally as well.

Our interviews showed that funding unproductive activities was generally considered a burden by the entrepreneurs whereas subsidizing community institutions and thereby generating stronger symbolic and social capital was not. County and township governments that lacked the funds to develop infrastructure especially encouraged entrepreneurs to make donations. The local authorities also attempted to promote the perception that entrepreneurs are exemplary actors in local development. However, moral obligations toward the clan still play a meaningful role in the entrepreneurs' lives and many of them perceived this obligation in a positive light. "The money we earn is not just our own," declared one entrepreneur, "it also belongs to the clan as a social community."[9] This perception captures the double role of the entrepreneur. On the one hand, the entrepreneur is a member of a kinship network; on the other hand, the entrepreneur has to consider the interests of his or her company and survive in the market. As the company's significance increases in the eyes of the entrepreneur, the clan and the package of traditional values that it represents decrease in importance. This generally has repercussions for the clan and its values.

Emile Durkheim suggests that division of labor is an important step in the development processes. Increasing the division of labor indicates that social structures are changing, and new forms of social solidarity and social order are developing. For Nuosu, the trend is increasingly toward forming social relationships beyond the immediate clan and village communities, which contributes to the intermingling of individuals and groups. One result of this intermingling is the creation of markets, competition among producers, and specialization among suppliers. What Durkheim calls "mechanical solidarity," as marked by a strong collective consciousness, starts to decline as communities become differentiated. Above all, entrepreneurs' newfound mobility and their increased migration into other areas or into cities weaken both social control and the cohesiveness of traditional social organizations. Many entrepreneurs feel that the clan does not play much of a role in their business activities and tends instead to be a burden. Such views illustrate a weakened collective consciousness and a growing process of individualization.

These trends fuel the development of organic solidarity, which is characterized by division of labor based on specialist and individual organizations and institutions (Durkheim 1992: 289). Both money and commercialization play important roles in this process of change. An "expansion of the self" accompanies the possession of money and its consequences include breaking away from traditional social ties and relationships. Though new forms of relationships and ties develop, these are associated less with the clan and more with social structures that transcend clan boundaries. Money creates institutions that go beyond the clan, i.e., larger business or commercial circles with interconnected interests, obligations, and dependencies (see Simmel 1994: 405ff.; Heinemann 1987b: 333–34). Our interviews demonstrate that many Nuosu entrepreneurs perceive the clan as diminishing in its social function. The strength of the clan's social role may depend on the decline or increase in its economic role. Our survey shows that slightly less than a third of the Nuosu entrepreneurs interviewed have business relations within the clan; more than two-thirds (69.1%) do not. This is not remarkable for a society in which market events and entrepreneurship have historically played only a marginal role. In fact, factors that transcend clans are becoming increasingly important for entrepreneurs. In their role as clan members, entrepreneurs face the following dilemma: they are obliged to take care of kin or clan members by providing jobs or material gifts, despite the fact that these people contribute little or nothing to the development of their firms, and this hinders them from operating effectively in the market. In this respect, the ethnic network of the clan is somewhat disadvantageous for entrepreneurs, who must minimize their sense of ethnic solidarity in order to survive financially.

Of the Nuosu entrepreneurs surveyed, 49.4 percent wished to increase their support of their clan; 33.3 percent viewed the clan as a reason for the backwardness of Nuosu entrepreneurs; 28.4 percent said they would support their clan if they had more money; 19.8 percent thought that supporting their clan was not important; 18.5 percent supported their clan through donations; 14.8 percent thought that supporting the clan was important for succeeding in business; and 2.5 percent thought that having relatives in high positions was important for succeeding in business.

For many Nuosu entrepreneurs, the clan plays a decreasing role in their decision making. The majority did not see supporting the clan as a life goal, and only a relatively low percentage expressed a desire to support their clan if they had more money. As many as a third explicitly felt that the burden of supporting the clan is partly responsible for the underdeveloped or "backward" state of Nuosu entrepreneurship. Entrepreneurs express ambivalent opinions about the clan. While many complained about the clan's burden-some nature, others felt that payments made in support of their clans distinguished them in a positive sense from the Han.

However, despite critical voices, Nuosu scholar Mgebbu Lunzy (Ma Erzi) explains the continued importance of the clans,

> Although entrepreneurs may argue otherwise, the clan is still significant to every individual. Even if entrepreneurs say they do not employ their own clan members, there will still be clan members in their company administration or in the security departments. Clan members are really the only people who can be trusted.[10]

The clans as institutions have also come to represent new ideals. An entrepreneur describes the clans' function in promoting equality:

> Within the clan one has to reach unity, otherwise nothing works anymore. Money does not play a decisive role; having money contributes only marginally. In the clan, we are all equal, even high-up cadres, because they are also clan members.[11]

This equality is somewhat of a fiction, if not because of the traditional social stratification of the past, then because of the economically elite status of the entrepreneurial stratum in the present. However, the idea of equality gives clan members the feeling of having an equal right to participate in clan activities. Every clan member has a vote at clan gatherings where difficult questions and problems are resolved through a process of consultation and discussion. Many entrepreneurs term this process "grass-roots democracy," with the interpretation that democracy has always been an important component of Nuosu society.

Another change, which we have not researched extensively, is in female entrepreneurs' roles and positions within their clan. Successful female entrepreneurs have become more self-confident and are increasingly accepted as independent clan personalities.[12] A female entrepreneur in Jinyang explained that until 1978, Nuosu women had generally been peasants or housewives. When she embarked on the process of starting her own business in 1994, the clan did not help her; she achieved everything through her own efforts. In her clan's defense, however, she noted it was much too poor to have supported her. A few years later, her clan had become a considerable burden on her; she transferred money, bought clothing, and paid for a number of children's basic needs and school attendance. On the other hand, her entrepreneurial activities had increased her prestige within the clan and people listened to her opinions. Before, she had never even visited Xichang, the prefectural capital. Since becoming an entrepreneur, she had traveled to the two most important cities in Southwest China—Chengdu and Kunming. However, despite such success stories, the prevailing opinion within the clans is that (Nuosu) women should not take part in business activities and that only "bad" women engage in self-employed work or open restaurants. Although traditionally females occasionally became shamans or leading clan figures, women today are still restricted from doing business.

ENTREPRENEURS AS CLAN HEADMEN

Entrepreneurs' positions within their clan improve if they are economically successful. Many larger entrepreneurs have effectively become clan leaders (N: *suyy* or *ssahxo*), giving rise to the popular saying, "A good company can make you a headman (Ch: *touren*)." Out of 81 Nuosu entrepreneurs, 27 admitted that they were popularly accepted as such "leaders"; either their opinions were decisive (Ch: *shuo le suan*), or they were invited to participate in making important decisions and sought for advice. Becoming a clan *touren* was not traditionally tied to particular rules about birth, descent, or membership. A *touren* was (and still is) not an elected person; he was a person whose character (intelligence, courage, wisdom, and trust) and abilities were widely accepted as superior and who automatically grew into the role of a leading figure.[13] However, there was also competition in becoming a *touren*; the candidate had to prove himself well versed and capable at mediation, warfare, handling relationships, including conflicts, with other clans and the local authorities, defense of clan property, and increasing clan wealth. Because increasing the clan's wealth enhanced its influence, in principle, the clan leader was the administrator of the clan's collective property. The more capable a person was in these arenas, the more rapidly he could obtain political leadership, though it was a competitive advantage to be the son of a renowned clan leader or to possess good connections and influence.

Because clan leadership was tied to political competition, not to mythological or religious concepts, the leader's power was traditionally legitimized by collective loyalty based on his demonstrated successful performance. The Nuosu clan leader thus resembled the Melanesian concept of "the big man" described in the introduction.

FIG. 8. *An entrepreneur of Han slave origins with her children, Zhaojue County*

FIG. 9. *A shopkeeper in one of her shops, Yanyuan County*

A study of the traditional functions of such clan leaders identifies three important preconditions for their general acceptance: courage and success in clan feuds; the ability to handle and efficiently mediate internal and external clan affairs; and the ability to accumulate wealth. In a sense, there are also three kinds of leadership—money (N: *suga*), law or mediation (N: *ndeggu*), and bravery and fighting (N: *ssakuo*).[14] Although the key to all three is the ability to handle civil and military matters well, economic success is not an entirely new criterion for evaluating clan leadership. However, the criteria for leadership today have been altered by social and economic transformations; the primary requirements for leadership now are skills in dealing with internal and external clan business and economic successes that contribute to the clan community's prosperity.

Many entrepreneurs differentiate between a *touren*, who is the face of the clan for the outside world, and a family manager, who runs the clan almost like a firm and takes care of its economic development. Some clans have begun to resemble companies, instead of companies coming to resemble clans. For example, entrepreneurs with internal leadership functions appear to take on the role of a clan manager rather than that of the traditional *touren*. This is precisely the situation that entrepreneurs are referring to when they say that they are not the clan leader but they make all the important decisions or are involved in making them.

The requisite for leadership today is for an entrepreneur to enjoy prestige or close connections within the clan. Someone whose father was a clan leader, for instance, or someone who is well rooted in a clan village, as are the rural entrepreneurs in Yanyuan County, would be a likely candidate for a leadership position. At the same time, becoming a clan leader also depends on whether an entrepreneur has contributed to infrastructure improvements in his home village, such as constructing schools, roads, water pipes, electricity channels, and clinics, or by instituting reforestation programs. Almost all Nuosu entrepreneurs who exercise clan leadership functions have made appropriate donations of goods. Another high-prestige activity appears to be to directly assist in reducing poverty. Entrepreneurs contribute to this effort by creating jobs and offering vocational training.

NON-KIN RELATIONS

Entrepreneurs build many different sets of relationships outside their clan or lineage. Business cooperation transcends clan boundaries and entrepreneurs often maintain relationships with people they know from past activities or jobs (as cadres, workers, etc.). Connections with friends and with people with whom they have shared experiences ("*tong* relationships") are especially important and will be explained in more detail in the following section. Even if the clan continues to be dominant in the social sphere, many entrepreneurs argue that friends and other people with whom they have non-kinship relationships now play important roles in accessing credit or business support. Some even complain that, in addition to the burden of supporting clan members, friends have become another burden. Others emphasize their village community's growing role in building social relationships insofar as these communities are not identical to the clan or lineage.

The role of clan-transcending networks is increasing, as is the role of "*tong* relationships." Commonalities (Ch: *tong*), represent shared experiences, which are the most important basis for social relationships (Ch: *guanxi*). Belonging to the same ethnic community is a central factor in social and *tong* relationships, but the *tongban* (classmate), *tongbao* (regional compatriot), *tonghang* (colleagues in a specialized field), *tongshi* (work colleague), *tongxiang* (from the same village or township), *tongxue* (schoolmate), etc., are also special relationships.

A private entrepreneur's networks include not only those with whom he has close relationships but also those who hold important positions, for example, as a manager or a cadre, and who can be of use to him. At the same time, *tong* relationships are not based purely on economic advantage but also on friendship and trust. Mutual assistance and support are understood as investments in the future and do not require direct service in exchange. The reciprocal obligation may become due at a later date, but may also never be realized.

For companies in urban areas, including county towns, relationships with classmates and former colleagues play a more significant role than for rural firms, where familial or village relationships carry more weight. Relationships between cadres who shared experiences in the same local Party organizations or Party schools are also very important. Whereas clan and kin relationships are born out of traditional Nuosu social structures, *tong* relationships emerge from Chinese institutional structures. The two relationship types blend in interesting ways in today's society, not just among entrepreneurs but also among cadres and intellectuals.

The increase in non-kin relationships establishes an imperative for consolidating a common, shared Nuosu identity as members of an ethnic group, not merely kin groups. A shared identity based on ethnic lines rather than clan lines is indeed in the process of growing, because social and economic changes and migration are weakening the clans' social grip on individuals. At the same time, a gradual process of *economization* is taking place within the clans. Clan socioeconomic functions continue to grow as families and clan members contribute capital and labor. Entrepreneurs aid in this process as well as in the process of forming clan-transcending bonds of solidarity, as mentioned above. Because the entrepreneurs see themselves as both clan members and as members of an (imagined) Nuosu entrepreneurial community, the ethnic group becomes a social space in which they expect solidarity, and ethnic solidarity among entrepreneurs reinforces ethnic identity. The new ethnic self-confidence has an impact on inter-ethnic relationships, as do easier access to cash, the acquisition of many new consumer goods, and the development of new skills and knowledge. Ethnic solidarity is forming in other areas of life as well and, in some cases, it extends beyond the Liangshan Yi (Nuosu) to other Yi groups from Yunnan or Guizhou.

INDIVIDUALIZATION

At the same time that ethnic solidarity is growing, a process of individualization is also emerging. Individualization is a crucial component of modernization processes and a significant element of social change. We found notable expressions of growing individualization.

Of the 78 Nuosu entrepreneurs in our survey, 86.4 percent emphasized a good future for their children as an important life goal; 85.2 percent thought commercial success depended on their own abilities; 77.8 percent gave high priority to having a happy family, 48.2 percent prioritized higher social prestige, 43.2 percent prioritized individual happiness; 20 percent considered an interest in self-employment to be the primary motivation for founding their company; and 19.7 percent declared that they individually would alter unfavorable decisions of local authorities.

Our interviews demonstrate that the entrepreneurs increasingly emphasize the well being of their own companies and their nuclear families. Entrepreneurship inherently requires a more individualistic outlook, implying a decreased focus on larger social frameworks such as clans, even if entrepreneurs have not been able to withdraw from their traditional social obligations. As table 4.8 shows, more than 40 percent of the Nuosu and almost 40 percent of the Han believed that individual happiness was an important goal in life. Only 14–15 percent (both Nuosu and Han) stated that it was not important to them. This is also a significant indication of growing individualism.

Of course, young people are generally more individualistic. A young Nuosu entrepreneur in his twenties declared,

I only believe in myself. I don't care about the "three representations" [Ch: *sange daibiao*] or anything like that! I need personal freedom—that's something I learned going to a private middle school in Chengdu. I believe the best way to get this is by becoming an entrepreneur.[15]

Young entrepreneurs with a high level of education and hence a stronger sense of alienation from Liangshan society (in the above case, through schooling outside Liangshan) show a higher degree of individualism. Although this scenario is not widespread in rural areas, it is increasing among young Nuosu, including young entrepreneurs, in Xichang and outside Liangshan.

ENTREPRENEURS AS AGENTS OF SOCIAL CHANGE

Although strong traditional ties (clan, kinship) retain their pivotal significance for entrepreneurs, a gradual shift toward strong post-traditional ties, such as *tong* relationships, is taking place in all the counties. This gradual change in (social) resources intensifies social and personal insecurities and generates deviant behavior in disoriented young people. However, social problems appear to be less serious where clan communities and traditions remain dominant, for instance, in Meigu, compared to counties where the sense of community has been weakened. In Meigu, the development of the private sector has been more successful than in many other counties and yet, interestingly, socioeconomic changes there do not seem to have weakened the clans.

Political or social uncertainty and unpredictability increase the economic functions of companies that employ an entrepreneur's clan members, or clan companies. So long as particular services are not publicly available (for instance, access to credit), kinship, *guanxi*, and networks serve as resources. Clan communities attempt to counteract the gradual erosion of their importance, as described above, through new organizational forms. In addition, the state, which struggled against the clans for many years, has discovered the clan's role as an instrument of social order and stability.

Without a doubt, the thinking of many Nuosu entrepreneurs is still rooted in a moral economy. Nuosu economic behavior is tied to non-economic relationships and concepts of social morality; market logic is not the decisive factor in entrepreneurial matters. Some even criticize the market economy for causing social norms to slacken. The transition from a moral economy to a market economy creates an ambiguous situation: social interaction and prestige are less and less determined by local morality, and goods and relationships become increasingly commercialized. Entrepreneurs are eventually forced to behave in rational ways dictated by the market if they want to survive, which is the trader's dilemma. Some of the entrepreneurs have recognized this dilemma, as shown by their desire to not employ clan members in their companies and their preference for helping clan members by providing money, donations, and material support.

Concurrently, the market creates new and separate value systems based on economic equality in the market, where the buyer and the seller meet on equal terms. These values are not based on the subordination of the individual to the group (clan) or on hierarchies on the basis of age and gender, though such non-economic characteristics can still be applied within religious communities, parties, and interest groups.

Entrepreneurs have increasingly become the pacemakers of progress. They not only reflect market conditions and technical progress but also develop significant prestige within their respective clans or ethnic communities. By not abandoning important elements of Nuosu culture, they promote the maintenance of culture and cultural renewal. However, processes of industrialization are separating economic activities from traditional family activities, and workplaces are becoming increasingly impersonal. At the same time, clan-transcending frameworks in business and everyday life are causing both entrepreneurs and their employees to think in terms of clan-transcending categories rather than clan structures. These frameworks facilitate the transition from a clan identity to an ethnic identity.

7

Entrepreneurs
and Ethnic Relations

....

How does ethnic entrepreneurship affect ethnic boundaries, concepts of ethnicity, new patterns of segregation, and ethnic competition? Our concern is not with the larger concept of ethnicity as used in ethnic mobilization but with an everyday concept of ethnicity; not with a group consciousness based on objective factors such as language and descent, but with ethnicity that is formed through contacts with other groups. How does a group think about itself? How do members of that group differentiate themselves from others? What do others think about them?

Scholars have devised both essentialist and constructivist concepts to address the question of ethnicity. In the essentialist vein, Bernhard Waldenfels writes, "Strangeness means not being affiliated with an us-group" (1997: 22). This "us-group" exists only in relation to the "others" from whom its members are considered naturally different, although the cultural characteristics that determine the lines of division may change or be changed over time. Members of us-groups are considered to have certain essential characteristics that mark them as insiders. However, because we are interested in everyday ethnicity, in our study of the effect of entrepreneurship on ethnic relations, we will use a constructivist concept of ethnicity, in which attribution is key to ethnic group formation. The concept of ethnicity we use does not, or does not only, emerge from objective factors, such as language and descent, and a group consciousness based on those, but rather from "social processes of attribution," which are formed through contact with others. Individuals attribute certain characteristics to themselves and other characteristics to others in order to identify members of their ethnic group, although the particular cultural characteristics used as dividing lines may change. An interactive process separates one person's ethnic group members from others. Frederik Barth has argued that socially relevant factors are more critical for membership than "objective" differences. Irrespective of how "objectively" similar or different one group is from another, if its members concertedly separate themselves from the other group, then they understand themselves to be members of a common group, different from the members of the other, and wish to be perceived as such (Barth 1981: 204).

EVERYDAY ETHNICITY AND ETHNIC BOUNDARIES

Statements made by Han and Nuosu entrepreneurs about each other demonstrate this "us-versus-them" mentality. However, Nuosu and Han entrepreneurs do not have uniform or homogeneous perceptions of their own or the other ethnic group, although stereotypes and prejudices are to be found among all the ethnic groups. Because of the differences between and among the ethnic groups, open contradictions and conflicts between the Han and the Nuosu are not easily recognizable to outsiders. Further, the Nuosu language partially serves as a medium of separation because it is not understood by the Han. Our interviews, therefore, focused on the question of identity as expressed through ethnic stereotypes. Many Nuosu believe that excessive alcohol consumption is an "ethnic characteristic" (*minzu tese*) that divides Nuosu and Han. The feeling of Nuosu ethnic solidarity intensifies notably with alcohol consumption, which also increases their self-confidence. When drinking, Nuosu more clearly formulate differences between themselves and the Han, more loudly criticize discrimination, and question the official view of history. The perceived differences between Han and Nuosu may be summarized as follows:

Han Perceptions of Yi Entrepreneurs

NEGATIVE	POSITIVE
Uneducated	Some are hardworking
Lazy	
Prone to heavy drinking	
Aggressive under the influence of alcohol	
Lack an understanding of the market	
Inefficient at business management	
Inconsistent commitment to business	

Lack a concern for labor
Nepotistic
Ignorant of the law
Closed-minded toward the outside
  world
Competitive only in drinking
Influenced by slave-owner social origins
Uncultured
Corrupt

Yi Perceptions of Han Entrepreneurs

NEGATIVE	POSITIVE
Concerned only with making money	Good management skills
Unconcerned with others' interests	
Disloyal	
Unwilling to spend for social purposes	
Most are bad	
More interested in reinvesting profits than in supporting lineage	
Less courageous and openhearted than Yi	
Less attentive to kinship (tracing ancestry to only the sixth generation, versus up to the twelfth generation for Yi)	
Selfish	
Mean	
Lacking compassion and concern for the poor	

Yi Perceptions of Yi Entrepreneurs

POSITIVE	NEGATIVE
Hardworking	Slow to adopt new practices
Patient	Neglect themselves while caring for others
Responsible toward family and lineage	Hindered in accumulating wealth by the emphasis on lineage
Upright and outspoken	Wasteful
Attentive to "face"	
Courageous and brave	
Willing to spend for social purposes	

Willing to use profits to support lineage

Paying taxes regularly

Attentive to customer service

Han Perceptions of Han Entrepreneurs

POSITIVE   NEGATIVE

More highly educated

Technologically superior

Future-oriented

Innovative

Exercise better judgment

More market-oriented

Entrepreneurs in most counties made similar statements about the kind of imagined differences between the two groups. They were asked how they would characterize entrepreneurs of the opposite group and/or of the same group. The stereotypes apply only to entrepreneurs of the opposite group but it seems that both groups have many of the same stereotypes about each other. As Barth has argued, the issue here is not determining objective differences; it is determining which differences "the actors themselves regard as significant" (1981: 203). We could also argue, as Stuart Hall does, that identity is always a structured representation of positive characteristics discerned through the narrow eye of the other's negative attributes (1994: 45). But it would be one-sided and incorrect to examine Nuosu and Han relations only from the perspective of boundaries. Various forms of mutually productive and supportive interrelationships must be analyzed in order to understand local ethnic interactions.

 The entrepreneurs' statements also illuminate different Han and Nuosu worldviews concerning their economic interpretations of society. One such difference is in terms of kinship. There is no difference of opinion about the fact that local Nuosu are more kin oriented than local Han; however, Nuosu evaluate this attribute positively, while Han evaluate it negatively. Furthermore, while Nuosu feel that the Han focus on economics is immoral, Han feel that Nuosu non-economic obligations are anti-business. The Han economic focus can be understood as a form of ethnocentrism (in Bourdieu's sense of the word, 1999: 206). Although non-economic interests and obligatory social behaviors are also significant to Han Chinese communities, whether in villages or clans, Han entrepreneurs criticize Nuosu economic attitudes because they do not correspond to their ideals of "modern" market relations and conditions. In this context, Han entrepreneurs define modern markets as being open, cosmopolitan, purely economically directed, and having standard business practices. It is significant that the Han entrepreneurs in Liangshan are mostly immigrants from outside Liangshan (or their offspring) and are now separated from their original communities.

However, the economically rational and calculating ability that Han entrepreneurs ascribe to themselves (and which many Nuosu entrepreneurs confirm) is an imaginary construct; Han entrepreneurs do not always behave in a manner governed by economic rationality. A good example is the issue of social relations and donations. As we discussed in chapter 6, more than half of the surveyed Han find social connections advantageous, even indispensable for their business lives, and most of them also fulfill social obligations by donating money primarily for social purposes but also to the government administration. Some Han entrepreneurs also send money to clan members from their native areas. This demonstrates that the boundary between Han and Nuosu on the grounds that Nuosu behave in non-rational, non-economic ways is maintained simply by prejudice. Since economic and social benefits are closely tied to each other, people strive not only for material profit but also for social recognition, prestige, status, and power. Striving to make a profit without considering the community promotes resentment and exclusion. Thus, both Nuosu and Han entrepreneurs attempt to acquire social capital in addition to generating economic capital. The difference is only in the intensity of the social element, and this is determined less by ethnic factors than by local factors; this means that the difference between Nuosu and Han entrepreneurs' ability to obtain economic and social capital is connected to the degree to which they are embedded in local social structures. As we have emphasized already, the Nuosu are more strongly embedded in their local environments.

Our concept of ethnicity includes an additional element, namely, critical self-reflection on the part of the ethnic minority. When distinguishing themselves from the Nuosu, Han express positive self-images, whereas many Nuosu entrepreneurs critically analyze their own ethnicity (see list above). The essentialist "us" of the Nuosu is conditional, and its homogeneity is therefore questionable. This self-critical reflection is one component of a process of political and social change that has required the Nuosu to adapt economically. Such criticism may also reflect the negative evaluation of the Nuosu in the Communist historiography.

Although both entrepreneur groups' statements exhibit prejudices and stereotypes, there are no unbridgeable contradictions between the two groups that could lead to violent conflict. This is because the private sector offers alternative options for employment and social ascent for both ethnic groups. In contrast, before the beginning of the economic reforms, the available jobs were predominantly in the state sector and careers as officials were available to Han but not to Nuosu.

Ethnicity is a form of interaction between cultural groups operating in a common context. As an organizational tool, ethnicity enables groups to maintain boundaries "despite an exchange of persons and information with other groups and individual social contacts between [the groups] . . . The maintenance of boundaries is the true marker of ethnicity" (Huschen and Richter 1991: 29; see also Cohen 1974: xiiff.; Jäggi 1993: 96ff.). Ethnicity also provides the potential for organizing and for marking boundaries, which contributes to maintaining ethnic group consciousness in spite of economic, social, and political cooperation that may transcend ethnic boundaries.

As noted previously, one of the key aspects of "everyday ethnicity" is marking boundaries between oneself and others. One of the larger Nuosu entrepreneurs talked to us in some detail about characteristics that distinguish the Nuosu from the Han. His statement is typical of wealthier entrepreneurs, who think in larger contexts. He elaborated at length on self-evaluation and the evaluation of others:

Most of the Han entrepreneurs around here come from places outside of Liangshan and bring their own workforce with them. Their workers have specialized knowledge and learn very quickly; they have an iron determination, and work with great precision. Amongst the Yi, these psychological characteristics are rather weak.

About 80 percent of Yi, but only 20 percent of the Han are not aware of important problems. On the other hand, Yi are courageous—they dare to do anything and let nothing worry them. Of course, this has to do with tradition, but it also has to do with the Yi entrepreneurs' low level of education. However, Han also know from a very early age what they want in life; Yi do not.

I would also say about 90 percent of the Han are sly and unscrupulous, whereas Yi are open and honest. Another thing about the Han is that ever since the Qing dynasty, they kow-tow when they are down, but when their status rises again, they forget those who have smoothed their path for them. Our county deputy director is a very good example. At every opportunity he crawls to the prefectural Party Secretary and flatters him with honey-sweet words. Nauseating! We Yi don't do that! We have a saying that in everything we do, we look 1,000 meters ahead. Han on the other hand, are always looking many kilometers ahead.

There is a difference in Yi and Han attitudes toward work as well. Yi are relatively quickly satisfied with what they have attained and then wish to sit back and relax. Han are restless, and they continuously desire to strive for more. Han are frugal; Yi throw their money out of the window with both hands. We all know that nothing works in China without social connections (Ch: *guanxi*). Han are the masters of this art. Since the Yi are not as well versed in this, Yi influence stops at the prefectural level.

To be quite frank, the Yi are only a small ethnic minority; Liangshan has an official Nuosu population of about 3 million. If we subtract those who, for whatever reason, have had themselves registered as Yi, but are actually not or no longer Yi, we reach a figure of about 2.5 million. Then they have to be subdivided into Black and White Yi as well as into various strata of slaves, into clans and lineages. What are the Yi, but just a loose pile of sand? To achieve unity amongst all Yi is very difficult; Yi have little power and strength, are dissimilar and without influence.

The Yi have lived in a closed-off world for a long time and know little about what goes on outside of it. Historically, a slave owner controlled a township at the most. What went on outside of that place was unknown to him. After the founding of the People's Republic, the Yi had the Han culture poured down their throats. Nowadays Yi don't even possess their own industry. Admittedly, Yi have their own script but its use is not widespread. Realistically, the future prospects are extremely gloomy.[1]

This entrepreneur expresses sentiments that many other larger and more educated entrepreneurs confirm. Although the Nuosu are courageous, open, and honest, their existence is in question, because they are backward in economic and educational terms, do not form an organized social unit, and have not been able to oppose the crushing superiority of the Han. Entrepreneurs think that the development of Nuosu entrepreneurship is important for these very reasons.

MARKET COMPETITION AND ECONOMIC SEGREGATION

Processes of social change, including the modernization process, promote competition based on ethnic boundaries, which stimulates ethnic mobilization. Rather than creating a social hierarchy between Han and Nuosu entrepreneurs, developing the private sector has led to ethnic competition. Thus, instead of creating a *hierarchical cultural division of labor*, competition has created a *segmented cultural division of labor*.[2]

In counties with a significant Nuosu majority, Han entrepreneurs feel themselves to be disadvantaged and discriminated against. Only 10 percent of the Han entrepreneurs in our survey feel that the local government respects their interests; some believe that the authorities protect Nuosu entrepreneurs and only further Nuosu interests. Some also declared that they suffer from fiscal discrimination. These perceptions affect Han entrepreneurs' business lives and commercial contacts, and further intensify Han feelings of resentment toward Nuosu.

On the other hand, twice as many Nuosu expressed ethnic resentment. For example, Nuosu entrepreneurs complained that Han entrepreneurs obtained credit more easily because the banks generally do not give loans to Nuosu. These kinds of conflicts arise when different ethnicities compete for cultural and economic hegemony within a particular space, and when a distinct difference in power exists between them. In this sense, Nuosu discrimination against the Han enhances Nuosu group identity and self-esteem.

Patterns of cultural, geographic, and economic segregation are created when social groups grow apart because of ethnic phenomena. For example, ethnic groups may create their own business networks (ethnic economies) or only employ members of their own ethnic communities. Although there are varying patterns of segregation in Liangshan Prefecture, we see two main trends. In some areas, ethnic segregation in employment is currently increasing. However, segregation is also decreasing due to prevailing market factors. Patterns of segregation exist in the spheres of employment, organization, and entrepreneurship.

State and large collective businesses generally employ Nuosu rather than Han personnel. However, in private companies, Han employ Nuosu workers only for performing secondary or "inferior" tasks. Nuosu entrepreneurs, in contrast, employ Han, if at all, in technical and professional positions; management and security positions, or those involving physical labor, are mostly reserved for Nuosu.

Table 7.1 illustrates the level of segregation in employment. Nuosu entrepreneurs appear to have a stronger preference for employing members of their own ethnic group for several reasons. Nuosu entrepreneurs are morally obliged to employ people from their own clan or village. Because trusting relationships exist between entrepreneurs and their clan or village members, the employees will accept situations that Han laborers would not stand

TABLE 7.1 Employment by Ethnicity

Employment type	Entrepreneurs	
Nuosu employing Nuosu only	55	(85.9%)
Nuosu employing Nuosu and Han	6	(9.4%)
Nuosu employing Han only	3	(4.7%)
Total	64	(100%)
Han employing Han only	28	(66.7%)
Han employing Nuosu and Han	9	(21.4%)
Han employing Nuosu only	5	(11.9%)
Total	42	(100%)

SOURCE: Author's survey, 1999–2002.

for, for instance, poor working conditions or delays in payment when the company is in financial difficulty. Nuosu workers can be paid lower wages and are willing to perform physically demanding, dirty, or dangerous tasks that the Han regard as "inferior" and are unwilling to do. Nuosu entrepreneurs also believe that shared ethnicity with their employees will allow them to get along better. Moreover, Han do not like to work for Nuosu entrepreneurs, which leads to employer–employee conflicts based on mutual prejudice. Finally, though to a lesser extent, Nuosu entrepreneurs also feel a social and ethnic obligation to employ disadvantaged people of their own ethnicity who may not be members of their own clans.

In counties in which Nuosu are the majority, local cadres exert pressure on Han entrepreneurs to employ Nuosu. A Han mine owner in Zhaojue noted that this has some positive effects: "Employing a large number of Yi brings me official recognition and many advantages. The local officials and the local population cause me fewer difficulties."[3] In areas where Nuosu are the majority, Han who will not put any Nuosu on their payroll are "punished" by being charged higher taxes and levies. Nuosu end up being hired to carry out the "inferior" work that Han are often not prepared to do themselves. A large percentage of the Han entrepreneurs whom we interviewed did not want to hire Nuosu because they felt Nuosu were lazy and rebellious, frequently did not show up for work, and, worst of all, possessed a low level of education and training. What made matters even worse in the opinion of the Han entrepreneurs was that Nuosu did not work harmoniously together and conflicts continually arose among them. However, in

FIG. 10. *Workers in a private enterprise, Yuexi County*

FIG. 11. *A rural Nuosu entrepreneur with his staff, Xide County*

one case, a Han businesswoman in Butuo employed mostly young Nuosu, partly because there were few Han personnel available (in both Butuo and Meigu) and partly because Nuosu made fewer demands than Han workers. As a precaution, however, she hired all of her Nuosu staff on a temporary basis, not for the long term.

There were also differences in hiring preference depending on the type of business and the level of specialized knowledge and technical capabilities required. For example, a Nuosu entrepreneur in Meigu told us that he employed mostly Han workers in building construction because they were technically more competent and worked with greater precision. He employed Nuosu in his brickworks business, where simpler skills were required. The Nuosu owner of a large restaurant in Xide argued that she preferred to employ Han waitstaff, because she found that they were friendlier to the customers.

Segregation in the employment sector is thus not of an absolute nature. Ethnic or kinship relations alone may not be the decisive factor. Nevertheless, hiring patterns are dominated by ethnic boundaries.

Nuosu and Han also showed a preference for segregating the interest organizations that represent the entrepreneurs. Although almost two-thirds of the Nuosu (65.4%) and more than four-fifths of the Han (85.4%) would like to see the formation of an autonomous, non-state interest organization for entrepreneurs, more than a fourth of both respondent groups (Nuosu 29.0%, Han 26.2%) are in favor of segregating the organizations along ethnic lines. Respondents in both ethnic groups apparently assume that they have divergent interests that can only be formulated and represented through separated associations. In the more developed counties of Mianning and Ganluo, over 80 percent were in favor of forming an independent association and almost half wished for separate Nuosu and Han associations. Increasing economic development may be responsible for the demand to establish separate organizations; however, this view can also be interpreted as an expression of ethnic competition within a segmented cultural division of labor.

On the other hand, despite seemingly rigid ethnic boundaries, business relations can transcend ethnic lines (see Olzak 1983: 356). Existing entrepreneur organizations bring business people of both ethnic groups together, enabling them to network and increasing their cooperation with each other. This somewhat weakens the segregation between different communities and lines of business. Ethnic relations that transcend clan divisions may also arise from this process.

Opportunities for the two ethnic groups to interact are more common in urban county towns than in rural areas, which means that ethnic boundaries are more fluid in these areas. More than two-thirds of both ethnic groups in urban county town rejected the idea of establishing entrepreneurial interest associations along ethnic lines, which may be an additional indication of flexible ethnic boundaries. However, there may be multiple reasons for this opinion: people may have had mixed feelings, they may have been confused regarding government policies, or perhaps they did not perceive their statements to be contradictory.

In the commercial sphere, there is also structural segregation, especially in more developed counties, such as Ganluo and Mianning. In these counties, 60 percent of the suppliers to Han entrepreneurs were Han, and 90 percent of the purchasers were state-owned, Han-managed companies. For the Nuosu, rural and Nuosu companies made up 45.5 percent of their suppliers, and Han firms made up an additional third (31.8%). However, irrespective of the ethnicity of their suppliers, half of the Nuosu companies sold their products to Han or to state companies. In less developed counties, this trend was less conspicuous. For Han enterprises in all counties, primary suppliers and customers were mainly private Han companies and included some state enterprises that were managed by Han. For Nuosu companies, the primary suppliers and customers were mostly private Nuosu companies, but the percentage of Nuosu suppliers and customers was close to the percentage of Han suppliers and customers. However, it is important to keep in mind that the limited selection of suppliers and customers in the less developed areas can affect these choices. Our figures demonstrate that market limitations and constraints bring entrepreneurs of both ethnic groups together on the market, thus diminishing segregation in business. They also reveal that the difficulty of accumulating capital perpetuates structural inequalities and that the more the market is developed, the more segregation becomes irrelevant.

Entrepreneurs have varying levels of social interaction with each other. Large percentages of both groups (Nuosu 42.0%, Han 42.9%) regularly have contact with other entrepreneurs, which may indicate that communication between entrepreneurs of both ethnic groups has increased, presumably initially among larger and better-educated business people. Entrepreneurial organizations also foster inter-ethnic interaction of Nuosu and Han entrepreneurs.

On the other hand, nearly half of the Nuosu (41.7%) and one-third of the Han (33.3%) never or rarely have any form of contact with other entrepreneurs, regardless of ethnicity. Still, 66.7 percent of the Han and 58.3 percent of the Nuosu stated that they had regular business or other types of relations with entrepreneurs from both groups. Such high percentages indicate that the spheres of business, ethnic, and kinship relationships are increasingly overlapping each other. More and more entrepreneurs have realized that contacts with entrepreneurs of other ethnic groups can give them access to information and networks otherwise unavailable to them in their own surroundings. However, there are still exceptions. In Ganluo and Mianning, not a single Han entrepreneur regularly communicated with Nuosu entrepreneurs. In contrast, Nuosu entrepreneurs had regular exchanges with both groups; 31 percent of the Han only interacted with other Han, while only 23.5 percent of the Nuosu had exclusively Nuosu business dealings. At the other extreme, only a single Han entrepreneur primarily interacted with Nuosu colleagues, in contrast to 19.8 percent of Nuosu entrepreneurs who primarily interacted with Han. This either indicates that Nuosu are more open-minded than a large percentage of Han, who are not interested in fostering contacts with Nuosu entrepreneurs, or that Nuosu simply have to interact with Han if they want to form business networks.

ETHNIC BOUNDARIES AND ETHNIC COMPETITION

In the past, the Nuosu were economically disadvantaged compared to the Han. In this respect, nothing has changed; the higher the percentage of Nuosu in a county population, the greater the poverty and the lower the incomes in that county. This is true even in Meigu, which has the highest percentage of Nuosu and had a higher economic performance than Butuo or Jinyang in recent years. Although it has been two decades since the government first authorized the establishment of private businesses, it has still not been possible to significantly increase the proportion of Nuosu who own companies in the private sector. They amounted to merely 9.2 percent in 1999. While the percentage of Nuosu in the private sector is higher in counties with a Nuosu majority, it is still much lower than the percentage of Nuosu within the population. For instance, in Zhaojue, where 97 percent of the population is Nuosu, only 45 percent of the individual firm owners are Nuosu. Since Han mostly employ other Han, in counties with a Nuosu majority, only a small percentage of Nuosu employees have found work in the private sector.

In Liangshan Prefecture, what we have termed a "cultural division of labor" is clearly recognizable. This term refers to the fact that businesses in the larger sectors of private industry are almost always run by Han, whereas Nuosu are more limited to businesses in the tertiary sector. In some areas, the percentage of Nuosu in the larger business sectors (construction, mining, and manufacturing) is significantly below 5 percent; in the tertiary sector (trade, catering, and services) it is a little over 10 percent. This suggests that Han entrepreneurs mostly run lines of business that require larger investments, more human capital and skills, and also generate larger profits. A larger percentage of Nuosu run small firms in the tertiary sector, which require fewer resources.

Ethnic competition is expressed in the close cooperation between certain Nuosu cadres and Nuosu entrepreneurs, who are attempting to utilize ethnic resources to counterbalance discrimination. This cooperation takes different forms; for example, the local authorities may give preference to Nuosu entrepreneurs by granting them advantages or by imposing special levies on Han entrepreneurs, especially on those who have migrated into the area.

One of the Nuosu entrepreneurs' most important resources is their home court advantage. Clan relationships, networks, and shared ethnicity facilitate company management and business relations—at least up to the prefectural level. Nuosu entrepreneurs also use any advantage they have in the competition for rights, privileges, and resources. These include Party membership, previous cadre positions, and activities such as serving as deputies of the People's Congresses or of the Political Consultative Conferences. Correspondingly, Nuosu participate differently in politics than Han do. Nuosu entrepreneurs try to solve problems by using their relationships and networks, whereas Han will use other methods such as making donations to officials. Because Han are the ethnic majority in China, open and direct discrimination against Han entrepreneurs might lead to intervention from the prefectural or provincial authorities. Nuosu entrepreneurs and cadres thus use subtle strategies for exerting political pressure or securing advantages over the Han. That Han entrepreneurs are more involved in the Sichuan Trade Union Association may be connected with this set of problems; if they are discriminated against in local areas, Han entrepreneurs may exert direct political pressure through the trade union.

Differing economic behaviors and different concepts of social and local obligations thus maintain ethnic boundaries despite the effects of social transformations. Many of the Nuosu entrepreneurs choose to become entrepreneurs due to blocked prospects of upward mobility because of their family status; as members of the former upper strata their path to social ascent was blocked or impeded due to political and cultural changes. This continues to create social barriers for Nuosu. Han and Nuosu entrepreneurs also have completely different collective memories and images. To the Han entrepreneurs, the Nuosu have risen from a backward-looking, slave-owning society and are primitive; most of the Nuosu entrepreneurs feel the Han are egocentric and ignorant and take no interest in Nuosu culture and development. Such sentiments arise partly due to the fact that many Han entrepreneurs only go to Liangshan to take advantage of the market opportunities there.

Ethnic boundaries are by no means only defined by actual or perceived cultural characteristics. Frederik Barth has stated that the ethnic boundaries that define a group are, " . . . of course social boundaries" (1981: 204). Very often, social differences merge with ethnic differences within people's consciousness to create ethnic boundaries. Some examples of social differences are disparities in educational level, differences in degrees of poverty and in living standards, or even differences in the motivations for becoming self-employed. The main motivation for Nuosu is the desire to increase their income and standard of living; Han, in contrast, aim for self-fulfillment. However, some differences undoubtedly have a social background and not an ethnic one, such as Han entrepreneurs' generally higher qualifications and level of specialized skills or knowledge. Thus, ethnic boundaries are caused by the perception of inequality in the Nuosu consciousness and by the perception of superiority in the consciousness of the Han.

In many respects, Nuosu and Han entrepreneurs develop the same or similar attitudes due to their focus on entrepreneurship; their thinking is not always ethnically influenced. Both groups desire a greater degree of economic and entrepreneurial liberty, both are of the opinion that entrepreneurs have to cooperate with each other and take part in politics in order to further their own interests, and both believe that a non-state organization is necessary for representing their interests. Both are dissatisfied with local government behavior toward their firms, albeit to differing degrees. In addition, there are major similarities in their life goals and attitudes as well as in their assessments of entrepreneurs' economic, social, and political positions in society. Both groups feel *guanxi* are important for economic success.

The market, in an economic sense, and activities in urban areas place entrepreneurs in situations with stronger communication contexts. The state has also promoted a form of integration that transcends ethnicity by making membership in the associations for entrepreneurs compulsory. This endeavor is emphasized by the fact that the most important entrepreneurial association, the Federation of Industry and Commerce, is subordinated to the Party's United Front Departments, which are responsible for integrating social, economic, and intellectual elites outside the Party. Of course, in counties officially below the poverty line, the ability of these associations to fulfill these tasks adequately is limited.

Though many entrepreneurs admit that the Federation of Industry and Commerce brings Nuosu and Han entrepreneurs into closer contact, in particular, business contacts appear to be developing in areas where Han and Nuosu live intermingled. However, only a few entrepreneurs were able to provide examples of close and trusting cooperation. This is also true for relationships between Han entrepreneurs and Nuosu officials. One of the exceptions is a Han owner of a copper mine in Zhaojue who has developed a close relationship with the local authorities. He primarily employs Nuosu workers, his vice-director is a Nuosu who has close contacts to local cadres, and he regularly invites a bimo to clear his factory of evil spirits. The Chairman of the Federation of Industry and Commerce of Zhaojue commented on his business, "Employing mainly Yi workers and respecting local Yi customs has given him recognition as well as many advantages from local officials and among the local Yi. Neither local cadres nor the local people give him any trouble."[4]

In summary, there exists a distinct "us-and-them" dichotomy between Nuosu and Han, as well as barriers based on prejudices and stereotypes. A cultural division of labor between Nuosu and Han entrepreneurs creates new ethnic tensions due to market competition. Han entrepreneurs believe they are locally disadvantaged and discriminated against; such negative perceptions affect their business lives and commercial contacts, thus intensifying their resentment of Nuosu. Among Nuosu entrepreneurs, ethnic resentments have developed along different lines. Nuosu feel they are discriminated against in translocal markets. They do not perceive discrimination by locally established (Han) industrial enterprises, in employment practices, in appointment procedures for Nuosu officials, or on the basis of cultural activities or ethnic customs. Although Yi entrepreneurship undoubtedly contributes to increased equality, the increasing ethnic resentment over access to markets, acquisition of local resources, economic competition, and various forms of segregation are significant factors affecting entrepreneurship.

8

Entrepreneurs
and Ethnic Identity

....

Nuosu entrepreneurs' discourse on questions of status and identity very often echo the arguments advanced by Yi researchers, whose work is well known in Liangshan. Entrepreneurs, a new economic and social elite, are helping shape a new Nuosu collective consciousness.

In addition to the obvious identity markers of time (Nuosu history) and space (Liangshan as "home"), economic success contributes to identity formation as well. Ethnic identity, which arises from proximity in a shared social space, is a collective process. The identity formation effect of entrepreneurship thus can take place only in interaction with other status groups. In this milieu, entrepreneurs are both carriers of ethnic symbols and agents of modernization who actively shape identity.

IDENTITY

Several different senses of the concept "identity" are relevant to the Nuosu situation: identity as a collective pattern, as proximity in a shared social space, as a warm loyalty or "us" feeling, and as a process.

In very general terms, identity refers to the ego-identity as a part of the collective identity. The individual identifies himself or herself with collective players based on imagined commonalities. These players—to use a modern term—can also be collectively understood as a cultural network. Through this identification, an individual finds his or her own identity as well as a pattern of orientation. This pattern molds a person's thinking and behavior, as well as his or her images of others and of the self. Ethnic identity refers "to the individual level of identification with a culturally defined collectivity" (Hutchinson and Smith 1996: 5).

However, identity is not simply a cognitive process, nor is it merely an invented or imagined process. It requires specific preconditions beyond cognition, in order for cognitive identifications to come into being at all. Ethnic identity is characterized by proximity to others within a shared social space. Blood (kin), territory, history, or myths, along with shared language, religion, and customs, form such nearness within a social space among the Liangshan Yi. Although these factors may appear to be constructs, in the consciousness of those concerned, they still represent commonalities by which one group discerns itself from another. The core factors of identity are the question of the differences from others, the continuity of these differences, feelings of self-appreciation as an ethnic community, and a common territory representing the body of this community. Stuart Hall, a cultural theoretician, stated that cultural identities are unstable points of identification or links that are formed within the discourse on history and culture. It is not a "being" but a "positioning" (Hall 1994: 30).

The concept of "circles of loyalty" is also helpful to our discussion of ethnic identity. Such circles consist of people with common belief and affiliation systems. Rosenberg differentiates between "warm" and "cold" loyalties. "Warm loyalty" refers to emotional relationships experienced as "natural," such as family, kinship, clan, or ethnic group relations. "Cold loyalties" are rational-artificial relationships with external organizations, such as parties, clubs and associations, and state institutions. Warm circles create closeness within a social or ethnic space in which the warmth or nearness is characterized by a proximity in behavior, historical memory, symbolism, and symbolic codes or languages (Rosenberg 2000). The shared language of the Nuosu is the primary vehicle for communicating the warmth, the loyalty, and the "us" feeling. As previously discussed, a group's distinction from "others," the "them" group (in this case, Han), is a central part of individual and collective identities in that group. Within this paradigm, identity formation is a kind of "warming up" of identity factors that were previously cold. If people experience a warm feeling for the "Yi nationality" or for China, the project of ethnicity building or nation building has succeeded profoundly.

New approaches to the study of identity are based on the idea of identity as a process, not as a static concept. Identities adapt to social changes and "learning" takes place during rapid processes of change. Reflections on a people's history, traditions, and future form new identities. Dittrich and Radtke argue that "identity consists in the ability to master continually new situations" (1990: 30). To put it concisely, an identity means that someone must identify with a group. The group is not only a perceived collective, it is also characterized by certain commonalities that generate a strong "us" feeling (warm loyalty). In applying such general identity concepts to Nuosu entrepreneurs, we find four important factors that affect the creation of identity among them. These include time and space as markers of an ethnic identity, economic success as part of a growing individual and ethnic self-consciousness, the dual role of entrepreneurs as carriers of ethnic symbols and as agents of modernization, and food and alcohol as identity generating markers.

TIME AND SPACE AS ETHNIC MARKERS

Time (Nuosu history) and space (Liangshan) are important markers of identity for Nuosu. In the following section, we will discuss the changing historical discourse among Yi scholars and the corresponding process among Nuosu entrepreneurs. We will also examine the concept of Liangshan as homeland and its role as a stimulus for entrepreneurs' efforts to develop their native areas.

The reconstruction of the Nuosu ethnic identity by Yi scholars and Nuosu entrepreneurs is an attempt to create a collective identity by combining historical, territorial, language, and ethnic factors and/or symbols (Eisenstadt 1996: 21). History (time) marks societies, their cognitive road maps, and their identities. Kolakowski correctly emphasizes that a historical memory is a precondition for national identity (1995: 53). Undoubtedly, historical events and processes can be constructed in retrospect and instrumentalized. In the 1950s, the Communist Party classified the Nuosu social structure as a "slave-owner society." By this act, Nuosu society was attributed with being historically backward and primitive in comparison to the Han, who had supposedly reached the higher stage of "feudalism." Classification as a slave-owner society has been institutionalized and is represented symbolically, for example, in the name "Nuosu Slave-owning Society Museum" in Xichang. This classification has also been part of educational socialization since the 1950s and many Nuosu, including entrepreneurs, have internalized it. In schools, students learn that their ethnic group is economically and culturally backward and inferior to Han culture (see Harrell and Bamo 1998). This is reflected, for instance, in a statement made by a leading county official during a welcoming speech given by the Butuo County leadership. He noted, "the traces of a slave-owning society are still relatively strong here [in Butuo]."[1] This is a symbolic expression of the attitude, "We are poor and backward here, and the customs of the local Nuosu are still very traditional."

Li and Harrell argue that the Nuosu describe their past in genealogical terms and less in terms of historical events. The Yi neither initiated nor controlled the study of "Yi history" as an area of knowledge (Li and Harrell 2001). This began to change in the 1980s, when Yi scholars started to question the cultural classifications developed by the Han; for instance, Wu Ga states, "the Chinese narrative of the Yi history and Yi ethnicity is a sinocentric view of history" (Wu Ga 1998: 46). The scholars have also put forward their own interpretations and theses; during times of social pluralization and political liberalization, people begin to question the construction of a national culture by those in power.

Numerous Yi scholars have assessed Yi history and culture from a completely new vantage point and have gained new insights. For example, it has been argued that the Yi were the earliest descendants of the Yuanmou people, whose fossils are the oldest to be found in Asia. The Yi would thus not only be the ancestors of the Han but also the oldest of "yellow race," including the Japanese, and they would be the ancestors of the Native Americans. Symbols found on 10,000-year-old ceramics excavated in northern Yunnan have been linked to the Yi script, which Yi scholars have also connected with the Banpo script, found on ceramics produced by an 8,000-year-old Neolithic culture and excavated in northwest China. The finds of the "Sanxingdui culture" in 1986, near Guanghan in Sichuan Province, date back to between 2,000 and 3,000 BCE and have also been associated with the Yi. Thus, Yi scholars argue that in addition to the assumed single center of old Chinese culture, there was another original cultural center that was the Yi. This conclusion has led to additional claims: the legendary emperors of the Xia, Zhou, and Qin dynasties were Yi ancestors; Taoism was created by the Yi; Laozi, the name of the founder of Taoist philosophy, is a Yi name and means "born in the year of the tiger," and so forth.[2]

It is not our intent, however, to evaluate the arguments of this discourse in a historical context. "History," argues Georg Elwert, "can at the same time be both false and productive. It is false or flawed as a historical report, but it is innovative as a model projected onto the past of what societal relationships should be" (2002: 33). In this vein, our interest lies in the conclusions that Yi scholars reach and in the arguments they use to make the following points. First, that the Yi were the ancestors of the "yellow race," including the Chinese, the Japanese, and Native Americans,[3] and, secondly, that the Yi script, which is approximately 10,000 years old, is the oldest script in the world. The argument follows that it is, therefore, also the progenitor of the Chinese script as well as of the scripts found in Mesopotamia, Egypt, India, and in the ancient Mediterranean.[4]

Yi scholars challenge the Han historical worldview by valuing their history and culture above Han history and culture. This is in significant contrast to the Han historical interpretation, which claims that the Han brought history and culture to other peoples, who were always socially and politically inferior to them. For example, in a book published in 2000 based on the work of the Yi scholar Liu Yaohan, Fu Shouzong argues that historical research has established that the cultures of the Yangzi River watershed, especially in Liangshan and other Yi areas in Yunnan, were considerably older than those of the Yellow River, where Chinese culture is commonly thought to have originated. Thus, he concludes, "the Yi lands are one of the cradles of Chinese culture and civilization" (Fu 2000: 6). According to these Yi authors, the Han descended from the Yi, and not vice versa. By challenging the claims of Chinese history per se, such writings fundamentally question the classification of the Yi as a historically backward "slave-owner society." Moreover, according to Li and Harrell, such interpretations of Yi history also extend a positive value to China and Chinese culture:

> Using the antiquity of Yi writing as a kind of Chinese writing, connected at least in its origins with Han writing, [helps] rescue China from the national shame of having invented writing later than certain other ancient civilizations (Li and Harrell 2001: 13).

In this way, the new historical identity of the Yi takes shape and claims uniqueness for itself. This identity is further expressed through scripts. A Yi poet noted that Guo Moruo (1892–1978), the greatest Chinese scholar of ancient scripts, was unable to decode the symbols on the Banpo ceramics, whereas a Yi bimo was able to recognize 54 of the 56 symbols (Harrell and Li 2003: 378). This reinforces the argument that Yi culture, not Han culture, is the oldest and has had the longest uninterrupted existence in the recorded history of the world. Anthony Smith uses the term "continuous perennialism" to refer to the claim that an ethnic group has continuously maintained its national identity for millennia. Such a claim is part of a constructed collective memory or, to use Eric Hobsbawm's term, an *invented tradition* that refers to history and historical events and is part of the collective identity (Smith 1999: 5). Not only entrepreneurs but also cadres, artists, and other members of the intellectual elite frequently refer to the historical elements mentioned above and unquestioningly declare them to be the objective truth. This is certainly a reaction to Han historical arguments and positions. Many Yi feel that Han arguments paint an incorrect picture of reality and are based on historical injustices and past acts of violence perpetrated by the Han.

We have given a few though rather detailed examples to demonstrate the reach of historical discourse in re-evaluating Yi history and reshaping Yi identity. This discourse manifests itself in the historical view held by Nuosu entrepreneurs who promote the same arguments, challenge the concept of the Nuosu as a slave-owner society, and reject the view that theirs was a cruel and exploitative society prior to the 1950s. They show pride in their ancient history, their script, and in bimo culture, which are for them clear signs of their superiority over the Han and Han culture. Statements made by Nuosu entrepreneurs during our interviews showed that this historical perspective has already been incorporated into local knowledge and is accepted as the truth.

However, some entrepreneurs have thoughts about history that go even further. They claim that their traditional culture was destroyed during the Democratic Reform in the mid-1950s and the Nuosu were brutally persecuted. They argue that, historically, Yunnan Province was actually Yi country. In the 1950s, because the Communist Party was afraid of the Yi, it separated them into various ethnic groups, working on the principle of "divide and conquer." Another entrepreneur pointed out that the Yi had possessed a large independent territory during the rule of the Yuan Dynasty (1271–1368); this area was reduced during the reign of the Ming Dynasty (1368–1644), leading to an uprising among the Yi in which 30,000 Yi were killed. At that time, many Yi fled into Liangshan. During the era of the Qing Dynasty (1644–1911), the Yi gained a greater degree of autonomy, which was preserved throughout the Nationalist regime; the Communists eliminated this autonomy.

During our interviews, entrepreneurs also referred to contemporary issues. Their ideas were stated in such a way as to create ethnic boundaries and can be understood as expressions of ethnicity. Although they are individual and not group statements, viewing them together reveals a common theme running through them.

> We Yi formerly had our own empire, the Nanzhao Empire. The bearers of this state were the Yi, not, as some historians falsely assume, the Bai. Only through violence was it possible to integrate us into China. (Entrepreneur from Ganluo)[5]

Traditionally, we did not have a slave-owner society. Up until 1956 we had a "production responsibility system" (Ch: *shengchan zerenzhi*).[6] Before the "Democratic Reform" [1956–1957] there was no poverty here; every family owned cattle and had enough to eat. That changed after the reforms. Our health care system was also much better than it is today. (Entrepreneur from Mianning)

The Han chopped down our trees [during the Great Leap Forward], and nowadays they accuse us of destroying the environment. The facts show who the real destroyers are. (Entrepreneur from Zhaojue)

Fifty percent of what the Han write about the Yi is complete nonsense. (Entrepreneur from Xichang)

It is true that opium was grown here, but it was only intended for sale to the Han. For the Yi, the use of opium was taboo. (Entrepreneur from Yanyuan)

In the middle of the city [Xichang] there is a large memorial in memory of the supposed blood-brotherhood between Marshall Liu Bocheng [of the Red Army during the Long March] and a leading Nuosu figure. [The blood brotherhood gave Liu permission to move unchecked through Yi areas.] In reality, Liu Bocheng paid the Yi protection money (Ch: *baohufei*) so that we would leave the Red Army in peace. That is a fact but nobody dares to say it openly. (Entrepreneur from Puge)

Historically, the Yi have never been ruled by anyone apart from the Communist Party. Just to be honest for once—we would be more developed by now if the Democratic Reforms hadn't happened. (Entrepreneur from Meigu)

Earlier, we did not want to have anything to do with the Han, and we avoided places where there were many of them. We believed they would bring us illnesses. (Entrepreneur from Butuo)

We are not concerned about whether these example statements represent the truth. They are used simply to illustrate several widespread sentiments among the Nuosu: that they have their own glorious history, which has been falsely interpreted and assessed by the Han; that the relatively harmonious social and economic order of the Yi was permanently disturbed by their integration into the socialist project; and that if they had had the opportunity, they would have developed better and more quickly by themselves.

Entrepreneurs' positive historical self-image and negative evaluation of other social groups promotes their own ethnic identity and self-confidence. However, this evaluation also helps them to come to terms with their devaluation through official historiography as well as to handle the injustices they have experienced since the 1950s. Entrepreneurs old enough to have experienced traditional Yi life noticeably idealize this society. The Yi have also experienced a loss of independence, especially by the defeat of the armed rebellion in the 1950s and the massive repression that followed, as well as by the liquidation of the upper class. They have therefore adopted a very resigned attitude and their thoughts have turned inwards. Entrepreneurs between the ages of 35 and 55 years are ambivalent about their role. On the one hand, they possess a strong bond with their own ethnic group; on the other hand, they have been massively exposed to Han culture and the political campaigns of the Mao era, which ripped Nuosu culture apart—discriminated against it, demonized it as backward, and destroyed it.

Entrepreneurship in a modern sense cannot non-exist in a slave-owner society; the emergence of Nuosu entrepreneurship could therefore be seen as an indicator that the "backwardness" of Nuosu society has finally ended. The entrepreneurs, as agents of modernity, are the avant-garde of the Nuosu and thus enjoy equality with the Han. One entrepreneur explained:

> The slave-society is a symbol of backwardness, and under conditions of backwardness, we Yi people did not develop the institution of entrepreneurship. Times have changed now. We already have a considerable number of Yi entrepreneurs and Yi officials. Why shouldn't we be able to modernize ourselves through the efforts of our own talented people?[7]

This sentiment is not only an indicator of processes of change, but also of an economic elite with a growing self-consciousness that contributes to reevaluating history and thus to altering Nuosu identity.

In addition to history (time), territory (space) is a concrete reference point for the Nuosu identity. What the Chinese term "Liangshan" (Cool Mountains), is for the Yi "Nuosu Muddi"—the Land of the Nuosu. They have settled this area for over a thousand years. A large proportion of the Yi in Yunnan and Guizhou see this region as the homeland of their forefathers and of all Yi (Harrell 2000b: 3ff.). Nuosu Muddi is therefore a "personal place," i.e., a territory that possesses a particular sense of closeness or unity for the Nuosu, to which they are drawn, and which they regard as their ethnic territory and cultural center. The beauty of the natural landscape and their feelings associated with the homeland are expressed in literature and songs, and also reflected in everyday symbolism. Mountain and animal symbols suffuse Yi religious imagery as well as patterns in traditional clothing and everyday commodities, such as dishes and bowls. Harrell fittingly termed these images "mountain patterns" (2000b).

For the majority of the entrepreneurs, the close relationship to the homeland is a driving force behind their modernizing endeavors. The "development and modernization" of Liangshan is an important part of their justification for increasing their entrepreneurial impact and giving "development aid" to their native villages in the form of infrastructure, education, and social benefits. An entrepreneur in Meigu stated:

> Of course, I am not able to develop the entire area of Liangshan, so I will contribute to my village first. I have funded the construction of the roads leading through my village, and I also intend to build a primary school here. It is not only the clan that counts, but also the village. If someone needs bricks for a new house in our village, I will provide them free of cost. If someone needs money to start a new business, I will support him economically. I want not only to develop my own business but to develop this village as well.[8]

A large entrepreneur in Yanyuan indicated a similar motivation for improving his native place:

> Without a doubt, I am the most important entrepreneur in this county. I have provided employment to Yi and to Han; I have contributed to local development by constructing roads, bridges, and schools and by providing electricity, medical care and running water. Thus, I have contributed to the prosperity of this formerly extremely poor area. Consequently, the relationship between the nationalities [Nuosu and Han] has improved a lot. The Yi used to steal from the Han and vice versa. Their relationship has changed, because I have arranged for both to prosper now. . . . Why did I return to this poor area even though my business was very successful in Xichang? I felt that we Yi are looked down upon and discriminated against by the Han. People who are poor are perceived as lazy. Others believe that we Yi are heavily involved in crime and are drug addicts. We can only change this image by striving to develop Liangshan and by generating new economic, social and political prestige and standing. I am determined to contribute to such a change![9]

Comments like these indicate that Nuosu Muddi as a personal and ethnic place is also a source of pride and a space of safety. The entrepreneurs know their way around Liangshan, and they are bound to various ethnic and social networks there. They view themselves as having a certain responsibility for Liangshan's development, which they trace back to ethnic components. Interview respondents identified a range of "invented" commonalities and circles of loyalty, which the majority applied to themselves in their role as *ethnic entrepreneurs*, not as individuals. Nuosu entrepreneurs see themselves as daring, socially responsible people who possess socially shared knowledge and who contribute to the development of their local and ethnic environments. They want to ensure the long-term existence of the Nuosu ethnic community by pioneering economic development and raising the educational standard in Liangshan.

ECONOMIC SUCCESS AND ETHNIC SELF-CONFIDENCE

Economic strength is an important prerequisite for increasing political autonomy. Because Liangshan Prefecture depends heavily on state subsidies, it can hardly become entirely self-sufficient. The subsidies give the state control over the development projects that it finances. Furthermore, a greater degree of autonomy presupposes that emerging social groups will have acquired sufficient power to negotiate with the state over social concerns. Intellectuals and entrepreneurs represent such strategic social groups.

The success of economic development processes is tied to ethnic competition and control of economic resources. The definition of ethnic identity through competition or as a process of confrontation is, therefore, an important economic consideration. Paul Brass has characterized the formation of ethnic identity as a process of threefold confrontation: a confrontation within the ethnic group for the control of material and symbolic resources; a confrontation between ethnic groups in the form of competition for rights, privileges, and resources; and a confrontation between the state and the groups that control it and local population groups on their territory (Brass 1985: 1).

In our study, the first process can be identified in the confrontation between Nuosu entrepreneurs and Nuosu cadres; the entrepreneurial stratum has begun to control both material and symbolic resources of the Nuosu, thus challenging traditional control by Nuosu cadres. The entrepreneurs' self-confidence in their new status as a strategic group is growing, and it is reflected in their role in society and in the economy. They show pride both in their entrepreneurship and in belonging to the stratum of entrepreneurs that has contributed so much to the development of "their" local communities. Such pride also promotes a consciousness of their own abilities and of the possibilities for success as an ethnic group. "We Yi have proven that we can become successful entrepreneurs—more successful than the Han," said one Yi entrepreneur.[10]

The second process of ethnic confrontation that Brass discusses is even more evident in Liangshan than the first. Ethnic resentment and segregation result from market competition. Past economic disadvantages of the Nuosu have caused the percentage of self-employed Nuosu to be markedly lower than the percentage of Nuosu within the population. There is a cultural division of labor, as we have seen—Han are employed in higher paying, more technical positions, and Nuosu have the more menial jobs. Some entrepreneurs make use of ethnic resources by working in close cooperation with Nuosu cadres in an attempt to counteract discrimination. Han entrepreneurs thus feel more strongly disadvantaged and discriminated against by local government officials, and resentful toward Nuosu entrepreneurs.

The third form of confrontation—that between the state and local population groups—is more complex to trace, insofar as the Nuosu are up against a state institution that controls not only Liangshan Prefecture but also the entire country. Confrontations are sparked both by questions of autonomy and by development politics. However, as far as development politics are concerned, nowadays, the "state" no longer moves development forward—entrepreneurs have taken the lead in realizing the development potential of the individual counties.

ENTREPRENEURS AS CARRIERS OF ETHNIC SYMBOLS AND AS AGENTS OF MODERNIZATION

Ernst Cassirer declared that people's understanding of the world and of the self consists of symbols; forming symbols and understanding them was for him the hallmark of being human (Cassirer 1994). Ethnic symbols bear ethnic messages, which serve an important function in creating ethnic identities—ethnic symbols thus may be said to form the key aspect of ethnicity. For Nuosu, ethnic dress, traditional wooden drinking vessels, wooden bowls, the traditional ethnic dish *tuotuorou* (lumps of boiled meat), drinking and love songs, local cigarettes and alcoholic beverages, the bimo as an ethnic institution, and traditional architecture are all important symbols. Primary schools founded by entrepreneurs and focusing on teaching the

Nuosu language and script also serve symbolic functions, representing ethnicity as expressed through collective transactions.

Every entrepreneur we interviewed wished to document his or her ethnic identity by putting on traditional clothing for the photographs, serving *tuotuorou*, and using wooden plates and spoons decorated with traditional patterns and symbols. These objects are found in every entrepreneur's household and function both as everyday commodities and as symbolic objects, in that they symbolize the difference between Han and Nuosu everyday life and demonstrate that the entrepreneur belongs to the Nuosu ethnic group. These objects therefore carry cultural codes for social identity and collective memory. Moreover, as this symbolism encompasses all clans and represents all Nuosu, the entrepreneur, as an imagined agent of modernity, carries on the symbolism of collective tradition as well.

Symbolic buildings and the decoration of personal space represent a person's status and identity as well. Larger entrepreneurs such as Ahou Muye from Meigu County, Jize Ji Amu from Yanyuan, and Jjike Jiajia from Ganluo have built new houses in traditional Nuosu style, with traditional interior furnishings—furniture bearing traditional symbolism, collected bimo texts, amulets, and fetishes. Jize Ji Amu lives in a large house built in the traditional style of *tusi* living quarters, with spartanly furnished interiors.[11] "I have furnished the interior area very meagerly so the local officials will not become envious," he explained. However, the indoor fireplace in Jize's house was made of high-quality stone from Leibo County, and spirits were served in silver Tibetan bowls from neighboring Muli County. His company's administrative building, several different department buildings, and buildings in the company's forested recreation area were all constructed in the traditional style. Items on company information boards were all written in Nuosu script, and only a few were also written in Chinese.

A Nuosu entrepreneur in Meigu County who manufactured traditional commodities from wood and leather echoed the opinions of many Nuosu when he stressed the superiority of his goods to Han-made products. His materials, including wood, leather, and natural paints, were organic and environmentally friendly, and thus his products were "green wares." He argued that since Nuosu everyday commodities were made of wood, they were less fragile and longer lasting in contrast to Han pottery.

Most restaurants in county towns are Han restaurants with Chinese food. A small number of restaurants offer Nuosu specialties and provide traditional Nuosu utensils for eating and drinking as well. Although nowadays ceramic crockery, glasses, and chopsticks are used in everyday life, guests who eat in

FIG. 12. *An entrepreneur and his family, Ganluo County*

FIG. 13. *An entrepreneur's "traditional" house, Meigu County*

entrepreneurs' homes are served in traditional Nuosu utensils: black, red, and yellow painted wooden cups instead of glasses, spoons with long stems instead of chopsticks, and wooden bowls instead of ceramic plates. Hosts explain with pride that this is Nuosu custom and a tradition. In spite of, or perhaps because of, the dominant use of Han-style commodities in everyday life, the use of Nuosu utensils for guests exudes a certain air of solemnity.[12]

As ethnic reference figures, both carriers of modernity and preservers of traditions, entrepreneurs define themselves through ideas of shared Nuosu ancestry, history, and culture. They share the perception of a commonly experienced cultural threat to their people and feel that their cultural lifestyle should be preserved. Entrepreneurs further define themselves through their shared language and script, as well as by declaring the bimo carriers of cultural, social, and symbolic capital, religious traditions, and traditions of cult and knowledge.

However, only a minority of the entrepreneurs, mainly the larger ones, believe that they are carriers and protectors of important traditional cultural elements. For many, the necessity of surviving in the market, their low educational level, and the pursuit of individual self-interests overwhelm such idealism. Overall, a somewhat pessimistic attitude prevails in reference to the backwardness of Nuosu economic development, the loss of language amongst the more educated and the young people, as well as in reference to Han political and cultural dominance.

Political socialization, especially among members of the CCP, and educational socialization in schools have created an internalized, crushed historical self-image and divided ethnic consciousness. Meanwhile, the use of the Nuosu language and script is also declining. Particularly in urban areas, Nuosu is becoming a private language and is only used for political propaganda or in literature and poetry. This is true to a much greater degree for local officials and Party members than for other Nuosu. At home, many families only speak standard Chinese, which of course is also the lingua franca of everyday, urban, public life. The children of the larger entrepreneurs, of the educated, and of the officials have switched to speaking mostly Chinese. Especially in Nuosu families in Xichang and in urban areas outside Liangshan, young people's use of the Nuosu language is decreasing dramatically. More and more of the entrepreneurs' children are being educated in elite schools in Xichang or being sent to schools outside the prefecture, where they only speak and learn standard Chinese. Consequently, one entrepreneur's view that the Nuosu and their "culture" have a gloomy future is certainly close to reality.

Up to this point, we have been referring to Nuosu entrepreneurs as agents of modernity. This is an ambiguous term. Modernity in the form of local development and social change is accompanied by modernity in the form of a threat to local customs, language, and culture. The entrepreneurs' "modernization" is manifested in a change in lifestyle and this new lifestyle has a tremendous impact on young people. Entrepreneurs set social and symbolic (ethnic) standards through the example of their prosperity, consumer behavior, habits, and lifestyles. For example, large entrepreneurs often drive more expensive cars than leading local officials. The local population evaluates expensive cars as a measure of an entrepreneur's success. For example, one Nuosu entrepreneur in Yanyuan bought a Chrysler Jeep from the United States despite the immense import tax. There are, however, strong local variations in consumer behavior. Not every entrepreneur pursues an extravagant lifestyle. Ostentatious consumption also varies between urban and rural areas and between larger and smaller entrepreneurs. In counties where entrepreneurs have higher incomes and more elegant lifestyles (such as Xichang, Ganluo, and Mianning), luxury is put on display (though only in Xichang, Chengdu, Kunming, or other cities outside Liangshan, not in the entrepreneurs' home counties). A growing number of Nuosu entrepreneurs have also been sending their children to expensive private schools outside Liangshan.

Large TV sets, refrigerators, washing machines, video recorders, stereo systems, air-conditioners, cars, video cameras, the newest mobile phones, comfortable apartments, and luxurious residential interiors (with modern Western furniture) are all important status symbols and, at the very least, signs of modest prosperity. Many large entrepreneurs own at least one house and often additional property. Because private entrepreneurs earn significantly above the average income, their expenditures are correspondingly high, reflecting their unmistakably higher standard of living.

Lifestyles, or patterns of behavior and tastes, also serve as significant social markers. Some lifestyles include what sociologists term "conspicuous consumption." Such lifestyles generate symbolic differences and form a "proper language" (Bourdieu 1998: 23, 24). They symbolize membership in a particular stratum or group and mark a boundary vis-à-vis others who do not belong to the group. The entrepreneurs display their lifestyles as an icon of their entrepreneurial achievements. Owning a house or an apartment and certain brands or styles of cars, such as limousines; consuming expensive brands of alcohol and cigarettes; installing expensive electronic consumer goods; regularly patronizing expensive restaurants and karaoke bars; as well as sometimes having attractive young girlfriends are recognized lifestyle components that identify an individual as a member of the new (ethnic) entrepreneurial stratum. This is true for both Nuosu and Han entrepreneurs. However, there is also a specific lifestyle among Nuosu entrepreneurs that includes building houses in the traditional Nuosu style, and symbolically collecting silverware, historic relics, or, in some cases, old and rare cultural objects.

Conspicuous consumption also shapes lifestyle in other ways. Eating together in expensive restaurants promotes the formation of entrepreneur networks and group consciousness among entrepreneurs who can regularly afford such luxuries. Gastro-politics are a way of building business relationships with officials and other important contact persons. They belong to a way of life for entrepreneurs who spend a considerable portion of their profits on hospitality. At the same time, however, gastro-politics contain and convey ideas about what it means to be a "guest," about group behavior, and about classifying the status of the entrepreneurs. This process forms values and a "social language" (Chang 1977: 248–49). Particularly in urban areas, brand awareness or going to certain recognized restaurants and amusement establishments serves less as a symbolic display of wealth and more as behavior that documents business success, self-confidence in status, and upward social mobility.

This style of consumption also affects non-entrepreneurial Nuosu. Entrepreneurs who live such lifestyles are role models, particularly for young people as well as for officials and small entrepreneurs. Increasing numbers of Nuosu seek this kind of lifestyle and believe that it can be achieved through entrepreneurial activity because of their expectations of the profits associated with entrepreneurism.

We did not interview non-entrepreneurs among the Nuosu to ask about their attitudes toward business people. There may be some envy and some may feel that entrepreneurs, like the *tusi* in the past, "live like Han." However, our impression is that the majority of the local Nuosu people, particularly the younger ones, admire the entrepreneurs' success and wealth, and intend to emulate them. Their admiration is strongly related to whether or not the successful entrepreneurs support their communities, whether they behave "like Han" or like Nuosu in terms of their customs, clothing, and lifestyle. There may also be a generation gap in people's assessment of entrepreneurs and their behavior—older people may partially reject them while younger people may support them.

As agents of modernity, Nuosu entrepreneurs thus contribute to shifts in attitudes and values. They are trendsetters and role models, for example,

FIG. 14. *Preparing* tuotuorou *for the research group
at the home of a Nuosu entrepreneur, Meigu County*

regarding prosperity, wealth, property, and luxury. They are also role models for behaviors and values concerning competition, economic freedoms, innovation, and market behavior, and they promote new structures as well, such as organizations representing their interests, local level public income structures, and the labor market.

A key characteristic of entrepreneurs is innovation. Innovation is not only an economic action, but also has to do with social change and with the reassessment of values. Entrepreneurs interpret values differently and question old patterns of thinking. The transformative nature of entrepreneurs as producers of change has been overlooked in the literature about them.

FOOD AND ALCOHOL AS MARKERS OF IDENTITY

For our interviews in rural areas, we were generally invited into homes and treated to the traditional rituals of hospitality. An animal (a sheep, a pig, or a cow) was slaughtered and eaten together, accompanied by generous amounts of alcohol. The dishes were always the same: *tuotuorou*, served with round, flat buckwheat cakes (N: *mgefu* or *mgamo*), garlic soup, and potatoes boiled with the skins.

Communal food and alcohol consumption serves a social function; eating the same dishes and drinking and smoking together create rapport and build community. Marcel Mauss has pointed out that gifts of food or invitations to share a meal are particularly binding social conventions (Mauss 1990: 27ff.) because food and drink are a form of communication as well as markers of a person's ethnic belonging and social position. Moreover, food and alcohol can define ethnic distinctions that can be used to mark boundaries between the Nuosu and the Han.

However, alcohol is often consumed excessively, particularly in public spaces. In our discussion, we will not treat alcohol as a pathological "problem" (as in "problem drinking") but rather as a socializing and equalizing phenomenon, as a "social act, performed in a recognized social context" (Douglas 1991b: 4). Dwight Heath has argued that alcoholism seems to be virtually absent, "even in many societies where drunkenness is frequent, highly esteemed, and actively sought" (Heath 1975: 76; see also Heath 1994: 357–61), and this is the case in Liangshan Yi society. In fact, Nuosu primarily drink in groups. Thus, alcohol is used to generate social capital, for instance, in the interest of initiating or developing social connections, network building, promoting social communication, or, when drinking with strangers, overcoming strangeness. It is an expression of hospitality, a form of interaction that unifies people and binds them together. To reject drinking is an affront that can break bonds. Some argue that the high mountain climate fosters the consumption of hard liquor. Others argue that the reasons for excessive alcohol consumption are the problems of adapting to processes of industrialization, urbanization, and de-peasantization, or to malfunctions of the political system (See, for example, Bennett 1985: 408; Chase 1985).

Yi scholar Pan Wenchao writes,

The alcohol culture of the Yi is a part of the outstanding Yi culture. Alcohol is a material carrier that reflects the make up of the production and life culture of the Yi. Politics, economics, military affairs, religion and an entire canon of customs cannot be separated from alcohol consumption. Alcohol has always been a part of Liangshan Nuosu life. There is a Nuosu proverb, "Spirits are as precious to the Yi as tea is to the Han." (2000: 1)

According to Pan Wenchao, liquor serves many important functions in Yi society. Drinking liquor together founds friendships, encourages relationships and the sharing of feelings, solidifies clan relationships and love relationships between the sexes, serves a ritual purpose at funerals and religious ceremonies, creates confidence, seals blood-brother relationships, cooperation and alliances, and settles conflicts and disputes. Liquor is also a restorative medium and a medicine (ibid.: 1).

Consuming alcohol also has a strong ritual aspect. Simply out of principle, people will urge others to drink, and to drink every glass in one shot. This is true regardless of a person's ethnicity and even for foreigners. Anyone who considers himself or herself a "real Yi" is forced to drink, irrespective of whether or not he or she enjoys drinking, or is healthy enough to do so. Dinner occasions in particular are used to drink as much alcohol as possible, and such occasions are frequent. The Liangshan Nuosu Yi perceive themselves as "*lao da*," the heartiest drinkers among all Yi groups, and look down on other Yi and Han on this account. Being able to hold one's drink is perceived as a sign of superiority, particularly in comparison to non-Yi, and as a part of the ethnic identity.

However, heavy drinking is an invented Nuosu tradition. It is a symbolic rule that "seeks to inculcate certain values and norms of behavior by repetition, which automatically implies continuity with the past" and establishes its own past by "quasi-obligatory repetition," Eric Hobsbawm argues (1984: 1, 2). In fact, widespread and excessive alcohol consumption is a "popular memory," to use Hobsbawm's term, and not at all "traditionally" conditioned, as Han and many Nuosu claim. In fact, the erosion of community authority, rituals, and solidarity have resulted in an increase in the uncontrolled consumption of alcohol. Opinions differ widely about the nature of this invented tradition. For example, one leading county functionary thought drinking alcohol was "*women minzu tese*"—a characteristic of our ethnicity. A Nuosu entrepreneur disputed this idea, pointing to the bad influence of the Han:

> The habit of always emptying a glass in one shot is a new custom adopted from the Han. In the past, this custom did not exist amongst the Yi. Young men would never dare to get drunk in the presence of their elders and would always only sip [Ch: *biaoshi*] their drinks. Spirits were only drunk on festive occasions such as marriages or funerals. It is wrong to say that downing a glass in one shot was an *Yi zu de guiju*—a general principle for the Yi.

Historically, traditional drinking behavior was bound by strict rules as demonstrated by such proverbs as, "The earth is ploughed from below to above; spirits are drunk from above to below." In other words, older and more highly placed people should be allowed to drink first. Another saying goes, "Spirits are for the old; meat is for the young" (Ma Xueliang 1989:

338–39). The limits to drinking are explicit in the saying, "He who drinks one bowl is a good fellow; he who drinks two bowls is a hero (N: *ssakuo*); he who drinks three bowls is a piece of dog-skin (N: *kenji*)."[13]

Today, however, alcohol plays an important role in establishing or creating social capital, as well as in strengthening Nuosu ethnic identity. The ritual of shared consumption strengthens the group's inward cohesion and delineates a boundary of ethnic exclusion from the Other (Han). From a social-psychological point of view, enjoying alcohol as a group can be considered "constructive drinking" (Douglas 1991a) because it encourages social integration and defuses latent conflicts. However, social decline and poverty often lead to increased alcohol consumption. A state of intoxication not only enables people to forget their everyday problems, it also stills hunger and causes a physical feeling of warmth. Studies in other parts of the world demonstrate that the use of alcohol among ethnic minorities is commonly a way of dealing with the feelings associated with social transformation, i.e., the danger of the disintegration of the group.

Nuosu, including Nuosu entrepreneurs, have multiple individual and collective identities. They are members of many different social groups: they are citizens of China and members of the Yi nationality, of the Nuosu-Yi in Liangshan, of particular Nuosu castes, clans, lineages, and village communities; they are members of the Party and/or the entrepreneurial stratum, and of other small social groups or associations. They are both Chinese entrepreneurs and "national minority" entrepreneurs. Although they can switch between the various identities and between different frames of reference and boundaries,[14] each identity is still bound into different circles of loyalty and warmth, which creates a hierarchy of identities within each individual's consciousness. There no such thing as a static identity; identities develop in dynamic processes. These multiple competing identities are unequal and exist in a disequilibrium that fundamentally challenges the consideration of the Nuosu and of Nuosu entrepreneurs as a homogenous group.

Conclusion

The Influence of Nuosu Entrepreneurs

....

Nuosu entrepreneurs operate simultaneously in the dual worlds of the Chinese state-market economy and Nuosu clan society. I turn in this concluding chapter to a summary of the effects of entrepreneurship on society, economy, and politics in Liangshan. I consider the effects of Nuosu entrepreneurship in three areas: economic development, Nuosu society and culture, and Nuosu identity and Nuosu-Han relations. Finally, I present some thoughts on the comparative relevance of the Nuosu case for understanding the role of ethnic entrepreneurs in general. At the outset, it is important to reiterate that although the market has created a new value system, the moral economy still has a strong impact on the market behavior of the Nuosu entrepreneurs; they still live in the dual worlds of individual profit-making and clan obligation. Nuosu see the market as a value-laden moral economy, whereas Han see the market as a rational, profitable field of economics. The fact that Han and Nuosu have different working concepts of the market shows that markets are cultural systems, represented differently through people's thoughts and actions. Entrepreneurship has not eliminated the division between these cultural systems, though it has blurred that division through the processes summarized below.

ECONOMIC DEVELOPMENT

This book is only marginally concerned with the economic function of private entrepreneurs although our research has shown that private entrepreneurs in Liangshan are essential resources for local economic development and as employers, as well as sources of county revenue. They change local economic structures and social institutions, and they finance social and economic development projects, such as infrastructure development and educational and health institutions. Thus, encouraging entrepreneur contributions is "a low-cost strategy for economic development, job creation, and technical innovation" (Ray 1988: 4). Encouraging ethnic (Nuosu) entrepreneurs is of particular advantage because they consider development activities as part of their social obligations and because they mostly hire Nuosu personnel. Entrepreneurs are therefore not only agents of economic change, but also of cultural and social change.[1]

SOCIETY AND CULTURE

Because of strong ties to their communities, Nuosu entrepreneurs do not act only in their own individual and material interests but in the interest of maintaining their social status; they respect social values and meet moral and social obligations toward their communities. Non-economic motives are thus important forces in their economic success. Due to underdeveloped market structures and institutions, the moral economy is clearly visible in Nuosu society. This economy is maintained by reciprocal obligations and by the clans who also maintain bonds and values within the community. However, growing market influences and social changes are eroding existing social structures. Entrepreneurs thus face the trader's dilemma of meeting social obligations on the one hand, and of pursuing entrepreneurial market interests on the other.

Our studies show that the primary identification of Nuosu, including Nuosu entrepreneurs, is not with the Nuosu or the Yi as a whole, but with their own clans and localities. In general, the heterogeneous community of the Liangshan Nuosu Yi shows different and sometimes contradicting degrees of identification and loyalty to the larger Yi nationality. However, apart from this, Nuosu entrepreneurs share some commonalities in their relations with their ethnic communities, their culture, and development. If entrepreneurs become aware of their function as social modernizers, they might also become important shapers of the future. A reference to the entire ethnic group would gradually replace the concern for particular clans; the moral economy would be defined less in terms of clans and would increasingly relate to Yi nationality as a whole. However, as James Scott (1976; 3–4, 167) and others have demonstrated, it is difficult to maintain a moral economy in which the actors' obligations are to a group as large as the Yi, or even the Liangshan Yi (Nuosu). The moral economy may, therefore, reestablish along different lines or fade out entirely.

As entrepreneurship, industry, commerce, and services were not part of the traditional Nuosu economy, individual and private businesses are new phenomena in Nuosu society. These phenomena are part of an "ethnic learning" process. The learning is ethnic, because it takes place collectively; it includes a large number of Nuosu in private economic frameworks and it concerns activities that go beyond the clan. As part of this learning process, nearly all the entrepreneurs we interviewed have come to recognize entrepreneurship as the precondition for economic development. In turn, economic development, along with education, is seen as the only way for the Nuosu to assert themselves and develop as an ethnic community, and as a group within the Yi nationality.

An ethnic group or members of the group can also learn lessons from the past that are important for the group's survival during the upheavals of modernization and social change. Part of ethnic learning is applying these lessons in ways that change or improve economic, social, and political behaviors, which, in turn, improve the group's chances of survival. However, ethnic learning also involves developing new concepts and policies in order to solve current and future problems. Learning is a process of adjusting to situational changes in which it is necessary to solve problems with new solutions that will be acceptable to ethnic stakeholders. Although the stakeholders only represent specific constituents of the total group (communities, clans, organizations, and elites), they are the players who are capable of learning. This implies that learning is not a single process but rather develops as a sequence of processes in which people acquire more and more knowledge and experience learning at different levels (Haas 1990: 25–26), as well as the need for certain key players, such as well-known ethnic-group representatives who have enough social standing to push these processes forward.

Nuosu entrepreneurship itself is an expression of ethnic learning in the form of a social group breaking with traditional economic ideas. The entrepreneurs are pioneers of a transformation from self-sufficiency to market-orientation, and from a clan-oriented to a community-oriented society. They are not so much carriers of tradition as they are bearers of modernity. They facilitate Nuosu society's adaptation to modernity, which takes place under the influence of the entrepreneurs rather than under pressure from the state.

There are two trends of changing loyalties among the Nuosu today. One trend is caused by the impact of the market and of entrepreneurship as systems of communication. Economic interactions between entrepreneurs and within the market generate circles of loyalty beyond families and clans. Nuosu ethnicity and status as an entrepreneur are emerging as new points of reference. The other trend is initiated by state and Party endeavors to bind successful entrepreneurs into non-local and trans-ethnic circles of loyalty. Becoming a member of entrepreneurial associations, the Party, parties, or mass organizations, or a deputy of a People's Congress or a Political Consultative Conference creates such bonds.

In China, trans-ethnic, sense-giving, eschatological ideologies such as the "Communist project" are now crumbling and eroding. Currently, the nationalist project is replacing the eschatological ideology. The Chinese nationalism of the Nuosu and of the Yi may actually be supported by Yi scholars' historical and cultural studies, which I analyzed in chapter 8. For example, if the Yi are the founders of Chinese culture, they are unlikely to want to separate from China. This may be why so much chauvinistic Yi history is allowed to be published, while Uighur or Tibetan revisionist histories are ruthlessly suppressed (see Harrell and Li 2003).

Despite state or Party efforts to win them over to new loyalties beyond their immediate warm relationships, entrepreneurs still play a double role in organizations where relationships are based on cold loyalty. On the one hand, ethnic entrepreneurs are Chinese citizens and the Party or the nation is a new identifying group worthy of their loyalty. On the other hand, they represent the interests of their ethnic communities in political organizations or associations.

Rather than being replaced by cold loyalties and trans-ethnic connections, traditional warm loyalties to ethnic groups and to the clan have experienced an intensified return. During our fieldwork, entrepreneurs defined themselves primarily as ethnic players with reference to their clan or ethnic group. They consistently prioritized local development and Nuosu Yi interests over references to higher circles of loyalty such as the province, the state, and the Party.

Rapid economic and social change and increasing individualization lead to increased social insecurity and a weakening of social bonds. This applies to the entrepreneurs and to the Nuosu as a whole. The result is a state of permanent insecurity among the Nuosu, which is only intensified by the erosion of their culture and language. Insofar as they belonged to a clan, Nuosu traditionally differentiated themselves from other people based on clan membership, not ethnicity. Thus, the clan was actually the main reference point for identity, and it remains a central element of Nuosu identity today.

Another part of Yi identity is the belief that Yi, especially the Liangshan Nuosu, are especially courageous, aggressive, and fear nothing. Courage and bravery have always been associated with common clan feuds, in which not a few have lost their lives. Angst played (and plays) only a small role within their community; the main source of angst is the threat of exclusion from the clan community. Heroism and heroic ideals have possessed (and still possess) an important place in socialization,[2] and psychological stability has been guaranteed by solidarity within the clan and not by religion or the promise of a better life after death.

Entrepreneurship offers an economic method of breaking down insecurity if it actually promotes economic development, creates jobs, and increases ethnic-entrepreneurial self-confidence. Socially conscious entrepreneurial strata could take care of social obligations that the clans are increasingly unable to meet. The entrepreneurial stratum also offers an answer to the ethic of heroism; not a few entrepreneurs argue that they display such virtues as gallantry and courage.

The clan still functions as a social organization offering social certainty and mutual support, and clan ties have become stronger through quasi-modern institutions. On the other hand, the clan still limits the formation of a shared (ethnic) consciousness amongst the Nuosu, as clan interests are prioritized over the interests of the Nuosu as an ethnic community. However, a clan-transcending consciousness has emerged despite such limitations, carried at least partially by the new wave of entrepreneurs. On the other hand, identities have become fragile due to the destabilization of the moral economy and the social and economic change. Moreover, the relative participatory equality generated by the clan is dissolving.

ETHNIC IDENTITY AND NUOSU-HAN RELATIONS

Ethnicity can be economically constructed and utilized for commercial gain. Granovetter has suggested that particular groups or persons may strategically use ethnic features and characteristics to maximize their income, solve economic problems, or ensure loyalty (Granovetter 1995: 148). For example, entrepreneurs wear traditional Nuosu garb, commission bimo to drive out spirits, or have Nuosu symbols placed on buildings and businesses in order to reinforce their ethnic employees' loyalty and to strengthen relationships with Nuosu clients and customers. In this context, cultural and symbolic capital is utilized toward economic ends.

The presence of differing ethnicity does not necessarily lead to ethnic conflicts. Peaceful and cooperative relationships between Nuosu and Han do exist. Conflicts only come about in the course of the modernization process when economic inequality increases, the battle for scarce resources intensifies, and the gulf between "us" and "them" (i.e., Nuosu and Han) widens.

The rise of entrepreneurship has begun to dissolve the cultural division of labor, which Hechter has classified as "internal colonialism" (Hechter 1975). The situation in which Han are employed in high-status occupations and exploit the Nuosu, who are employed in low-status occupations, has been changing. In spite of having different economic starting points, Nuosu and Han have equal opportunities for becoming self-employed. Furthermore, Nuosu entrepreneurs are standing up for their ethnicity by dispelling the dominant negative images historically developed by the Han and thereby dismissing the accompanying norms.

The notion of "reactive ethnicity" seems most suitable as the cause of ethnic entrepreneurship amongst the Nuosu. A reactive ethnicity originates from Nuosu experiences of economic discrimination and the perceived necessity of ensuring their ethnic group's survival. It is also a reaction to cultural and political discrimination. Previously, companies were established and run primarily by Han Chinese, and the workforce consisted of Han personnel from other regions. Economic development thus is a way of ensuring ethnic survival and counteracting discrimination by promoting upward mobility and assisting Nuosu in climbing political ladders.

However, it would be inaccurate to regard Nuosu entrepreneurship simply as a form of reactive ethnicity because its reactive nature is only in response to development. Entrepreneurship is also an active modernization force working in the interest of maintaining and developing the Nuosu and their culture, and it also creates the ability to shape local development rather than merely react to development. Entrepreneurship also has a passive function, namely the effects of entrepreneurs' lifestyles and social image on the other members of Nuosu society. Scarman argues that ethnic entrepreneurship and a greater involvement in business contributes to community stability, as it allows ethnic minorities to participate more in society, economically as well as politically (1982: 16–68; see also Mars and Ward 1984: 1). It has not been proven whether this is true for the Nuosu.

Ethnicity is not the only or essential factor in ethnic entrepreneurship. It is quite possible that some Nuosu will become entrepreneurs without being in situations where there are ethnic interactions. On one level, ethnic entrepreneurs are nothing but entrepreneurs first and foremost; the economic and entrepreneurial interests they share with other entrepreneurs may be greater than their differences along ethnic lines.

Unlike in Tibet or Xinjiang, there is no hard ethno-nationalism among the Yi in general or among the Nuosu entrepreneurs in Liangshan, in the form of striving for a separate state or for special status within the People's

Republic of China. However, soft ethno-nationalism is widespread and is characterized by a desire for expanded autonomy and for the classification of the autonomous prefecture (Ch: *zizhizhou*) as an autonomous province (Ch: *zizhiqu*). However, cultural nationalism is even more common and its goal is to maintain and support script and language traditions while recognizing modernization as the precondition for revaluing traditional culture and the ethnic group. There is, undoubtedly, a desire for respect as an important population within the Chinese nation. Yi ethnic consciousness in this sense is like African-American ethnic consciousness. The Yi are as unambiguously Chinese (in the national sense of Chinese as *Zhongguo ren*) as African Americans are Americans. However, both populations believe that they are not accorded the respect due to first-class citizens of China and the United States, respectively. The Yi strive to correct this through cultural politics and through ethnic entrepreneurship.

The emergence of ethnic entrepreneurship does not necessarily generate ethnic mobilization and ethno-nationalism. However, this could be the case if an ethnic group and its entrepreneurs are discriminated against or disadvantaged in trans-regional markets. In this case, ethnic entrepreneurs could be tempted to instrumentalize and mobilize ethnic tensions and prejudices for their own interests. In the final analysis, however, conflicts may be reduced or prevented by equal opportunity and "affirmative action" policies. Thomas Meyer writes, "fair dealings on the part of differing cultural identities with each other, that is, a constructive politics of identity, presupposes equality as the main motive for actions." This in turn entails "fairness in access to the core opportunities of social life and political power as well as mutual recognition and respect" (Meyer 2002: 34). In this context, entrepreneurship forms a basis for equal treatment, albeit primarily within the market. It promotes local development, creates a socially aware business elite, and strengthens Yi identity. Nevertheless, entrepreneurship in Liangshan is still unstable, as its development depends to a large degree on the local bureaucracy. Realistically, legal safeguards and well-aimed assistance programs are needed in order to better protect and support the growth of this very promising aspect of Yi social development.

RELEVANCE OF THE NUOSU CASE

Our conclusions bring us to an important question. What is the relevance of our findings for China's ethnic groups or for policy? Entrepreneurship is probably one of the most effective ways to integrate ethnic minorities into the local and national economy. At the same time, as an integrating and stabilizing element, it may also be an important factor for poverty allevia-tion. However, China's ethnic communities differ in their economic dis-positions. Some ethnicities have strong merchant, trading, and craftsman traditions, such as the Uighurs or Hui. Others were traditionally farmers, herdsmen, or hunters and gatherers. Some ethnic groups are primary eth-nic groups, behaving as closed communities within the larger Han society. Other ethnic groups are secondary groups, and have historically participated in Han society economically and politically.[3]

The Liangshan Yi used to be a primary ethnic group, and some member groups in the mountains still are. By means of ethnic integration, particu-larly in urban areas (including county towns), a large share of the Nuosu has become a secondary ethnic group, though both ways of life continue to exist. Entrepreneurs cannot exist under secluded and remote conditions; they have to have access to the market. Therefore, they function as carriers of the transformation into a secondary ethnic group.

In multi-ethnic states, minority ethnic communities develop different social and political strategies for survival, such as isolation or accommo-dation, where the latter involves participation in Han social and political domains. Other strategies include communalism (communal control in areas where an ethnic group constitutes the majority), autonomism (particularly on cultural and political issues), separatism, and irredentism (see Smith 1981: 15–17 for more details). In terms of entrepreneurship, accommodation appears to be the most appropriate strategy for acting according to market logics. Government officials might strive for communalism or even stronger autonomism, but the choice of a specific strategic behavior or even a com-bination of different strategies depends on the ethnic community's distinct historical, social, economic, and political setting. Hence, different ethnic groups turn to different strategies. Social changes leading to stronger social mobility and stratification may even generate different strategies among different strata or regional communities within one ethnic group; therefore, it would obviously be inappropriate to make arguments that claim to be true for all ethnic communities within China.

Entrepreneurs are a crucial part of economic, social, and political pro-cesses in all ethnic communities. However, changes in social and institu-tional settings affect not only a given minority ethnic group but the relationship and interaction of that group with the dominant group. The rela-tionships among the different *minzu* in China are changing as well, though in different directions, oscillating between isolation or separatism and accommodation or integration. As demonstrated in this book through the example of Nuosu society and Nuosu entrepreneurs in Liangshan, the entrepreneurial economic elite that is emerging has a strong self-consciousness which contributes to the strengthening of the group's ethnic identity and its modern ethnicity, while functioning as an agent of development and modernization. Future research on entrepreneurship among other ethnic communities in China will allow us to review the arguments presented here and to explore the contribution of ethnic entrepreneurship to nationwide social and institutional change.

NOTES

INTRODUCTION

1. In this and following instances, the title Liangshan Prefecture refers to Liang-shan Yi Autonomous Prefecture.

2. Most of these Tibetans are not Tibetans in the sense in which we use the term, but rather members of Qiang-speaking groups such as Ersu, Duoxu, Nameze, and Prmi.

3. See Heberer 1984: 239–64 for details from the early 1980s.

4. For more on the economic situation in Liangshan, see Heberer 2001b.

5. See Heinrich 1992, 1994; Bieszcz-Kaiser, Lungwitz, and Preusche 1994; Wright, Filatotchev, and Buck 1996; Engerer 1997; Lissjutkina 1997; Siehl 1998; Zschoch 1998.

6. See Lütkenhorst and Reinhardt 1993; Sloane 1999; Susan Young 1995; Menkhoff and Gerke 2002; Dickson 2003; Heberer 2003b.

7. See also Peter Chen and Evers 1978; Hsiao 1993; Robison and Goodman 1996; Jones 1998; Rüland 1998; in a critical vein, see Bell, Brown, Jayasuriya, and Jones 1995.

8. Some of the most important work on the private sector includes Zhang Xuwu, Li, and Xie 1994, 1996; Zhongguo siyou qiyezhu jieceng yanjiu ketizu 1994; Zhang Fuchi and Guo 1997; He Zhenguo 1997; Wu Guangbin 1998; Zhongguo qiyejia diaocha xitong 1998a, 1998b; Zhang Houyi and Ming 2000; Li Ding and Bao 2000; Zhang Houyi, Ming, and He 2002; Zhang Houyi, Ming, and Liang 2002; Zou Tieli 2003. In recent years there has been an emphasis on the crucial role of the private sector in developing minority areas, see, for example, Xiao Zhuoji 2000; Wei Xianjin 2001.

9. See Wang Xingrang 1991; Nie 1997; Liu Jianming 1998; Tang Hao 1998; Wang Kuirong 1998; Xing 1999; Wu Jianguo 2003.

10. Managers of state and collective enterprises, i.e., those in the sphere of "intrapreneurship" (innovative managers), are not included in my use of the term.

Carsrud, Olm, and Eddy 1986: 367–68 make a similar argument about not collaps-
ing the two spheres.

11. Granovetter 1985; Carruthers and Babb 2000: 7ff.; Granovetter and Swedberg
2001.

12. On the economic theory of entrepreneurship, see, for instance, Casson 1982.

13. Dangschat 1998: 21; Samers 1998; Scherr 2000: 411.

14. For instance, both Uighurs and Hui have long valued entrepreneurship
whereas Mongols have traditionally disdained trade as parasitic.

15. See Gongshang xingzheng guanli tongji huibian 2001: 47.

16. See Nee 1989; Schak 1994; Heberer and Taubmann 1998; Heberer 1999;
Heberer 2001a; Fan, Heberer, and Taubman 2006.

17. For some recently published, detailed studies on Chinese entrepreneurship,
see Dickson 2003; Heberer 2003b; Krug 2004.

18. The term "cadre" (Ch: *ganbu*) has two meanings. In one sense, it comprises
all Party officials, civil servants in administrative institutions and public organizations, as well as members of the army. In the second sense, "cadre" stands for persons in leadership positions. One has to differentiate between Party cadres,
administrative cadres, and military cadres. As the term covers all Party leaders—
state leaders as much as village cadres or policemen—it does not stand for a homogeneous group. To become a cadre who is a civil servant paid by the state (state cadre),
someone would have to be put on the official staffing schedule by the appropriate
personnel offices. Organization departments are responsible for the Party cadres.
State cadres are paid out of the official household expenditure. Their salaries are
part of the regular budget, approved by the local People's Congresses, whereas the
other rural cadres have to be paid by extra-budgetary means.

19. The social and political roles played by the "others," i.e., by ethnic minorities, has meanwhile become a topic of research in China. See, for instance, Zhou
Daming and Qin 2003.

20. For instance, Yang Zhong (2003: 8–9), who has conducted research in Han
areas, has argued that in the eyes of the rural population local officials primarily
were perceived as representatives of the central government in Beijing.

21. See Barth 1963; for the relationship between industrialization and ethnicity,
see Hechter 1976.

22. This analysis does not include the questionnaires from Leibo County. This
is because our Chinese partners had used a different questionnaire in Leibo than
the one we used in other counties, and, further, no interviews were conducted there,
so that we did not obtain the information necessary for an in-depth analysis. Our
analysis in this volume, therefore, is based on the 123 interviews that we carried out
together with our Chinese colleagues.

1. See Lu Hui's (2001) material on the Jiddu and Bibbu in Jinyang, for example.

2. I am grateful to Stevan Harrell for this information.

3. For more on ethnic classification in China, see Mullaney 2004 and Mackerras 2004.

4. Anderson 1993: 15. Wu Ga 1998 shows that though "Yi" is a constructed official term, most people classified as Yi share particular commonalities in culture and modes of thinking. Also see Pan Jiao 1998.

5. See, for instance, the case of the persecution of a Nuosu scholar's father, in Mgebbu Lunzy and Stevan Harrell 2003.

6. Interview, Zhaojue County, 16 August 1981.

7. See, among others, Wang Geliu 1997; He Gaowa 1997; Ma Wenyu 1997; Wu Zongjin 1998: 167ff.; Hao 1998: 241ff.; Shen Guiping and Shi 1998: 136ff.; Wang Yongwu 1998.

8. The law was published in *Renmin Ribao,* 2 March 2001.

9. Zhonghua Renmin Gongheguo minzu quyu zizhifa xiugai jianyi gao 1998.

10. Progressive development from primitive society to slave-owning, feudal, capitalist, and socialist society.

11. He Yaohua 1998, for instance, speaks of different histories—an official Chinese one and various versions offered by the Yi, differing according to strata or Yi group.

12. The interviews with the Yi scholars were conducted in Beijing and Kunming in October 1998; the informants asked not to be named.

13. See, for example, Lü Qing 1996: 59–65.

14. See *Minzu* 11, 1998: 24. Hou Yuangao 2001 provides an excellent overview of the economic and political problems in the Liangshan area since the 1950s.

2 | THE LIANGSHAN ECONOMIC SETTING
AND PRIVATE ENTREPRENEURS

1. See Lin Yaohua 1961: 84–96, 1995: 60–70 for more on this.

2. See Liangshan Yizu nuli shehui 1982: 46ff.; Sichuan sheng Liangshan Yizu shehui lishi diaocha 1985: 2–15ff.; Sichuan sheng liangshan Yizu shehui diaocha ziliao xuanjuan 1987: 91ff.; Ma Xueliang 1989: 301ff.

3. Hill 1998b: 41ff. and 2001: 1038; Liangshan Yizu nuli shehui 1982: 61ff.

4. See, for instance, Sha 1990 and 1992.

5. Discussion in Jinyang County, 22 August 2002. The so-called laziness of the Yi, which Han officials complain about, is in fact not extraordinary. Marshall Sahlins

has shown that the majority of hunter and gatherer societies can subsist with working two and a half days a week (Sahlins 2000: 95ff.). Also, women work harder than
men, and we think that the stereotypes of Yi laziness are based on the Han looking
only at Nuosu men and holding them in disdain.

6. Compare this, for instance, with the question, "Why do nations have unproductive cultures?" (Porter 2000: 22), which is in fact a moral and pejorative
evaluation.

7. Private conversation with Mgebbu Lunzy, Düsseldorf, 18 November 2001.

8. Both counties had less than 25 percent Nuosu population.

9. Interview with a Yi scholar, Ganluo County, 19 August 1999.

10. This information was provided by the Bureau for Administration of Industry and Commerce of the Liangshan Autonomous Prefecture in Xichang, on 24
August 1999.

11. According to official classifications, urban here means businesses located in
the city of Xichang, in the county seats (county towns), or in towns with urban status (Ch: *zhen*).

12. Rural laborers do indeed migrate into the urban areas, but until now, they
do so less with the intention to reside for a long period than to obtain a higher income
in order to support their families and acquire starting capital for self-employment
in their home area.

13. Bureau for Administration of Industry and Commerce of Liangshan
Prefecture.

3 | PRIVATE SECTOR DEVELOPMENT IN NINE LIANGSHAN COUNTIES

1. Discussion with the county government and the Party Secretary of Jinyang
County, 22 August 2002.

2. In *Minzu* August 2002: 9.

3. Zhaojue xianzhi 1999. On traditional economic structures of Zhaojue county,
see Sichuan sheng liangshan Yizu shehui diaocha ziliao xuanjuan 1987: 155ff. and
291ff.

4. Jiang, Lu, and Dan 1996: 193. For more details on the situation of education
in Zhaojue County, see Heberer 2001b: 224–25.

5. See Bai Shige 2001 for a case study on AIDS in Zhaojue County.

6. See the report of the investigation in Zhaojue xian Yizu quan 1999: 291ff.

7. Zhaojue xian Yizu quan 1999: 141. For a case study on prostitution in
Xichang, see Kang, Yang, and Zhang 2001.

8. See the investigative report Lai and Mujie 1996.

9. More in Butuo xianzhi 1993. On traditional economic structures of Butuo County, see Sichuan sheng liangshan Yizu shehui diaocha ziliao xuanjuan 1987: 192ff.

10. Interview, Butuo County, 31 August 2001. The interviewee preferred to remain anonymous.

11. Interview, Butuo County, 2 September 2001.

12. Meigu xianzhi 1996. On traditional economic structures of Meigu County, see Sichuan sheng Liangshan Yizu shehui diaocha ziliao xuanjuan 1987: 89ff.

13. The Institute of Bimo Research in Meigu (Ch: Bimo Wenhua Yanjiusuo) in Meigu estimated that there are 8,400 bimo in Meigu, including students. However, Wei Anduo 2000: 13–14 and *Minzu* October 2002: 46–47 suggest that there are only about 6,000 of them.

14. See Ganluo xianzhi 1996. On traditional economic structures of Ganluo County, see Sichuan sheng liangshan Yizu shehui diaocha ziliao xuanjuan 1987: 219ff.

15. Interview, Ganluo County, 13 August 1999.

16. Interview, Ganluo County, 14 August 1999.

17. "Guanyu wo xian geti, siying jingji fazhan qingkuang de diaocha baogao" (investigation report on the development of individual and private economy in our county). Report delivered to the Political Consultative Conference of Zhaojue County, 25 August 1998.

18. Interview, Jinyang County, 22 August 2002.

4 | COMPARATIVE PROFILES OF NUOSU AND HAN ENTREPRENEURS

1. See Heberer 2003b for findings from surveys in other regions.

2. Government or state cadres (Ch: *guojia ganbu*) are included in the official staff plan of the state and their salary is paid by the state.

3. Discussion in Yanyuan County, 26 August 2000.

4. Wu Jinghua is the highest ranking Yi in the Party hierarchy. Among other positions, he was vice minister of the State Nationalities' Commission and Party Secretary of Tibet.

5. For a more detailed biography, see Stevan Harrell, "Nuosu Lacquerware: A Traditional Craft and Its Recent Transformations" http://faculty.washington.edu/stevehar/lacquer.html; accessed on 30 May 2006. A Chinese version of this essay has been published in Harrell 2000a. See also the chapter on lacquerware in Harrell, Bamo, and Ma Erzi 2000: 31–36.

1. These figures are from our survey conducted in the period 1999–2002.

2. Li Ding and Bao 2000: 363. According to a 2002 official national survey of 2.03 million private-business owners conducted by Communist Party United Front Work Department, the All China Federation of Industry and Commerce, and the China Private Economy Research Institute, 29.9 percent of the owners were Communist Party members; see Lawrence 2003: 30.

3. *Zhonguo Gongshang Bao*, 19 May, 26 May, and 16 June 2000.

4. Interview, Butuo Cuonty, 2 September 2001.

5. Discussion with officials of the Bureau for the Administration of Industry and Commerce, Mianning County, 19 August 1999.

6. This was demonstrated in Heberer 2001a: 381ff.

7. Also see Oi 1989; Yang Jingchu 1994; Yan 1996; Kipnis 1997; Gold 2002.

8. Interview, Puge County, 16 September 2001.

9. Interview, Xichang County, 27 August 2002.

10. See, for example, a contribution of the Organizational Department of the Central Committee of the CCP, Lingdao weihe bang dakuan (Why do leading officials help the rich?) in: *Jingji Ribao* (Economic Daily), 6 December 1995; Yin 1996: 11–15; Shi and Pang 1996: 210–36.

1. We differentiate between "clan," a unilineal kin group claiming descent from a common ancestor, "lineages" as branches of descents from a common ancestor (i.e., branches of a clan), and "kin" (groups of persons related by blood).

2. To work without wages in order to support clan members economically is a tradition among Yi clans; see, for instance, Ma Erzi 2001.

3. Li Fang made a similar observation; see Li Fang 1998: 168ff.

4. This movement from family or clan business to more corporate business models is probably nearly universal as business grows.

5. See Yao and Wang 2002 and Huang Xiangyuan 2000; Wang Yang 2002 and Huang Yan 2002 argue against the claim that employing clan members reduces a company's troubles in times of crisis.

6. See also Krüsselberg 1986: 184–85. Employing family or clan members who are less industrious or lazy is socially evaluated as positive behavior, as it enables the persons in question to become fully accepted members of their group.

7. This was true for every county and during the entire survey period, 1999–2002.

8. Interview, Mianning County, 17 August 1999.

9. Discussion in Mianning County, 15 August 1999.

10. Discussion with Ma Erzi in Mianning, 17 August 1999.

11. Discussion in Mianning County, 17 August 1999.

12. For more on the change in women's role during the reform era, see Wu Ga 1997, 2001.

13. For more on the role of the headman, see Liu Yu 2001: 116–17.

14. I am grateful to Stevan Harrell for this information.

15. Interview, Xichang County, 23 August 2002.

7 | ENTREPRENEURS AND ETHNIC RELATIONS

1. Interview, Puge County, 16 September 2001.

2. See Hechter 1975, 1978; Medrano 1994; Kunovich and Hodson 2002. On the theory of ethnic competition, see Barth 1969.

3. Interview, Zhaojue County, 18 August 2000.

4. Interview, Zhaojue County, 20 August 2000.

8 | ENTREPRENEURS AND ETHNIC IDENTITY

1. Interview, Butuo County, 31 August 2001.

2. Pan Jiao 1998; Liu Yaohan 1985a, 1985b, and 1992; Ma Xueliang 1987, 1989; Yang Jilin and Shen 1992; Qiesa 2002; Bai Xingfa 2002.

3. A similar perspective is put forward by Yi scholar Qiesa Wuniu (2002), who argues that in ancient China there existed two civilizations, one in the catchment area of the Yellow River, considered by Han to be their place of origin, the other one in the catchment area of the Yangzi River, considered by Yi to be their place of origin. Such a statement challenges Han history.

4. See Li and Harrell 2001; Gelong 1996: 15ff.; Wu Gu 2001; and Harrell and Li 2003.

5. Arguments like this one were frequently cited and refer not only to the Yi as an ethnic group and minzu but include also minzu who do not belong to the Yi groups such as the Bai, the Naxi, the Lisu, the Lahu, the Jinuo, and the Hani, i.e., groups that do not perceive themselves as part of a larger "Yi nationality" but are perceived by the Yi as belonging to their ethnic group.

6. The production responsibility system has been part and parcel of the reform effort in rural areas since 1979. The claim that such a system had existed in the Nuosu

areas prior to 1956 implies that the traditional agricultural production system of the Nuosu was more sophisticated than the one in Han areas.

7. Interview, Xichang County, 27 August 2002.

8. Interview, Meigu County, 6 September 2001.

9. Interview, Yanyuan County, 26 August 2000.

10. Interview, Puge County, 16 September 2001

11. Tusi were appointed hereditary headmen in the Yuan, Ming, and Qing Dynasties.

12. Parallel cases are found in Harrell 2001b: 183–88.

13. I am grateful to Stevan Harrell for this information.

14. On the process of switching identities, see Elwert 2002: 35–37.

CONCLUSION

1. Frederik Barth (1967: 664) was among the first to state this view.

2. For more details on this, see Liu Yu 2001.

3. See Francis 1976: 167–71 and 209–13 and Riggs 1994.

BIBLIOGRAPHY

Aldrich, Howard E., and Roger Waldinger

    1990   "Ethnicity and Entrepreneurship." *Annual Review of Sociology* 16: 111–35.

Aldrich, Howard E., Trevor P. Jones, and David McEvoy

    1984   "Ethnic Advantage and Minority Business Development." In Robin Ward and Richard Jenkins, eds., *Ethnic Communities in Business: Strategies for Economic Survival*, 189–210. Cambridge: Cambridge University Press.

Aldrich, Howard E., and Catherine Zimmer

    1986   "Entrepreneurship through Social Networks." In Donald Sexton and Raymond Smilor, eds., *The Art and Science of Entrepreneurship*, 3–23. Cambridge, Mass.: Ballinger Publishing Co.

Amit, Raphael, and Eitan Muller

    1996   "'Push'- und 'Pull'-Unternehmertum" (Push and pull entrepreneurship). *Zeitschrift für Klein- und Mittelunternehmen* 2 (44): 90–103.

Anderson, Benedict

    1993   *Die Erfindung der Nation: Zur Karriere eines folgenreichen Konzepts* (Imagined communities: Reflections on the origins and spread of nationalism). Frankfurt: Campus.

Arnold, Thomas Clay

    2001   "Rethinking Moral Economy." *American Political Science Review* 1: 85–95.

Auster, Ellen, and Howard Aldrich

    1984   "Small Business Vulnerability, Ethnic Enclaves and Ethnic Enterprises." In Robin Ward and Richard Jenkins, eds., *Ethnic Communities in Business: Strategies for Economic Survival*, 38–54. Cambridge: Cambridge University Press.

Axelsson, B., and G. Easton

    1992   (eds.) *Industrial Networks: A View of Reality*. London and New York: Routledge.

Bai Shige

    2001   "Zhaojue xian zhuhe xiang xingbing aicibing xianzhuang diaocha" (Investigation into the present situation of venereal disease and Aids in Zhuhe township of Zhaojue County). *Liangshan Minzu Yanjiu* 11: 217–26.

Bai Xingfa

    2002   *Yizu wenhua shi* (A cultural history of the Yi nationality). Kunming: Yunnan minzu chubanshe.

Bailey, Stephen J.

    1999   *Local Government Economics: Principles and Practice*. Houndmills and London: MacMillan.

Bajie Rihuo

    2001   "Liangshan Yizu xianzai de jingji sikao he xingwei" (Economic thought and actions of Liangshan Yi today). *Liangshan Minzu Yanjiu* 11: 46–63.

Bamo Ayi

    1997   "Lun Liangshan Yizu bimo jieceng de tezheng" (On particularities of the Bimo strata among the Liangshan Yi). In Dai Jingxia, ed., *Zhongguo Yixue* (Yi Studies in China), 37–50. Beijing: Minzu chubanshe.

    1998   "Zhongguo Liangshan Yizu shehui zhong de bimo" (The Bimo of the Yi society in Liangshan). Paper presented at the 2nd International Conference on Yi Studies, 19–23 June 1998, Trier University, Center for East Asian and Pacific Studies.

    2001   "On the Nature and Transmission of *Bimo* Knowledge in Liangshan." In Stevan Harrell, ed., *Perspectives on the Yi of Southwest China*, 118–31. Berkeley: University of California Press.

Baqie Rihuo

    1998   "Yizu chuantong jiating yu dangjin shehui fazhan" (Traditional Yi families and current social development). Paper presented at the 2nd International Conference on Yi Studies, 19–23 June 1998, Trier University, Center for East Asian and Pacific Studies.

Barth, Frederik

    1963   *The Role of the Entrepreneur in Social Change in Northern Norway*. Bergen, Oslo: Norwegian University Press.

    1967   "On the Study of Social Change." *American Anthropologist* 6: 661–69.

    1969   *Ethnic Groups and Boundaries*. Bergen, Oslo: Norwegian University Press.

    1981   *Process and Form in Social Life: Selected Essays of Frederik Barth, Vol. 1*. London and Boston: Routledge and Kegan Paul.

Bell, Daniel A., David Brown, Kanishka Jayasuriya, and David M. Jones

    1995   (eds.) *Towards Illiberal Democracy in Pacific Asia*. New York: St. Martin's Press.

Bennett, Linda A.

1985 "Ethnography, Alcohol, and South-Central European Societies: An Introduction." *East European Quarterly* 4: 385–413.

Berger, Brigitte

1991a (ed.) *The Culture of Entrepreneurship*. San Francisco: Institute for Contemporary Studies Press.

1991b "The Culture of Modern Entrepreneurship." In Brigitte Berger, ed., *The Culture of Entrepreneurship*, 13–32. San Francisco: Institute for Contemporary Studies Press.

Berghoff, Hartmut

1991 *Englische Unternehmer 1870–1914* (English entrepreneurs 1870–1914). Göttingen: Vandenhoeck and Rupprecht.

Berlin, Isaiah

1995 *Das krumme Holz der Humanität* (The crooked timber of humanity: Chapters in the history of ideas). Frankfurt/M.: Suhrkamp.

Bieszcz-Kaiser, Antonina, Ralph-Elmar Lungwitz, and Evelyn Preusche

1994 (eds.) *Transformation–Privatisierung–Akteure: Wandel von Eigentum in Mittel und Osteuropa* (Transformation—privatization—actors: The change of ownership in Middle and Eastern Europe). München, Mering: Hampp.

Biggart, Nicole W.

1997 "Explaining Asian Economic Organization: Toward a Weberian Institutional Perspective." In N. W. Biggart, Gary G. Hamilton, and Marco Orrú, eds., *The Economic Organization of East Asian Capitalism*, 3–32. Thousand Oaks, Calif.: Sage.

Birley, Sue

1996 "Start-ups." In Paul Burns and Jim Dewhurst, eds., *Small Business and Entrepreneurship*, 20–39. Houndmills and London: MacMillan and St. Martin's Press.

Birley, Sue, and Ian C. MacMillan

1995 (eds.) *International Entrepreneurship*. London and New York: Routledge.

1997 *Entrepreneurship in a Global Context*. London and New York: Routledge.

Blim, Michael

2000 "Capitalisms in Late Modernity." *Annual Review of Anthropology* 29: 25–38.

Bonacich, Edna

1973 "A Theory of Middleman Minorities." *American Sociological Review* 38: 583–94.

Bourdieu, Pierre

1998 *Praktische Vernunft: Zur Theorie des Handelns* (Practical reason: On the theory of action). Frankfurt/M.: Suhrkamp.

1999 *Sozialer Sinn: Kritik der theoretischen Vernunft* (Social sense: Critique of the-oretical reason). Frankfurt/M.: Suhrkamp.

Bowen II, J. Ray, and David C. Rose
1998 "On the Absence of Privately Owned, Publicly Traded Corporations in China: The Kirby Puzzle." *The Journal of Asian Studies* 2: 442–52.

Bradley, David
2001 "Language Policy for the Yi." In Stevan Harrell, ed., *Perspectives on the Yi of Southwest China*, 195–213. Berkeley: University of California Press.

Brandtstätter, Susanne
2000 "Elias in China: 'Civilizing Process,' Kinship and Customary Law in the Chi-nese Countryside." Working Paper No. 6, Max Planck Institute for Social Anthropology, Halle and Saale: Max-Planck-Gesellschaft.

Brass, Paul R.
1985 *Ethnic Groups and the State*. London: Sage.

Breton, Raymond
1964 "Institutional Completeness of Ethnic Communities and the Personal Relations of Immigrants." *The American Journal of Sociology* 70: 193–205.

Brown, Melissa J.
1996 (ed.) *Negotiating Ethnicities in China and Taiwan*. Berkeley: University of California, Institute of East Asian Studies.

Burns, Paul, and Jim Dewhurst
1996 (eds.) *Small Business and Entrepreneurship*. Basingstoke, London: MacMil-lan and St. Martin's Press.

Butuo xianzhi
1993 *Butuo xianzhi* (Butuo county annals). Beijing: Zhongguo jiancai gongye chubanshe.

Carruthers, Bruce G., and Sarah L. Babb
2000 *Economy/Society: Markets, Meanings, and Social Structure*. Thousand Oaks: Pine Forge Press.

Carsrud, Alan L., Kenneth W. Olm, and George G. Eddy
1986 "Entrepreneurship: Research in Quest of a Paradigm." In Donald Sexton and Raymond Smilor, eds., *The Art and Science of Entrepreneurship*, 367–78. Cambridge, Mass.: Ballinger Publishing Co.

Cassirer, Ernst
1994 *Philosophie der Symbolischen Formen, Erster Teil: Die Sprache* (Philosophy of symbolic forms, part I: Language). Darmstadt: Wissenschaftliche Buchgesellschaft.

Casson, Mark
1982 *The Entrepreneur*. Oxford: Martin Robertson.

1990 (ed.) *Entrepreneurship*. Aldershot and Brookfield, VT: Edward Elgar.

1995 *Entrepreneurship and Business Culture*. Aldershot and Brookfield, VT: Edward Elgar.

Chang, K. C.

1977 (ed.) *Food in Chinese Culture: Anthropological and Historical Perspectives*. New Haven: Yale University Press.

Chase, Charlotte

1985 "Alcohol Consumption: An Indication of System Malfunction in Contemporary Poland." *East European Quarterly* 4: 415–29.

Chen Jinluo, Wu Chongze, Yang Henggen, and Duoji Cairang

1998 (eds.) Shetuan guanli gongzuo (Administration of social associations). Beijing: Zhongguo shehui chubanshe.

Chen Lipeng

1998 "Guanyu wo guo minzu lifa xianzhuang de sikao" (On the current situation of the law on nationalities in our country). In *Guizhou Minzu Yanjiu* 3: 15–18.

Chen, Peter S. J., and Hans-Dieter Evers

1978 (eds.) *Studies in ASEAN Sociology: Urban Society and Social Change*. Singapore: Chopmen Enterprises.

Cohen, Abner

1974 (ed.) *Urban Ethnicity*. London and New York: Tavistock Publications.

Collins, Kathleen

2004 "The Logic of Clan Politics: Evidence from the Central Asian Trajectories. *World Politics* 56: 224–61.

Dangdai Liangshan

1992 *Dangdai Liangshan* (Contemporary Liangshan). Chengdu: Bashu shushe chubanshe.

Dangschat, Jens S.

1998 "Warum ziehen sich Gegensätze nicht an? Zu einer Mehrebenen-Theorie ethnischer und rassistischer Konflikte um den städtischen Raum" (Why don't opposites attract? On a multi-level theory of ethnic and racist conflicts about urban space). In Wilhelm Heitmeyer, Rainer Dollase, and Otto Backes, eds., *Die Krise der Städte*, 9–20. Frankfurt/M.: Suhrkamp.

Dickson, Bruce J.

2003 *Red Capitalists in China: The Party, Private Entrepreneurs, and Prospects for Political Change*. Cambridge: Cambridge University Press.

Dittrich, Eckhard J., and Frank-Olaf Radtke

1990 (eds.) *Ethnizität: Wissenschaft und Minderheiten* (Ethnicity: Science and minorities). Opladen: Westdeutscher Verlag.

Douglas, Mary

  1991a (ed.) *Constructive Drinking: Perspectives on Drink from Anthropology*. Cambridge and Paris: Cambridge University Press and Editions de la Maison des Sciences de l'Homme.

  1991b "A Distinctive Anthropological Perspective." In Mary Douglas, ed., *Constructive Drinking: Perspectives on Drink from Anthropology*, 3–15. Cambridge and Paris: Cambridge University Press and Editions de la Maison des Sciences de l'Homme.

Durkheim, Emile

  1992 *Über soziale Arbeitsteilung* (Division of labour in society). Frankfurt/M.: Suhrkamp.

  1998 *Die elementaren Formen des religiösen Lebens* (The elementary forms of religious life). Frankfurt/M.: Suhrkamp.

Eisenstadt, Shmuel Noah

  1996 "Die Konstruktion nationaler Identitäten in vergleichender Perspektive" (The construction of national identities in a comparative perspective). In Bernhard Giesen, ed., *Nationale und kulturelle Identität: Studien zur Entwicklung des kollektiven Bewusstseins in der Neuzeit*, 21–38. Frankfurt/M.: Suhrkamp.

Elias, Norbert, and John L. Scotson

  1990 *Etablierte und Außenseiter* (The established and the outsiders). Frankfurt/M.: Suhrkamp.

Elwert, Georg

  2002 "Switching Identity Discourses: Primordial Emotions and the Social Construction of We-Groups." In Günther Schlee, ed., *Imagined Differences: Hatred and the Construction of Identity*, 33–56. Münster and New York: Lit Verlag and Palgrave.

Engerer, Hella

  1997 *Eigentum in der Transformation: Grenzen der Privatisierung in Mittel- und Osteuropa* (Ownership in processes of transformation: Limits of privatization in Middle and Eastern Europe). Berlin: Duncker and Humblot.

Evers, Hans-Dieter

  1994 "The 'Traders' Dilemma.'" In Hans-Dieter Evers and Heiko Schrader, eds., *The Moral Economy of Trade: Ethnicity and Developing Markets*, 7–14. London and New York: Routledge.

  1995 "The Changing Culture of Markets." Working Paper No. 239, Sociology of Development Research Centre, Bielefeld: University of Bielefeld.

Evers, Hans-Dieter, and Heiko Schrader

  1994 (eds.) *The Moral Economy of Trade: Ethnicity and Developing Markets*. London and New York: Routledge.

Fan, Jie, Thomas Heberer, and Wolfgang Taubman
  2006 *Rural China: Economic and Social Change in the Late Twentieth Century.* Armonk, N.Y.: M. E. Sharpe.

Finch, John
  1997 "From Proletarian to Entrepreneur to Big Man: The Story of Noya." *Oceania* 68: 123–33.

Firth, Raymond
  1978 (ed.) *Themes in Economic Anthropology.* London: Tavistock Publications.

Frances, Jennifer, Rosalind Levacic, Jeremy Mitchell, and Grahame Thompson
  1991 "Introduction." In Grahame Thompson, Jennifer Frances, Rosalind Levacic, and Jeremy Mitchell, eds., *Markets, Hierarchies, and Networks: The Coordination of Social Life*, 1–19. London: Sage.

Francis, Emerich K.
  1976 *Interethnic Relations: An Essay in Sociological Theory.* New York: Elsevier.

Freire, Paulo
  1971 *Pädagogik der Unterdrückten* (Pedagogy of the Oppressed). Stuttgart: Kreuz Verlag.

Fu Shouzong
  2000 "Zhonghua minzuxue he minzu shi yanjiu de xin chengguo" (New Successes in the research of China's ethnology and ethnic histories). *Yizu Wenhua* 3: 1–7.

Fukui, Haruhiro
  2000 "Introduction: On the Significance of Informal Politics." In Lowell Dittmer, H. Fukui, and Peter N. S. Lee, eds., *Informal Politics in East Asia*, 1–21. Cambridge: Cambridge University Press.

Gabler
  1984 *Wirtschaftslexikon 11* (Encyclopedia of economics 11). Auflage, Wiesbaden: Gabler.

Gaga Erri
  2001 "Minzhu gaige yiqian Liangshan Yizu de jingji xingwei" (Economic actions of Liangshan Yi before Democratic Reforms). *Liangshan Minzu Yanjiu* 11: 26–45.

Gaha Shizhe
  1998 "Bimo yu Yizu de rentongxing" (Bimo and Yi identity). Paper presented at the 2nd International Conference on Yi Studies, 19–23 June 1998, Trier University, Center for East Asian and Pacific Studies.

Ganluo xianzhi
  1996 *Ganluo xianzhi* (Ganluo county annals). Chengdu: Sichuan renmin chubanshe.

Geertz, Clifford

1963 *Peddlers and Princes.* Chicago and London: University of Chicago Press.

1973 "Thick Description: Toward an Interpretive Theory of Culture." In C. Geertz, *The Interpretation of Cultures: Selected Essays,* 3–30. New York: Basic Books.

1983 *Local Knowledge.* Hammersmith and London: Fontana Press.

1999 *Dichte Beschreibung* (Thick description). Frankfurt/M.: Suhrkamp.

Gelong Ahong

1996 *Yizu gudai shi yanjiu* (Research on the ancient history of the Yi). Kunming: Yunnan minzu chubanshe.

Giddens, Anthony

1995 *Konsequenzen der Moderne* (The consequences of modernity). Frankfurt/M.: Suhrkamp.

Gladney, Dru C.

1991 *Muslim Chinese: Ethnic Nationalism in the People's Republic.* Cambridge, Mass., and London: Harvard University Press.

1998a *Ethnic Identity in China: The Making of a Muslim Minority Nationality.* Fort Worth, Tex.: Harcourt Brace College Pub.

1998b "Getting Rich Is Not So Glorious." In Robert W. Hefner, ed., *Market Cultures: Society and Morality in the New Asia Capitalism,* 104–25. Boulder, CO, and Oxford: Westview.

Gold, Thomas B.

2002 (ed.) *Social Connections in China: Institutions, Culture, and the Changing Nature of Guanxi.* Cambridge: Cambridge University Press.

Goodman, David S. G.

2003 "New Entrepreneurs in Reform China, Economic Growth and Social Change in Taiyuan, Shanxi." In Heidi Dahles and Tooto van den Muijzenberg, eds., *Capital and Knowledge in Asia: Changing Power Relations,* 187–97. London and New York: RoutledgeCurzon.

Gongshang xingzheng guanli tongji huibian

1989– Gongshang xingzheng guanli tongji huibian (Collection of Statistics of the
2001 Administration of Industry and Commerce). Beijing: Guojia gongshang xingzheng guanliju bangongshi.

Granovetter, Mark

1973 "The Strength of Weak Ties." *American Journal of Sociology* 68, May: 1360–80.

1974 *Getting a Job: A Study of Contacts and Careers.* Cambridge, Mass.: Harvard University Press.

1985 "Economic Action and Social Structure: The Problem of Embeddedness." *American Journal of Sociology* 3: 481–510.

1995 "The Economic Sociology of Firms and Entrepreneurs." In Alejandro

Portes, ed., *The Economic Sociology of Immigration: Essays on Networks, Ethnicity, and Entrepreneurship*. New York: Russell Sage Foundation.

Granovetter, Mark, and Richard Swedberg

2001 (eds.) *The Sociology of Economic Life*. Boulder, Col., and Oxford: Westview.

Greenfield, Sidney M., Arnold Strickon

1986 (eds.) *Entrepreneurship and Social Change*. Lanham, N.Y., and London: University Press of America.

Guanyu wo xian geti, siying jingji fazhan qingkuang de diaocha baogao (Investigation report on the development of individual and private economy in our county). Report delivered to the Political Consultative Conference of Zhaojue County, 25 August 1998.

Gur-Ze'er, Ilan, and Ilan Pappé

2003 "Beyond the Destruction of the Other's Collective Memory: Blueprints for a Palestinan/Israeli Dialogue." *Theory, Culture & Society* 1.

Ha, Kien Nghi

2000 "Ethnizität, Differenz und Hybridität in der Migration: Eine postkoloniale Perspektive" (Ethnicity, difference, and hybridity in migration: A postcolonial perspective). *Prokla, Schwerpunktheft Ethnisierung und Ökonomie* 3: 377–97.

Haas, Ernst B.

1990 *When Knowledge Is Power. Three Models of Change in International Organizations*. Berkeley: University of California Press.

Habermas, Tilmann

1999 *Geliebte Objekte: Symbole und Instrumente der Identitätsbildung* (Beloved objects: Symbols and tools of identity construction). Frankfurt/M.: Suhrkamp.

Hagen, Everett

1962 *On the Theory of Social Change: How Economic Growth Begins*. Homewood, Ill.: Dorsey Press.

Halbwachs, Maurice

1985 *Das kollektive Gedächtnis* (Collective memory). Frankfurt/M.: Suhrkamp.

Hall, Stuart

1992 "The Question of Cultural Identity." In Stuart Hall, David Held, and Tony McGrew, eds., *Modernity and Its Futures*, 274–316. Cambridge and Oxford: Polity Press in association with the Open University.

1994 (ed.) *Rassismus und kulturelle Identität* (Racism and cultural identity). *Ausgewählte Schriften 2*. Hamburg: Argument Verlag.

Hall, Stuart, and du Gay, Paul

1996 (eds.) *Questions of Cultural Identity*. London: Sage.

Hansen, Mette Halskov

   1999 *Lessons in Being Chinese: Minority Education and Ethnic Identity in Southwest China.* Seattle and London: University of Washington Press.

Hao Shiyuan

   1998 *Zhongguo de minzu yu minzu wenti: Lun Zhongguo Gongchandang jiejue minzu wenti de lilun yu shijian* (China's nationalities und the nationalities' question: Theory and practise of the CCP in order to solve the nationalities question). Nanchang: Jiangxi renmin chubanshe.

Harrell, Stevan

   1990 "Ethnicity, Local Interests, and the State: Yi Communities in Southwest China." *Comparative Studies in Society and History* 3: 515–48.

   1995a "Languages Defining Ethnicity in Southwest China." In Lola Romanucci-Ross and George DeVos, eds., *Ethnic Identity: Creation, Conflict, and Accommodation,* 97–114. London: Alta Mira Press.

   1995b "Introduction: Civilizing Projects and the Reaction to Them." In Stevan Harrell, ed., *Cultural Encounters on China's Ethnic Frontiers,* 3–36. Seattle and London: University of Washington Press.

   1995c "The History of the History of the Yi." In Stevan Harrell, ed., *Cultural Encounters on China's Ethnic Frontiers,* 363–91. Seattle and London: University of Washington Press.

   1998 "From Ethnic Group to Minzu (and back again?): Yi Identity in the People's Republic." Paper presented at the 2nd International Conference on Yi Studies, 19–23 June 1998, Trier University, Center for East Asian and Pacific Studies.

   2000a *Tianye zhong de zuqun guanxi yu minzu rentong: Zhongguo Xinan Yizu shequ kaocha yanjiu* (Field studies of ethnicity and ethnic identity: Yi communities of Southwest China). Nanning: Guangxi renmin chubanshe.

   2000b "The Survival of Yi Culture." In Stevan Harrell, Bamo Qubumo, Ma Erzi, *Mountain Patterns: The Survival of Culture in China,* 3–9. Seattle and London: University of Washington Press.

   2001a (ed.) *Perspectives on the Yi of Southwest China.* Berkeley: University of California Press.

   2001b *Ways of Being Ethnic in Southwest China.* Seattle and London: University of Washington Press.

Harrell, Stevan, and Bamo Ayi

   1998 "Combining Ethnic Heritage and National Unity: A Paradox of Nuosu (Yi) Language Textbooks in China." *Bulletin of Concerned Asian Scholars* 2: 62–71.

Harrell, Stevan, and Li Yongxiang

2003 "The History of the History of the Yi. Part II." *Modern China* 29, no. 3, July: 362–96.

Harrell, Stevan, Bamo Qubumo, and Ma Erzi

2000 *Mountain Patterns: The Survival of Culture in China.* Seattle and London: University of Washington Press.

Hayami, Yujiro, and Toshihiko Kawagoe

1993 *The Agrarian Origins of Commerce and Industry.* New York, Basingstoke: MacMillan Press and St. Martin's Press.

He Baogang and Guo Yingjie

2000 *Nationalism, National Identity and Democratization in China.* Aldershot and Brookfield, VT: Ashgate.

He Gaowa

1997 "Tan minzu zizhi difangnei minzu guanxi de weihu yu fazhan" (On the protection and development of nationalities' relationships within autonomous regions of nationalities). *Nei Menggu Shehui Kexue* (Social Sciences of Inner Mongolia) 6: 77–82.

He Mingwei

1995 "Liangshan zhou minzu ganbu xianzhuang he xuqiu yuce yanjiu" (Study on the current situation and prognosis on the demand of minorities' cadres in Liangshan Autonomous Prefecture). *Minzu Yanjiu* (Nationalities Studies) 3: 10–18.

He Yaohua

1998 "The Latest Trend on the Compilation of the History of the Yi People in China." Paper presented at the 2nd International Conference on Yi Studies, 19–23 June 1998, Trier University, Center for East Asian and Pacific Studies.

He Zhenguo

1997 (ed.) *Shehuizhuyi yu siying jingji* (Socialism and private economy). Changsha: Hunan renmin chubanshe.

Heath, Dwight

1975 "A critical review of ethnographic studies of alcohol use." *Research Advances in Alcohol and Drug Problems* 2.

1994 "Agricultural Changes and Drinking Among the Bolivian Camba: A Longitudinal View of the Aftermath of a Revolution." *Human Organization* 53, no. 4: 357–61.

Heberer, Thomas

1984 *Nationalitätenpolitik und Entwicklungspolitik in den Gebieten nationaler Min-*

derheiten in China (Nationalities policies and development policies in China's national minorities' areas). Bremen: Universität Bremen.

1987   (ed.) *Ethnic Minorities in China: Tradition and Transformation.* Aachen: Rader Verlag.

1989   *China and Its National Minorities: Autonomy or Assimilation?* Armonk, N.Y., and London: Sharpe.

1991   *Korruption in China: Analyse eines politischen, Ökonomischen und sozialen Problems* (Corruption in China: Analysis of a political, economic, and social problem). Opladen: Westdeutscher Verlag.

1999   "Entrepreneurs as Social Actors: Privatization and Social Change in China and Vietnam." Duisburg Working Papers on East Asian Studies, no. 21. Duisburg: Institute of East Asian Studies.

2000a "Some Considerations on China's Minorities in the 21st Century: Conflict or Conciliation?" Duisburg Working Papers on East Asian Studies, no. 31. Duisburg: Institute for East Asian Studies.

2000b "Chuyu shichang xingwei, shehui daode he minzu zerengan zhijian de minzu qiyejia" (Ethnic entrepreneurs between market behavior, social morality, and ethnic responsibility). *Liangshan Minzu Yanjiu* (Liangshan Nationalities Studies): 23–40.

2001a *Unternehmer als Strategische Gruppen: Zur sozialen und politischen Funktion von Unternehmern in China und Vietnam* (Entrepreneurs as strategic groups: On the social and political function of entrepreneurs in China and Vietnam). Hamburg: Schriftenreihe des Instituts für Asienkunde.

2001b "Nationalities Conflict and Ethnicity in the People's Republic of China, with Special Reference to the Yi in the Liangshan Yi Autonomous Prefecture." In Stevan Harrell, ed., *Perspectives on the Yi of Southwest China*, 214–37. Berkeley: University of California Press.

2001c "Die Nationalitätenfrage am Beginn des 21. Jahrhunderts. Konfliktursachen, ethnische Reaktionen, Lösungsansätze und Konfliktprävention" (The nationalities question at the outset of the 21st century: Causes of conflict, approaches of conflict solution, and conflict prevention). In Gunter Schubert, ed., *China: Konturen einer Übergangsgesellschaft auf dem Weg in das 21. Jahrhundert*, 81–134. Hamburg: Mitteilungen des Instituts für Asienkunde.

2002   "The role of private entrepreneurship for social and political change in the People's Republic of China and Vietnam." In Thomas Menkhoff and Solvay Gerke, eds., *Chinese Entrepreneurship and Asian Business Networks*, 100–28. London and New York: Routledge.

2003a "Entrepreneurs in China and Vietnam as Strategic Players in Social and Political Change." *The Journal of Communist Studies and Transitional Politics* 19 no. 1, March 2003: 64–79.

2003b *Private Entrepreneurs in China and Vietnam: Social and Political Functioning of Strategic Groups*. Leiden: Brill.

2003c "Strategic Groups and State Capacity: The Case of the Private Entrepreneurs." *China Perspectives* 46, March–April: 4–14.

2003d *Zuo wei zhanlüe qunti de qiyejia: Zhongguo siying qiyejia de shehui yu zhengzhi gongneng yanjiu* (Entrepreneurs as strategic groups: A study on the social and political function of China's private entrepreneurs). Beijing: Zhongyang bianyi chubanshe.

2005 "Ethnic Entrepreneurship and Ethnic Identity: A Case Study among the Liangshan Yi (Nuosu) in China. *The China Quarterly*, no. 182, June 2005: 407–27.

Heberer, Thomas, and Wolfgang Taubmann

1998 *Chinas Ländliche Gesellschaft im Umbruch: Urbanisierung und sozial-Ökonomischer Wandel* (China's rural society in upheaval: Urbanization and socioeconomic change). Opladen: Westdeutscher Verlag.

Hechter, Michael

1975 *Internal Colonialism: The Celtic Fringe in British National Development, 1536–1966*. London: Routledge and Kegan Paul.

1976 "Ethnicity and Industrialization: On the Proliferation of the Cultural Division of Labor." *Ethnicity* 3: 214–24.

1978 "Group Formation and the Cultural Division of Labour." *American Journal of Sociology* 84: 293–318.

Heinemann, Klaus

1987a (ed.) *Soziologie wirtschaftlichen Handelns* (Sociology of economic acting). Special issue, *Kölner Zeitschrift für Soziologie und Sozialpsychologie* 28. Opladen: Westdeutscher Verlag.

1987b "Soziologie des Geldes" (Sociology of money). In Klaus Heinemann, ed., *Soziologie wirtschaftlichen Handelns*, 322–38. Opladen: Westdeutscher Verlag.

Heinrich, Ralph P.

1992 "Privatisierung in Polen, Ungarn und der CSFR: Eine Bestandsaufnahme" (Privatization in Poland, Hungary, and the CSFR: An inventory). *Die Weltwirtschaft* 43: 295–316.

1994 "Privatisierung in ehemaligen Planwirtschaften: Eine positive Theorie" (Privatization in former planned economies). In Antonina Bieszcz-Kaiser, Ralph-Elmar Lungwitz, and Evelyn Preusche, eds., *Transformation–Privatisierung–Akteure: Wandel von Eigentum in Mittel und Osteuropa*, 44–72. München, Mering: Hampp.

Hill, Ann Maxwell

1998a "Historical Consciousness of Slavery Among Yi in Xiao Liangshan." Paper presented at the 2nd International Conference on Yi Studies, 19–23 June 1998, Trier University, Center for East Asian and Pacific Studies.

1998b *Merchants and Migrants: Trade and Ethnicity among Yunnanese Chinese in Southeast Asia.* Yale Southeast Asia Series, monograph 47. New Haven: Yale University Southeast Asia Studies.

2001 "Captives, Kin, and Slaves in Xiao Liangshan." *The Journal of Asian Studies* 4: 1033–49.

Hill, Ann Maxwell, and Eric Diehl

2001 "A Comparative Approach to Lineages among the Xiao Liangshan Nuosu and Han." In Stevan Harrell, ed., *Perspectives on the Yi of Southwest China,* 51–67. Berkeley: University of California Press.

Hobsbawm, Eric J.

1984 "Introduction: Inventing Traditions." In Eric Hobsbawm and Terence Ranger, eds., *The Invention of Tradition,* 1–14. Cambridge: Cambridge University Press.

Hou Yuangao

2001 "Chuan Dian Da xiao Liangshan Yizu diqu shehui wenhua bianqian zhong de minzu guanxi" (Ethnic relationship during the process of social and cultural change in the Greater and Lesser Liangshan Area of the Yi in Sichuan and Yunnan). *Liangshan Minzu Yanjiu* (Liangshan Nationalities Research): 116–30.

Hsiao, Hsin-Huang M.

1993 (ed.) *Discovery of the Middle Classes in East Asia.* Taipei Institute of Ethnology: Academia Sinica.

Hu Angang, Wang Shaoguang, and Kang Xiaoguang

1995 *Zhongguo diqu chaju baogao* (Regional disparities in China). Shenyang: Liaoning renmin chubanshe.

Huang Xiangyuan

2000 "Jiazu qiye de shengli haishi xiandai qiye de shengli" (Victory of clan enterprises or of modern enterprises). *Zhongguo Qiyejia* (Chinese Entrepreneurs) 4: 28–30.

Huang Yan

2002 "Jiazu qiye jianjian luowu" (Clan enterprises should gradually retreat). *Zhongguo Gongshang Bao,* 16 October.

Huschen, Andreas, and Detlef Richter

1991 "Ethnische Gruppe und Nation" (Ethnic groups and the nation). *Antimilitarismus Information,* Heft 12, December.

Hutchinson, John, and Anthony D. Smith

1996 (eds.) *Ethnicity*. Oxford and New York: Oxford University Press.

Iredale, Robyn, Naran Bilik, and Fei Guo

2003 (eds.) *China's Minorities on the Move: Selected Case Studies*. Armonk, N.Y., and London: M.E. Sharpe.

Jäggi, Christian J.

1993 *Nationalismus und ethnische Minderheiten* (Nationalism and ethnic minorities). Zürich: Orell Füsli.

Jenkins, Richard

1984 "Ethnic Minorities in Business: A Research Agenda." In Robin Ward and Richard Jenkins, eds., *Ethnic Communities in Business: Strategies for Economic Survival*, 231–38. Cambridge: Cambridge University Press.

Jia Ting, Wang Dekuan, and Tang Baoling

1987 "Dui Liaoning siren qiye de diaocha yu sikao" (Investigation and analysis of private enterprises in Liaoning). *Shehuixue Yanjiu* (*Studies in sociology*) 6: 28–32.

Jiang Liu, Lu Xueyi, and Dan Tianlun, eds.

1996 *1995–1996 nian Zhongguo shehui xingshi fenxi yu yuce* (Prognosis and analysis of the social situation in China in the years 1995 and 1996). Beijing: Zhongguo shehui kexue chubanshe.

Jike Quri

1999 "Lun Liangshan Yizu pinkun yuanyin, xianzhuang ji fupin duice" (Reasons and current situation of the poverty of the Yi in Liangshan and poverty alleviation policies). *Liangshan Yixue* (Yi Studies of Liangshan) 10: 39–44.

Jingji Ribao (Economic Daily), 6 December 1995 (from chapter 5).

Jinyang xian renmin zhengfu (Government of Jinyang County)

2001 *Jinyang xian nongcun fupin kaifa guihua* (Master plan for the development of Jinyang County and its poverty alleviation program). Jinyang: Government of Jinyang County.

Jinyang xianzhi

2000 *Jinyang xianzhi* (Jinyang county annals). Beijing: Fangzhi chubanshe.

Jones, David M.

1998 "Democratization, Civil Society and Illiberal Middle Class Culture in Pacific Asia." *Comparative Politics* 30, no. 2, January 1997–1998: 147–70.

Kang Hua, Yang Shengmei, and Zhang Ming

2001 "Xichang wule changsuo de danmian Yingxiang" (Bad effects of public places of entertainment in Xichang). *Liangshan Minzu Yanjiu* 11: 227–32.

Kaup, Katherine Palmer

2000 *Creating the Zhuang: Ethnic Politics in China*. Boulder, Col.: Lynne Rienner.

Kent, Calvin A.

1984a "The Rediscovery of the Entrepreneur." In Calvin A. Kent, ed., *The Environment for Entrepreneurship*, 1–19. Lexington, Mass.: Lexington Books.

1984b (ed.) *The Environment for Entrepreneurship*. Lexington, Toronto: Lexington Books.

Keyes, Charles

2002 "'The Peoples of Asia': Science and Politics in the Classification of Ethnic Groups in Thailand, China, and Vietnam." Presidential address, *The Journal of Asian Studies* 4: 1163–203.

Kipnis, Andrew B.

1997 *Producing Guanxi: Sentiment, Self, and Subculture in a North China Village.* Durham, N.C.: Duke University Press.

Kirzner, Israel M.

1984 "The Entrepreneurial Process." In Calvin A. Kent, ed., *The Environment for Entrepreneurship*, 41–58. Lexington, Mass.: Lexington Books.

Kolakowski, Leszek

1995 "Über kollektive Identität" (On collective identity). In Krzysztof Michalski, ed., *Identität im Wandel*, 47–60. Stuttgart: Klett-Cotta.

Kraemer, Klaus

1997 *Der Markt der Gesellschaft: Zu einer soziologischen Theorie der Marktgesellschaft* (The market of society: On a sociological theory of market economy). Opladen: Westdeutscher Verlag.

Krüsselberg, Hans-Günter

1986 "Ökonomik der Familie" (Economics of family). In Klaus Heinemann, ed., *Soziologie wirtschaftlichen Handelns*, 168–192. Opladen: Westdeutscher Verlag.

Krug, Barbara

2004 *China's Rational Entrepreneurs: The Development of the New Private Sector.* London and New York: RoutledgeCurzon.

Kunovich, Robert M., and Randy Hodson

2002 "Ethnic Diversity, Segregation, and Inequality: A Structural Model of Ethnic Prejudice in Bosnia and Croatia." *The Sociological Quarterly* 2: 185–212.

Lageman, Bernhard, Werner Friedrich, Werner Döhrn, Alena Brüstle, Norbert Heyl, Marco Puxi, and Friederike Welter

1994 *Aufbau mittelständischer Strukturen in Polen, Ungarn, der Tschechischen Republik und der Slowakischen Republik: Untersuchungen des Rheinisch-Westfälischen Instituts für Wirtschaftsforschung* (The construction of medium-sized entrepreneurial structures in Poland, Hungary, the Czech Republic, and Slovakia: Investigation of the Rheinisch-Westfaelisches Institute of Economic Research), Heft 11. Essen: Rheinisch-Westfälischen Instituts für Wirtschaftsforschung.

Lai Yi and Mujie Keha

1996 "Xianshi de minzu xin wenti" (Real new ethnic problems). *Xinan Minzu Xueyuan Xuebao* (Journal of the Southwestern University for Nationalities) 5: 66–72.

Lauda, Janet T.

1991 "Culture and Entrepreneurship in Less-Developed Countries: Ethnic Trading Networks as Economic Organizations. In Brigitte Berger, ed., *The Culture of Entrepreneurship*, 53–72. San Francisco: Institute for Contemporary Studies Press.

Lavoie, Don

1991 "The Discovery and Interpretation of Profit Opportunities: Culture and the Kirznerian Entrepreneur." In Brigitte Berger, ed., *The Culture of Entrepreneurship*, 33–52. San Francisco: Institute for Contemporary Studies Press.

Lawrence, Susan V.

2003 "The Wrangle over a Right to Riches." *Far Eastern Economic Review* 27, March: 28–31.

Lei Yun, Lu Weixian, and Mao Letang

1999 *Xibu shaoshu minzu diqu de xiangzhen jingji guanli* (Administration of town and township economy in Western China's ethnic minorities areas). Kunming: Yunnan jiaoyu chubanshe.

Letamendia, Francisco

2000 *Game of Mirrors: Centre-Periphery National Conflicts.* Aldershot and Brookfield, VT: Ashgate.

Li Ding and Bao Yujun

2000 (eds.) *Zhongguo siying jingji nianjian* (Yearbook of China's Private Economy). Beijing: Huawen chubanshe.

Li Fang

1998 "The Social Organization of Entrepreneurship: The Rise of Private Firms in China." Ph.D. diss., University of Michigan, Ann Arbor.

Li Peilin and Wang Chunguang

1993 *Xin shehui jiegou de shengchang dian: Xiangzhen qiye shehui jiaohuan lun* (The emergence of new social structures: On social exchange of rural enterprises). Jinan: Shandong renmin chubanshe.

Li Wenhua

2000 "Xibu da kaifa yu Yiqu fazhan yanjiu" (Studies on the opening of the western region and development of the Yi). *Xinan Minzu Xueyuan Xuebao*

(Journal of the Southwestern University for Nationalities), special issue, "Yi Studies": 8–12.

Li Xingxing

    2000 "Jisu bianqian zhong de Liangshan Yizu" (The rapid change of the Liangshan Yi). Paper presented at the 3rd International Conference on Yi Studies, Shilin Yi Autonomous County, 4–7 September.

Li Xingxing, Luo Yong, Ma Erzi, Li Jin, Luo Liangzhao, and Li Shaoming

    1997 *Liangshan: Da Xinan kaifa de zhi gaodian* (Liangshan: Highlight of the development of Southwest-China). Chengdu: Sichuan minzu chubanshe.

Li Yongxiang and Stevan Harrell

    2001 "The History of the History of the Yi, Part II." Preprints No.1, International Workshop on Yi Studies. Cambridge, Mass.: Harvard-Yenching Institute.

Liangshan tongji nianjian

    2001 *Liangshan tongji nianjian* (Statistical Yearbook of Liangshan). Xichang: Liangshan tongji ju.

Liangshan Yizu nuli shehui

    1982 *Liangshan Yizu nuli shehui* (Slave society of the Liangshan Yi). Beijing: Renmin chubanshe.

Liangshan Yizu zizhizhou gaikuang

    1985 *Liangshan Yizu zizhizhou gaikuang* (Situation of Liangshan Yi Autonomous Prefecture). Chengdu: Sichuan minzu chubanshe.

Light, Ivan

    1973 *Ethnic Enterprise in America: Business and Welfare Among Chinese, Japanese and Blacks.* Berkeley: University of California Press.

    1987 "Unternehmer und Unternehmertum ethnischer Gruppen" (Entrepreneurs and entrepreneurship of ethnic groups). In Klaus Heinemann, ed., *Soziologie wirtschaftlichen Handelns*, 193–215. Opladen: Westdeutscher Verlag.

Light, Ivan, and Stavros Karageorgis

    1994 "The Ethnic Economy." In Neil Smelser and Richard Swedberg, eds., *The Handbook of Economic Sociology*, 647–71. Princeton, N.J.: Princeton University Press.

Light, Ivan, and Carolyn Rosenstein

    1995 "Expanding the Interaction Theory of Entrepreneurship." In Alejandro Portes, ed., *The Economic Sociology of Immigration: Essays on Networks, Ethnicity, and Entrepreneurship*, 166–212. New York: Russell Sage Foundation.

Lin Yaohua

    1961 *The Lolo of Liang Shan.* New Haven: HRAF Press.

    1995 *Liangshan Yijia de jubian* (Tremendous changes among the Liangshan Yi). Beijing: Shangwu Yinshuguan.

Lissjutkina, Larissa

1997 "Die 'neureichen Russen': Zur Typologie der Unternehmerschaft" (Russia's "new rich": Towards a typology of entrepreneurship). In Anton Sterbling and Heinz Zipprian, eds., *Max Weber und Osteuropa*, 167–80. Hamburg: Kraemer.

Litzinger, Ralph A.

2000 *Other Chinas: The Yao and the Politics of National Belonging*. Durham, N.C.: Duke University Press.

Liu Jianming

1998 "Lun minzu diqu fei guoyou jingji de fazhan" (On the development of non-state ethnic economy). *Nei Menggu Shehui Kexue* (Social Sciences of Inner Mongolia) 3: 94–97.

Liu Yaohan

1985a *Zhongguo wenming yuantou xintan: Daojia yu Yizu huyu guan* (A new approach to the origin of Chinese civilization: Daoism and the Yi's concept of tiger's cosmos). Kunming: Yunnan renmin chubanshe.

1985b "Yizu wenhua yanjiu congshu zongxu" (General introduction to the book series Studies on the Yi culture). In Chuxiong Research Centre of Yi Culture, ed., *Yizu wenhua yanjiu wenji* (Collection of articles on studies on the Yi culture), 1–15. Kunming: Yunnan minzu chubanshe.

1985c "Yizu wenhua . . . (Collection of articles on the study of the Yi culture), 26–104.

1992 "Zongxu" (General introduction). In Yang Jilin and Shen Pulian, eds., *Zhongguo Yizu hu wenhua* (Tiger culture of China's Yi nationality), 1–27. Kunming: Yunnan renmin chubanshe.

1993 "'Yizu wenhua yanjiu congshu' zongxu" (General introduction to the series of Yi cultural studies). In Pu Zhen, ed., *The Philosophy of Daoist Chaos and the Yi's Myth of the World Creation*, 1–27. Kunming: Yunnan renmin chubanshe.

Liu Yu

2001 "Searching for the Heroic Age of the Yi People in Liangshan." In Stevan Harrell, ed., *Perspectives on the Yi of Southwest China*, 104–17. Berkeley: University of California Press.

Long Jianmin

1988 *Shichang qiyuan lun* (On the origin of markets). Kunming: Yunnan renmin chubanshe.

Lu Hui

1998 "Multiple Identity of the Yi Nationality in China." Paper presented at the 2nd International Conference on Yi Studies, 19–23 June 1998, Trier University, Center for East Asian and Pacific Studies.

2001 "Preferential Bilateral-Cross-Cousin Marriage among the Nuosu in Liangshan." In Stevan Harrell, ed., *Perspectives on the Yi of Southwest China*, 68–80. Berkeley: University of California Press.

Lü Qing

1996 "Shilun minzu shehuixue de yanjiu keti" (Research topics on sociology of nationalities). *Xibei Minzu Xueyuan Xuebao* (Journal of the Northwestern Nationalities Institute) 1: 59–65.

Luhmann, Niklas

1994 *Die Wirtschaft der Gesellschaft* (The economy of society). Frankfurt/M.: Suhrkamp.

1999 *Funktion und Folgen formaler Organisation* (Function and effects of formal organizations). Berlin: Duncker and Humblot.

Luohong Zige

2001 "Liangshan Yizu shehui de jingji biange" (Economic Changes of Liangshan Yi Society). *Liangshan Minzu Yanjiu* (Liangshan Nationalities Studies): 1–9.

Lütkenhorst, Wilfried, and Jürgen Reinhardt

1993 "The Increasing Role of the Private Sector in Asian Industrial Development." *Intereconomics*, January–February: 22–30.

Ma Erzi

2001 "Liangshan Yizu jiazhi he hunyin guoqu he xianzai de jingji gongneng" (Former and current economic function of clans and marriage among the Liangshan Yi). *Liangshan Minzu Yanjiu* (Liangshan Nationalities Studies): 10–25.

Ma Lilan

1998 *Pingdeng yu fazhan: Lun xin shiqi minzu diqu jingji shehui fazhan de ruogan guanxi* (Equality and development: On crucial relationships of economic and social development in nationalities' areas in the new period). Beijing: Minzu chubanshe.

Ma Linying

1999 "Dui Liangshan Yiqu xidu fandu wenti de xianzhuang diaocha" (Investigation on the problem and situation of drug consuming and drug trafficking in the Yi areas of Liangshan). *Xinan Minzu Xueyuan Xuebao* (Journal of the Southwestern University for Nationalities), special issue: 316–18.

2000 "Liangshan dupin wenti xianzhuang, yueshi ji duice yanjiu" (Study on the current situation, tendency and policies toward drugs problems in Liangshan). *Xinan Minzu Xueyuan Xuebao* (Journal of the Southwestern University for Nationalities), special issue, "Yi Studies": 119–24.

Ma Wenyu

1997 "Dui jinyibu wanshan wo guo minzu quyu zizhi zhidu de sikao" (Considerations on further improvement of the system of autonomy in our country). *Nei Menggu Shehui Kexue* (Social Sciences of Inner Mongolia) 6: 83–86.

Ma Xueliang

1987 "Yanjiu Yiwen guji, fayang Yizu wenhua" (Study ancient Yi scripts, develop Yi culture). *Xinan minzu yanjiu, Yizu zhuanji* (Special collection on the Yi, Studies on Nationalities in Southwest China), 428–40. Kunming: Yunnan renmin chubanshe.

Ma Xueliang

1989 (ed.) *Yizu wenhua shi* (History of the Yi culture). Shanghai: Shanghai renmin chubanshe.

Mackerras, Colin

1994 *China's Minorities: Integration and Modernization in the Twentieth Century.* Hong Kong: Oxford University Press.

1995 *China's Minority Cultures: Identities and Integration since 1912.* Melbourne: Longman and St. Martin's Press.

2002 "Ethnic minorities in China." In Colin Mackerras, ed., *Ethnicity in Asia,* 15–47. London and New York: RoutledgeCurzon.

2004 "Conclusion: Some Major Issues in Ethnic Classification." *China Information,* July: 303–13.

Mars, Gerald, and Robin Ward

1984 "Ethnic Business Development in Britain: Opportunities and Resources." In Robin Ward and Richard Jenkins, eds., *Ethnic Communities in Business: Strategies for Economic Survival,* 1–19. Cambridge: Cambridge University Press.

Mauss, Marcel

1990 *Die Gabe: Form und Funktion des Austauschs in archaischen Gesellschaften* (The Gift: Form and function of exchange in archaic societies). Frankfurt/M.: Suhrkamp.

Medrano, Juan Díez

1994 "The Effects of Ethnic Segregation and Ethnic Competition on Political Mobilization in the Basque Country." *American Sociological Review* 59: 873–89.

Meigu xianzhi

1996 *Meigu xianzhi* (Meigu county annals). Chengdu: Sichuan renmin chubanshe.

Menkhoff, Thomas, and Solvay Gerke

2002 (eds.) *Chinese Entrepreneurship and Asian Business Networks.* London and New York: RoutledgeCurzon.

Merton, Robert K.

1957 *Social Theory and Social Structure.* Glencoe, Ill.: The Free Press.

Meyer, Thomas

2002   *Identitätspolitik: Vom Missbrauch kultureller Unterschiede* (Identity politics: The misuse of cultural differences). Frankfurt/M.: Suhrkamp.

Mgebbu Lunzy (Ma Erzi) and Stevan Harrell

2003   "Nuosu and Neighboring Ethnic Groups: Ethnic Groups and Ethnic Relations in the Eyes and Ears of Three Generations of the Mgebbu Clan." *Asian Ethnicity* 4, no. 1, March: 129–45.

Mianning xianzhi

1994   *Mianning xianzhi* (Mianning county annals). Chengdu: Sichuan renmin chubanshe.

Mullaney, Thomas S.

2004   "Ethnic Classification Writ Large: The 1954 Yunnan Province Ethnic Classification Project and Its Foundations in Republican-Era Taxonomic Thought." *China Information* 18, July: 207–41.

Nee, Victor

1989   "Peasant Entrepreneurship and the Politics of Regulation in China." In Victor Nee and David Stark, eds., *Remaking the Economic Institutions of Socialism: China and Eastern Europe*, 169–207. Stanford: Stanford University Press.

Nie Yuanfei

1997   "Zhuoyan renli ziyuan kaifa, cujin fei gongyouzhi jingji fazhan" (From the perspective of developing labor resources promote the development of non-public ownership economy). *Minzu Gongzuo* (Nationalities Work) 12: 3–6.

Nimkoff, M. F.

1960   "Is the Joint Family an Obstacle to Industrialization?" *International Journal of Comparative Sociology* 1: 109–18.

Nohria, N., and R. G. Eccles

1992   (eds.) *Networks and Organizations: Structure, Form and Action.* Cambridge, Mass.: Harvard Business School Press.

Odgaard, Ole

1990–   "Inadequate and Inaccurate Chinese Statistics: The Case of Private Rural
1991   Enterprises." *China Information* 5: 29–38.

Oesterdiekhoff, Georg W.

1993   *Unternehmerisches Handeln und gesellschaftliche Entwicklung: Eine Theorie unternehmerischer Institutionen und Handlungsstrukturen* (Entrepreneurial acting and social development: A theory of entrepreneurial institutions and structures of acting). Opladen: Westdeutscher Verlag.

Oi, Jean

1989 *State and Peasant in Contemporary China: The Political Economy of Village Government*. Berkeley: University of California Press.

Olzak, Susan

1983 "Contemporary Ethnic Mobilization." *Annual Review of Sociology* 9: 355–74.

1986 "A Competition Model in Ethnic Collective Action in American Cities." In Susan Olzak and Joane Nagel, eds., *Competitive Ethnic Relations*, 17–46. Orlando, Fla., and San Diego: Academic Press.

Olzak, Susan, and Joane Nagel

1986 (eds.) *Competitive Ethnic Relations*. Orlando, Fla., and San Diego: Academic Press.

Pan Jiao

1997 "The Maintenance of the Lolo Caste Idea in Socialist China." *Inner Asia: Occasional Papers* 2, no. 1: 108–27.

1998 "Minzu rentong lilun ji Yi zu rentong de jiangou" (Theories of ethnic identity and the making of the Yi). Paper presented at the 2nd International Conference on Yi Studies, 19–23 June 1998, Trier University, Center for East Asian and Pacific Studies.

Pan Wenchao

2000 "Liangshan Yizu jiu wenhua" (The culture of alcohol among the Liangshan Yi). Paper presented at the 3rd International Conference on Yi Studies, Shilin Yi Autonomous County, 4–7 September.

Parsons, Talcott

1975 *Gesellschaften* (Societies). Frankfurt/M.: Suhrkamp.

Parsons, Talcott, and Neil J. Smelser

1972 *Economy and Society: A Study in the Integration of Economic and Social Theory*. London: Routledge.

Pierenkemper, Toni

1979 *Die Westfälischen Schwerindustriellen 1852–1913: Soziale Struktur und unternehmerischer Erfolg* (Westphalian heavy industry entrepreneurs 1852–1913: Social structure and entrepreneurial success). Göttingen: Vandenhoeck and Rupprecht.

Polanyi, Karl

1977a *The Great Transformation: Politische und Ökonomische Ursprünge von Gesellschaften und Wirtschaftssystemen* (The great transformation: Political and economic origins of societies and economic systems). Wien: Europaverlag.

1977b *The Livelihood of Man*. Edited by Harry W. Pearson. New York, San Francisco, London: Academic Press.

Porter, Michael E.
  2000 "Attitudes, Values, Beliefs, and the Microeconomics of Prosperity." In Lawrence E. Harrison and Samuel Huntington, eds., *Culture Matters: How Values Shape Human Progress*, 14–28. New York: Basic Books.

Portes, Alejandro
  1995a (ed.) *The Economic Sociology of Immigration: Essays on Networks, Ethnicity, and Entrepreneurship*. New York: Russell Sage Foundation.
  1995b "Economic Sociology and the Sociology of Immigration: A Conceptual Overview." In Alejandro Portes, ed., *The Economic Sociology of Immigration: Essays on Networks, Ethnicity, and Entrepreneurship*, 1–41. New York: Russell Sage Foundation.

Portes, Alejandro, and Julia Sensenbrenner
  2001 "Embeddedness and Immigration: Notes on the Social Determinants of Economic Action." In Mark Granovetter and Richard Swedberg, eds., *The Sociology of Economic Life*, 112–35. Boulder, Col.: Westview.

Powell, Walter W., and Laurel Smith-Doerr
  1994 "Networks and Economic Life." In Neil Smelser and Richard Swedberg, eds., *The Handbook of Economic Sociology*, 368–402. Princeton, N.J.: Princeton University Press.

Puge xianzhi
  1992 *Puge xianzhi* (Puge county annals). Chengdu: Sichuan daxue chubanshe.

Qiesa Wuniu
  2002 *Yizu gudai wenming shi* (History of the ancient civilization of the Yi). Beijing: Minzu chubanshe.

Qin Nanyang
  1999 "Lun siying qiyezhu de zhengzhi canyu" (Political participation of private entrepreneurs). In Zhang Houyi and Ming Lizhi, eds., *Zhongguo siying qiye fazhan baogao 1999* (Development report on China's private enterprises of 1999). Beijing: Shehui kexue wenxian chubanshe.

Qubishimei and Yang Liping
  1992 "Liangshan zhou pinkun wenti de duice yanjiu" (Studies on the problem of poverty in Liangshan Prefecture and ways of solving them). *Liangshan Minzu Yanjiu* (Liangshan Nationalities Studies): 31–39.

Ray, Dennis
  1988 "The Role of Entrepreneurship in Economic Development." *Entrepreneurship and Economic Development: Journal of Development Planning* 18: 3–17.

Reese, Pat Ray, and Howard E. Aldrich
  1995 "Entrepreneurial Networks and Business Performance." In Sue Birley and

Ian MacMillan, eds., *International Entrepreneurship*, 109–23. London and New York: Routledge.

Riggs, Fred W.

1994 "Ethnonationalism, industralism, and the modern state." *Third World Quarterly* 15, no. 4, December: 583–612.

Robison, Richard, and David Goodman

1996 (eds.) *The New Rich in Asia*. London, New York: Routledge.

Rhodes, R. A. W.

1999 *Control and Power in Central-Local Government Relations*. Aldershot, VT: Ashgate.

Romanucci-Ross, Lola, and George DeVos

1995 (eds.) *Ethnic Identity: Creation, Conflict, and Accomodation*. London: Alta Mira Press.

Rosenberg, Göran

2000 "Wärmekreise der Politik: Recht, Loyalität, Emotion in post-ethnischen Gesellschaften" (Circles of heat in politics: Law, loyalty, emotion in post-ethnic societies). *Lettre* 48: 4–8.

Rosenthal, Elisabeth

2001 "A Poor Ethnic Enclave in China is Shadowed by Drugs and HIV." *New York Times*, 21 December.

Rüegg-Sturm, Johannes

1998 "Neuere Systemtheorie und unternehmerischer Wandel" (Recent system theory and entrepreneurial change). *Die Unternehmung* 1: 2–17.

Rüland, Jürgen

1998 "Janusköpfige Mittelschichten in Südostasien" (Janus-faced middle strata in Southeast Asia). Paper presented at the conference "Middle Strata and Democracy: Social Mobility and Political Transformation," 9 October. Joint Conference of the Konrad-Adenauer-Foundation and the Institute of Political and Administrative Sciences, Rostock University.

Safran, William

1998 (ed.) *Nationalism and Ethnoregional Identities in China*. London and Portland, Ore.: Frank Cass.

Sahlins, Marshall

1963 "Poor Man, Rich Man, Big-Man, Chief: Political Types in Melanesia and Polynesia." *Comparative Studies in Society and History* 5: 285–303.

1974 *Stone Age Economics*. London and New York: Routledge.

2000 *Culture in Practice: Selected Essays*. New York: Zone Books.

Bibliography

Samers, Michael

    1998   "Immigration, 'Ethnic Minorities,' and 'Social Exclusion' in the European Union: A Critical Perspective." *Geoforum* 2: 123–44.

Sassen, Sakia

    1991   *The Global City*. Princeton, N.J.: Princeton University Press.

Scarman, Lord

    1982   "The Bristol Disorder, 10–12 April 1981," in *The Scarman Report*. New York: Penguin.

Schak, David

    1994   (ed.) *Entrepreneurship, Economic Growth and Social Change: The Transformation of Southern China*. Queensland, Aus.: Griffith University.

Schein, Lousa

    2000   *Minority Rules: The Miao and the Feminine in China's Cultural Politics*. Durham, N.C.: Duke University Press.

Scherr, Albert

    2000   "Ethnisierung als Resource und Praxis" (Ethnisation as resource and practice). *Prokla* 3: 399–414.

Schiel, Tilman

    1994   "The traders' dilemma." In Hans-Dieter Evers and Heiko Schrader, eds., *The Moral Economy of Trade: Ethnicity and Developing Markets*, 15–26. London, New York: Routledge.

Schlee, Günther

    2002   (ed.) *Imagined Differences: Hatred and the Construction of Identity*. Münster: Lit Verlag and New York: Palgrave.

Schoenhals, Martin

    2001   "Education and Ethnicity among the Liangshan Yi." In Stevan Harrell, ed., *Perspectives on the Yi of Southwest China*, 238–255. Berkeley: University of California Press.

Schubert, Gunter

    2002   *Chinas Kampf um die Nation: Dimensionen nationalistischen Denkens in der VR China, Taiwan und Hongkong an der Jahrtausendwende* (China's Fight for the Nation: Dimensions of nationalistic thinking in the PR of China, Taiwan, and Hongkong at the turn of the millenium). Hamburg: Mitteilungen des Instituts für Asienkunde.

Schumann, Dirk

    1992   *Bayerns Unternehmer in Gesellschaft und Staat 1834–1914* (Bavarian entrepreneurs in society and state 1834–1914). Göttingen: Vandenhoeck and Ruprecht.

Schumpeter, Joseph A.

    1928   "Unternehmer" (Entrepreneurs). In Ludwig Elster, Adolf Weber, and

Friedrich Wieser, eds., *Handwörterbuch der Staatswissenschaft* 8, 476–87. Jena: Fischer.

1987a *Theorie der wirtschaftlichen Entwicklung* (The theory of economic development). Berlin: Duncker and Humblot.

1987b *Beiträge zur Sozialökonomik* (Contributions to social economics). Edited by Stephan Böhm. Wien, Köln, Graz: Böhlau

Scott, James

1976 *The Moral Economy of the Peasants: Rebellion and Subsistence in Southeast Asia.* New Haven and London: Yale University Press.

Sexton, Donald, and Raymond Smilor

1986 (eds.) *The Art and Science of Entrepreneurship.* Cambridge, Mass.: Ballinger Publishing Co.

Sha Guangrong

1990 "Qian shu jiefang qian Ganluo de wazi maimai" (Transactions of slaves in Ganluo prior to liberation). *Yizu Wenhua* (Yi Nationality Culture) 19: 75–81.

1992 "Zhongzhi yapian gei Ganluo Yizu dailai de zainan" (Calamities among Yi of Ganluo brought by opium cultivation). *Yizu Wenhua* (Yi Nationality Culture) 21: 105–8.

Shen Guiping and Shi Yazhou

1998 *Minzu zhengce kexue daolun: Dangdai Zhongguo minzu zhengce lilun yanjiu* (Guidebook through political science of nationalities: Studies on the theory of nationalities policy in contemporary China). Beijing: Zhongyang minzu daxue chubanshe.

Shen Jun

1997 "Feifa zuzhi 'mentuhui' huodong weihai da" (Large harm done by illegal activities of sects). *Minzu* (Nationalities) 8: 35.

Shi Zhongwen and Pang Yi

1996 Paomo jingji, toushi Zhongguo de disan zhi yan (Bubble economy, view on China with the eyes of a third person). Beijing.

Sichuan sheng Liangshan Yizu shehui diaocha ziliao xuanjuan

1987 *Sichuan sheng Liangshan Yizu shehui diaocha ziliao xuanjuan* (Selection of investigation material on the Yi society of Liangshan in Sichuan province). Chengdu: Sichuan sheng shehui kexueyuan chubanshe.

Sichuan sheng Liangshan Yizu shehui lishi diaocha

1985 *Sichuan sheng Liangshan Yizu shehui lishi diaocha* (Investigation on the history of the Yi of Liangshan in Sichuan province). Chengdu: Sichuan sheng shehui kexueyuan chubanshe.

Siehl, Elke

1998 *Privatisierung in Rußland: Institutioneller Wandel in ausgewählten Regionen*

(Privatization in Russia: Institutional change in selected regions). Leverkusen: Gabler and Deutscher Universitätsverlag.

Silverman, S.

1976   "Ethnicity as adaptation: Strategies and systems." *Reviews in Anthropology* 3: 626–36.

Simmel, Georg

1994   *Philosophie des Geldes* (The philosophy of money). Frankfurt/M.: Suhrkamp.

Sloane, Patricia

1999   *Islam, Modernity, and Entrepreneurship among the Malays.* New York: St. Martin's Press.

Smelser, Neil, and Richard Swedberg

1994   (eds.) *The Handbook of Economic Sociology.* Princeton, N.J.: Princeton University Press.

Smith, Anthony D.

1981   *The Ethnic Revival.* Cambridge: Cambridge University Press.

1999   *Myths and Memories of the Nation.* Oxford: Oxford University Press

Smith, Joanne N.

2002   "'Making Culture Matter': Symbolic, Spatial and Social Boundaries between Uyghurs and Han Chinese." *Asian Ethnicity* 2: 53–74.

Sollors, Werner

1996   (ed.) *Theories of Ethnicity: A Classical Reader.* Houndmills and London: MacMillan Press.

Sombart, Werner

1987   *Der moderne Kapitalismus* (Modern capitalism). 3 vols. München, Berlin: Deutscher Taschenbuch-Verlag.

Song Tao

1998   "Wanshan yu fazhan minzu quyu zizhi zhidu de sikao" (Considerations on the perfection and development of the system of regional autonomy of nationalities). *Guangbo Dianshi Daxue Xuebao* (Journal of the University of Broadcast and Television) 3: 65–68.

Su Keming, Liangshan Yizu daode yanjiu

1997   *Su Keming, Liangshan Yizu daode yanjiu* (Studies on ethics of the Yi in Liangshan). Chengdu: Sichuan daxue chubanshe.

Sun Qingyou

1997   "Da Liangshan de 'xingxiang fupin'" (Support to overcome poverty in the Great Liangshan). *Minzu Tuanjie* (Unity of Nationalities) 2: 61–62.

Szelenyi, Ivan

1988   *Socialist Entrepreneurs: Embourgeoisement in Rural Hungary.* Cambridge and Oxford: Polity Press.

Tang Hao

1998 "Zhiyue minzu diqu fei gongyouzhi jingji fazhan de fei jingji Yinsu" (Non-economic factors which restrict the non-public ownership economy in ethnic areas). *Guizhou Minzu Yanjiu* (Nationalities Studies of Guizhou) 3: 57–59.

Tang Xing

2002 *Zuqun, wenhua yu jiaoyu* (Ethnicity, culture, and education). Beijing: Minzu chubanshe.

Tang Yunjin

2002 "Wo guo xibu diqu minying qiye dangqian mianlin de fazhan jiyu fenxi" (Analysis of the current situation of development of people-run enterprises in the western part of our country). *Xinan Minzu Xueyuan Xuebao* 12:81–83.

Tapp, Nicholas

2002 "In Defence of the Archaic: A Reconsideration of the 1950s Ethnic Classification Project in China." *Asian Ethnicity* 3, no. 1: 62–84.

Thompson, Grahame, Jennifer Frances, Rosalind Levacic, and Jeremy Mitchell

1991 (eds.) *Markets, Hierarchies and Networks: The Coordination of Social Life.* London, Newbury Park, New Delhi: Sage.

Tibi, Bassam

1985 *Der Islam und das Problem der kulturellen Bewältigung sozialen Wandels* (Islam and the problem of cultural coping with social change). Frankfurt/M.: Suhrkamp.

Trenk, Marin

1991 "'Dein Reichtum ist dein Ruin': Zum Stand der Forschung über afrikanische Unternehmer und wirtschaftliche Entwicklung" (Your wealth is your ruin: On the state of research on African entrepreneurs and economic development). *Anthropos* 86: 501–16.

Turner, Mark

1999 (ed.) *Central-Local Relations in Asia-Pacific: Convergence or Divergence.* Houndmills and London: MacMillan and St. Martin's Press.

Waldenfels, Bernhard

1997 *Topographie des Fremden* (Topography of the strange). Frankfurt/M.: Suhrkamp.

Waldmann, Peter, and Georg Elwert

1989 (ed.) *Ethnizität im Wandel* (Changing ethnicity). Saarbrücken: Breitenbach.

Walzer, Michael

1996 *Lokale Kritik, globale Standards* (Thick and thin: Moral arguments at home and abroad). Hamburg: Rotbuch.

1999 *Vernunft, Politik und Leidenschaft* (Reason, politics, and passion). Frankfurt/
      M.: Suhrkamp.
Wang Geliu
   1997 "Guanyu zizhiquan he youhui zhengce tanxi" (On autonomy rights and pref-
         erence policies). *Minzu Yanjiu* (Nationalities Studies) 5: 28–35.
Wang Kuirong
   1998 "Dui bianjiang minzu pinkun diqu fazhan fei gongyouzhi jingji de sikao"
         (Reflections on the non-public ownership economy in poverty areas of
         nationalities at the borders). *Chuangzao* (Creativity) 2: 35–36.
Wang Luping
   1992 "Shilun Yizu chuantong de jingji jiazhi guan" (On the traditional economic
         values of Yi nationality). *Xinan Minzu Xueyuan Xuebao* (Journal of the
         Southwestern University for Nationalities) 4: 47–51.
Wang Wenyuan
   2001 (ed.) *Liangshan nianjian 2000* (Liangshan Yearbook 2000). Xichang: Keji
         chubanshe.
Wang Xingrang
   1991 (ed.) *Shaoshu minzu geti shangye de jueqi* (The growth of trade among Chi-
         nese ethnic minorities). Beijing: Zhongguo shangye chubanshe.
Wang Yang
   2002 "Jiazu qiye Yinggai tichang" (Clan enterprises should be promoted). *Zhong-
         guo Gongshang Bao*, 16 October.
Wang Yongwu
   1998 "Shilun wo guo minzufa shishi jiandu jizhi de xianzhuang, wenti ji duice"
         (Current situation, problems, and reaction toward the system of supervi-
         sion in terms of nationalities' laws). *Xinan Minzu Xueyuan Xuebao* (Journal
         of the Southwestern Nationalities Institute) 1: 39–45.
Wank, David L.
   1995 "Bureaucratic Patronage and Private Business: Changing Networks of
         Power in Urban China." In Andrew G. Walder, ed., *The Waning of the Com-
         munist State: Economic Origin of Political Decline in China and Hungary*,
         53–183. Berkeley: University of California Press.
Ward, Robin, and Richard Jenkins
   1984 (eds.) *Ethnic Communities in Business: Strategies for Economic Survival*. Cam-
         bridge: Cambridge University Press.
Wei Anduo
   2000 "Yizu shi kaifa Zhongguo xibu de xianqu" (The Yi nationality is the fore-
         runner of the development of China's western areas). *Liangshan Daxue Xue-
         bao* (Journal of Liangshan University) 4: 13–18.

Wei Xianjin

    2001 "Minzu diqu feigong ruan huanjing ji dai jiaqiang" (We must urgently strengthen the weak environment of the non-state sector in nationalities areas). *Zhongguo Gongshang Bao* (China's newspaper for industry and commerce), 26 October.

Weir, Margaret, and Theda Skocpol

    1985 "State Structures and the Possibilities for 'Keynesian' Responses to the Great Depression in Sweden, Britain and the United States." In Peter Evans, Dietrich Rueschemeyer, and Theda Skocpol, eds., *Bringing the State Back In*, 107–68. Cambridge: Cambridge University Press.

Wen Jun and Hu Angang

    2003 "Minzu yu fazhan: Xin de xiandaihua Zhuigan" (Nationalities and development: striving for a new modernization). *Xinan Minzu Xueyuan Xuebao* (Journal of the Southwestern Nationalities Institute) 2: 1–12.

Werhahn, Peter H.

    1990 *Der Unternehmer: Seine Ökonomische Funktion und gesellschaftspolitische Verantwortung*. Trier: Paulinus.

White, Lynn T.

    1998 *Unstately Power, Vol. I: Local Causes of China's Economic Reforms*. Armonk, N.Y., and London: M.E. Sharpe.

Williams, Dee Mack

    1998 "Alcohol Indulgence in a Mongolian Community of China." *Bulletin of Concerned Asian Scholars* 30, no. 1, January: 13–22.

Wilmsen, Edwin N., and Patrick McAllister

    1996 (eds.) *The Politics of Difference: Ethnic Premises in a World of Power*. Chicago and London: The University of Chicago Press.

Wong, Siu-Lun

    1991 "Modernisation and Chinese Cultural Traditions in Hong Kong." In H. Tai, ed., *Confucianism and Economic Development: An Oriental Alternative*, 166–94. Washington, DC: The Washington Institute for Values in Public Policy.

Woodman, Sophia

    1999 "Less Dressed Up as More? Promoting Non-Profit-Making Organizations by Regulating Away Freedom of Association." *China Perspectives*, no. 2, March–April: 17–27.

Wright, Mike, Igor Filatotchev, and Trevor Buck

    1996 "Entrepreneurs and Privatized Firms in Russia and Ukraine: Evidence on Performance." *Frontiers of Entrepreneurship Research* 20: 644–68.

Wugashinuimo Louwu (Han: Wu Ga)

    1997 "Gender Issues in Government Minority Development Policies: Four Communities in Ninglang County, Yunnan Province." PhD diss., University of Michigan, Ann Arbor.

1998 "Discovering and Re-discovering Yi Identity: Shared Identity Narratives from the Classics of Yunnan, Sichuan, Guizhou and Guangxi." Paper presented at the 2nd International Conference on Yi Studies, 19–23 June 1998, Trier University, Center for East Asian and Pacific Studies.

2001 "Yi Women's Economic Role in Ninglang, Yunnan, under the Reforms." In Stevan Harrell, ed., *Perspectives on the Yi of Southwest China*, 256–66. Berkeley: University of California Press.

Wu Gu

2001 "Reconstructing Yi History from Yi Records.' In Stevan Harrell, ed., *Perspectives on the Yi of Southwest China*, 21–34. Berkeley: University of California Press.

Wu Guangbin

1998 *Zhongguo dangdai qiyejia chengzhang yanjiu* (Studies on the emerging of entrepreneurs in contemporary China). Xi'an: Shaanxi renmin chubanshe.

Wu Jianguo

2003 "Shilun Zangqu xiandaihua zhong de suoyouzhi jiegou wenti: Yi Xizang yu Sichuan Zangqu wei li" (On the problem of ownership structure in the process of modernization in Tibetan areas: With Tibetan areas in Tibet and Sichuan as examples). *Minzu Yanjiu* (Nationalities Studies) 2: 79–85.

Wu Jingzhong

1998 "Sichuan shaoshu minzu diqu geti siying jingji de fazhan ji tedian" (Development and characteristics of the individual economy in the minority areas in Sichuan province). Paper presented at the 2nd International Conference on Yi Studies, 19–23 June 1998, Trier University, Center for East Asian and Pacific Studies.

Wu Zongjin

1998 *Minzu fazhi de lilun yu shijian* (Theory and practice of the system of nationalities' rights). Beijing: Zhongguo minzhu fazhi chubanshe.

Xiao Lixin

2002 "Minzu pinkun diqu fupin kaifa yu renwen suzhi de tigao" (Anti-poverty alleviation in poor areas of nationalities and improvement of the quality of human resources). *Xinan Minzu Xueyuan Xuebao* (Journal of the southwestern university for nationalities) 10: 10–11.

Xiao Zhuoji

2000 "Xiang mian xin shiji de zhanlüexing jueze" (Strategic selection in the face of a new century). *Renmin Ribao* (People's daily), 9 March.

Xide xianzhi

1992 *Xide xianzhi* (Xide county annals). Chengdu: Dianzi keji chubanshe.

Xing Lijie

1999 "Jieqian guowai jingyan, zhenxing minzu diqu zhong xiao qiye" (Use the experiences abroad for the development of small and medium-sized enterprises). *Zhongyang Minzu Daxue* (Journal of the Central University for Nationalities) 1: 40–43.

Xu Xinxin

2000 "Cong zhiye pingjia yu zeye quxiang kan Zhongguo shehui jiegou bianqian" (From the assessment of occupational prestige and choice of occupation look at China's process of social change). *Shehuixue Yanjiu* 3: 67–85.

Xu Zurong and Yang Dandan

2003 "Jiakuai pinkun diqu geti siying jingji fazhan de zhengce jianyi" (Political recommendation in terms of accelerating the development of individual and private economy in poverty areas) *Qiushi* 1: 45–46.

Yan, Yunxiang

1996 *The Flow of Gifts: Reciprocity and Social Networks in a Chinese Village*. Stanford: Stanford University Press.

Yang Hui

1995 "Lun Liangshan Yizu qiye guanli ganbu de peiyang" (On the training of Yi management cadres in Liangshan). *Xinan Minzu Xueyuan Xuebao* (Journal of the Southwestern Nationalities Institute) 3: 50–53.

Yang Jilin and Shen Pulian

1992 *Zhongguo Yizu hu wenhua* (Tiger culture of China's Yi nationality). Kunming: Yunnan renmin chubanshe.

Yang Jingchu

1994 "Shehuizhuyi shichang jingji yu minzu guanxi de jige wenti" (Socialist market economy and some questions concerning the relations between nationalities). *Minzu Yanjiu* (Nationalities Studies) 5: 1–9.

Yang, Keming

2004 "Institutional Holes and Entrepreneurship in China." *The Sociological Review* 52, no. 3: 371–89.

Yang, Mayfair Mei-hui

1994 *Gifts, Banquets and the Art of Social Relationships in China*. Ithaca, N.Y.: Cornell University Press.

Yanyuan xianzhi

2000 *Yanyuan xianzhi* (Yanyuan county annals). Chengdu: Sichuan minzu chubanshe.

Yao Xiantao and Wang Lianjuan

2002 *Zhongguo jiazu qiye: Xianzhuang, wenti yu duice* (China's clan enterprises: Current situation, problems, and policies). Beijing: Qiye guanli chubanshe.

Yin Zhengkun

1996 "Shilun fubai chengyin ji jienue tujing" (Discussion on the reasons for corruption and ways of solution). *Huazhong Ligong Daxue Xuebao* (Journal of Central China Technical University) 2: 11–15.

Yizu jianshi

1987 *Yizu jianshi* (Short history of the Yi). Kunming: Yunnan renmin chubanshe.

Yizu wenhua yanjiu wenji

1985 *Yizu wenhua yanjiu wenji* (Collection of articles on the study of the Yi culture). Kunming: Yunnan renmin chubanshe.

Young, Frank W.

1971 "A Macrosociological Interpretation of Entrepreneurship." In Peter Kilby, ed., *Entrepreneurship and Economic Development*, 139–49. New York: Collier-Macmillan.

Young, Susan

1995 *Private Business and Economic Reform in China*. Armonk, N.Y., and London: M.E. Sharpe.

Yu, Tony Fu-Lai

2001 *Firms, Governments and Economic Change: An Entrepreneurial Perspective*. Cheltenham and Northampton, U.K.: Edward Elgar.

Yue Chaishen and Yuan Li

1998 "'Minzu quyu zizhifa' shishi baozhang wenti yanjiu" (Study on the protection of the 'Law on regional autonomy for nationalities'). *Xinan Minzu Xueyuan Xuebao* (Journal of the Southwestern Nationalities Institute) 5: 126–33.

Zhang Fuchi and Guo Yuqin

1997 (eds.) *Qiyejia jingshen* (Entrepreneur's spirit). Beijing: Qiye guanli chubanshe.

Zhang Houyi and Ming Lizhi

2000 (eds.) *Zhongguo siying qiye fazhan baogao 1999* (Development report on China's private enterprises of 1999). Beijing: Shehui kexue wenxian chubanshe.

Zhang Houyi, Ming Lizhi, and He Jiaan

2002 (eds.) *Siying qiye yu shichang jingji* (Private enterprises and the market economy). Beijing: Shehui kexue wenxian chubanshe.

Zhang Houyi, Ming Lizhi, and Liang Chuanyun

2002 (eds.) *Zhongguo siying qiye fazhan baogao*, no. 3, 2001. (Development report on China's private entrepreneurs). Beijing: Shehui kexue wenxian chubanshe.

Zhang Jianhua

   1998   *Yi zu shehui de zhengzhi yu junshi* (Politics and military of Yi society). Kun-
          ming: Yunnan minzu chubanshe.

Zhang Jianshi

   2002   "Liangshan Yizu chuantong qi Yi wenhua de bianqian" (The change of tra-
          ditional lacquer technique culture of Yi people in Liangshan). *Xinan Minzu
          Xueyuan Xuebao* 12: 42–53.

Zhang Xuwu, Li Ding, and Xie Minggan, eds.

   1994   *Zhongguo siying jingji nianjian* (Yearbook of the Chinese private economy).
          Hongkong: Xianggang jingji chubanshe.

   1996   *Zhongguo siying jingji nianjian* (Yearbook of the Chinese private economy).
          Beijing: Zhonghua gongshang lianhe chubanshe.

Zhao Xianren

   2000   (ed.) *Zhongguo shaoshu minzu diqu jingji fazhan baogao 1999* (Report on
          the regional economic development of China's ethnic minorities). Beijing:
          Minzu chubanshe.

Zhaojue xian Yizu quan

   1999   *Zhaojue xian Yizu quan* (Collection on Yi nationality, Zhaojue County).
          Edited by the Institute of Nationalities Studies, Chinese Academy of Social
          Sciences. Beijing: Minzu chubanshe.

Zhaojue xianzhi

   1999   *Zhaojue xianzhi* (Zhaojue county annals). Chengdu: Sichuan cishu chubanshe.

Zhong, Yang

   2003   *Local Government and Politics in China: Challenges from Below.* Armonk,
          N.Y., and London: M.E. Sharpe.

Zhonggong Meigu xianwei wenjian

   1998   *Zhonggong Meigu xianwei wenjian* (Document of the Party committee of
          the CCP of Meigu County), no. 53.

Zhongguo gongshangye lianhehui zhangcheng

   1997   (Statute of the Chinese Association of Industry and Commerce). Chengdu:
          Sichuan sheng gongshangye lianhehui and Sichuan sheng shanghui.

Zhongguo qiyejia diaocha xitong

   1998a (ed.) *Zhongguo qiye jingying guanlizhe chengzhang yu fazhan zhuanti diaocha
          baogao* (Special report on the training and development of Chinese enter-
          prise managers). Beijing: Jingji kexue chubanshe.

   1998b *Zhongguo qiyejia duiwu chengzhang yu fazhan baogao* (Report on the training
          and development of Chinese enterpreneurs). Beijing: Jingji kexue chubanshe.

Zhongguo siyou qiyezhu jieceng yanjiu ketizu

   1994   "Wo guo siyou qiye de jingying zhuangkuang yu siyou qiyezhu de quanti

tezheng" (Management situation of private enterprises and group characteristics of private entrepreneurs). *Zhongguo Shehui Kexue* (Social Sciences
of China) 4: 60–76.

"Zhonghua Renmin Gongheguo minzu quyu zizhifa" xiugai jianyi gao

  1996   "'Zhonghua Renmin Gongheguo minzu quyu zizhifa' xiugai jianyi gao"
         (Proposal on the revision of the "Law on regional autonomy of nationali-
         ties of the PR of China"). *Xinan Minzu Xueyuan Xuebao* (Journal of the
         Southwestern Nationalities Institute) 1: 34–38.

Zhou Daming and Qin Hongzeng

  2003   "Canyu yu fazhan: dangdai renleixue dui "tazhe" de guanhuai" (Participa-
         tory development: The concern for "others" by contemporary anthropol-
         ogy). *Minzu Yanjiu* (Nationalities Studies) 5: 44–50.

Zhou Ping

  1997   "Shaoshu minzu zhengzhi canyu fenxi" (Analysis of political participation
         of national minorities). *Yunnan Shehui Kexue* (Social Sciences of Yunnan)
         5: 68–74.

Zhou Xinhua and Xia Dasheng

  1995   "Minzu diqu nongcun shehui zhi'an wenti jianYi" (Suggestions in regards
         to security in rural areas of the nationalities' areas). *Zhongnan Minzu
         Xueyuan Xuebao* (Journal of the Central-South Nationalities Institute) 6:
         30–32.

Zou Tieli

  2003   *Zhongguo Gongchandang yu siying jingji* (The Communist Party of China
         and the economy). Beijing: Zhonggong dangshi chubanshe.

Zschoch, Barbara

  1998   *Entwicklung von Kleinunternehmen in Rußland* (Development of small-scale
         entrepreneurs in Russia). Frankfurt/M.: Peter Lang.

INDEX

The letter *f* following a page number denotes a figure.
The letter *t* following a page number denotes a table.

Jjike clan, 8, 158
juvenile crime, 56

kin networks, 137, 152–54, 160
kinship, 173, 220n1
Kolakowski, Leszek, 188
Kunming, 200

Lageman, Bernhard, 14
language, 187
laoxiang, 106
laziness, 96, 178, 194, 217n5
leadership types, 165
legal system, 143–44
Leibo County: discrimination against
   Nuosu in, 79; Nuosu entrepreneurs
   in, 83, 99; as research location, 24–
   25, 216n22
Li Fang, 21, 137, 220n3
Li Yongxiang, 189–90
Liangshan Prefecture: dependence on
   state subsidies, 195; divisions of, 43–
   44; economic development in, 44–
   50; emergence of entrepreneurship
   in, 19; founding of, 42; income disparity among counties in, 49t; instability of entrepreneurship in, 212; as
   marker for ethnic identity, 186, 188; as
   Nuosu Muddi, 193–94; politics in, 22;
   as poor region, 10–11; statistics on, 9
Liangshan Ribao (newspaper), 11, 66
life goals, 110–13
Light, Ivan, 17–18
Lin Biao, 29
Liu Bocheng, 192
Liu Yaohan, 190
lobby groups, 133–35
local government: debt, 11; economic
   policy, 122–23; entrepreneurial dissatisfaction with, 144–46; health care,
   6; performance of, 121–22; political
   participation patterns, 123–24; sani-

tation inspections, 4; state interven-
   tion, 123
Loho clan, 155
loyalties, 187
Lugu Lake, 72
Luhmann, Niklas, 151
Luojing Mountain, 71, 101

Ma Linying, 56
Mabian Autonomous County, 9, 43
Mao Zedong, 94
market competition: ethnic relations
   and, 23, 176–77, 196; Nuosu cooperation and, 183, 185
market economy, 113, 114t, 115–17, 173–
   74, 206
matsutake mushrooms, 96
Mauss, Marcel, 22, 203
mechanical solidarity, 160
media, 143t
Meigu County: *bimo* numbers in, 60,
   219n13; development successes in,
   81; dissatisfaction with local government, 146; entrepreneurial
   biographies from, 97, 99, 102–5;
   entrepreneurs' development aid, 194;
   government exploitation of business,
   78–80; interest associations in, 131,
   133; number of businesses in, 60–
   63; Nuosu entrepreneurs in, 83, 198f;
   as research location, 24–25; strength
   of traditional ties in, 168; tax breaks
   for business in, 63–64, 74–75; as Yi
   cultural center, 60, 64
Melanesians, 17
Meyer, Thomas, 212
mgajie caste, 26
mgamo, 202
Mgebbu Lunzy, 35, 42
mgefu, 202
Mianning County: cross-cultural social
   interactions, 182; dissatisfaction with

United Front Departments, 128, 130, 132–33, 184
unregistered enterprises, 20–21

value introjection, 150–51, 156

Waldenfels, Bernhard, 170
Walzer, Michael, 7, 35
Wank, David, 138
warm loyalties, 187, 209
weak ties, 137–41, 148
wealth, 27, 41–42, 115, 157
White Yi, 26, 176
women entrepreneurs, 162–63, 164f
workers' prestige, 119
Wu Jinghua, 101, 219n4

Xia Dynasty, 189
xiangzhen enterprises. *See* town and township enterprises
Xichang: clan branch associations in, 155; discrimination against Nuosu in, 78–79; entrepreneurial biographies from, 109; incorporation into Liangshan of, 42–44; individualization in, 168; ostentatious consumption in, 200; private sector concentration in, 48
Xide County: entrepreneur and staff in, 179f; entrepreneurial biographies from, 104; private sector in, 73–74; as research location, 24–25
Xinjiang, 211

Yala people, 28
Yanbian County, 43
Yanyuan County: entrepreneurial biographies from, 93–97, 98f, 109–10;

entrepreneurs as clan leaders, 165; entrepreneurs' development aid in, 194; interest associations in, 131; mining/agriculture as economic bases of, 72–75; ostentatious consumption in, 200; private sector in, 74; as research location, 24–25
Yi people: alcohol use by, 5; class system of, 26; as courageous, 209; effect of entrepreneurial class on, 22; guerrilla actions by, 28–29, 99; as Han ancestors, 189; history of, 188–93; populations of, 8, 191, 221n5; seen as lazy, 96, 178, 194, 217n5; seen as oldest East Asians, 189; seen as undeveloped by Han, 34–35, 188; socialist reforms among, 27–31; as underrepresented in employment, 13. *See also* Nuosu people; script of the Nuosu/Yi
Young, Frank, 18
Yuan Dynasty, 191
Yuexi County, 108, 179f
Yunnan province, 8, 167

Zangzu. *See* Tibetans
Zhaojue County: cross-cultural cooperation in, 185; dissatisfaction with public security, 146–47; drugs and crime in, 55–56; education in, 78; entrepreneurial biographies from, 106–7; HIV infection in, 55; interest associations in, 131–32; poverty in, 50, 55, 64; private sector development in, 55–57, 58t, 74; religious sects in, 56–57; report on core issues facing businesses in, 76–81; as research location, 24–25; Yi in Chengdu, 36
Zhou Dynasty, 189